KU-260-650

Dotter of her Father's Eyes

Mary M Talbot
Bryan Talbot

Jonathan Cape • London

To our granddotters:
Tabitha and Madeline

LIBRARY SERVICES FOR SCHOOLS	
38003044831055	
Bertrams	17/12/2013
	£14.99
LSS	

Acknowledgements

Laura Atherton, Stephen Atherton, Chaz Brenchley,
Rob Curley, Donald Farnworth, Dan Franklin, Dave Gibson,
Dr Mel Gibson, Stephen Holland, Dez Skinn, Dr Angela Smith,
Alwyn Talbot, Kristell Talbot, Robyn Talbot, Chris Warner

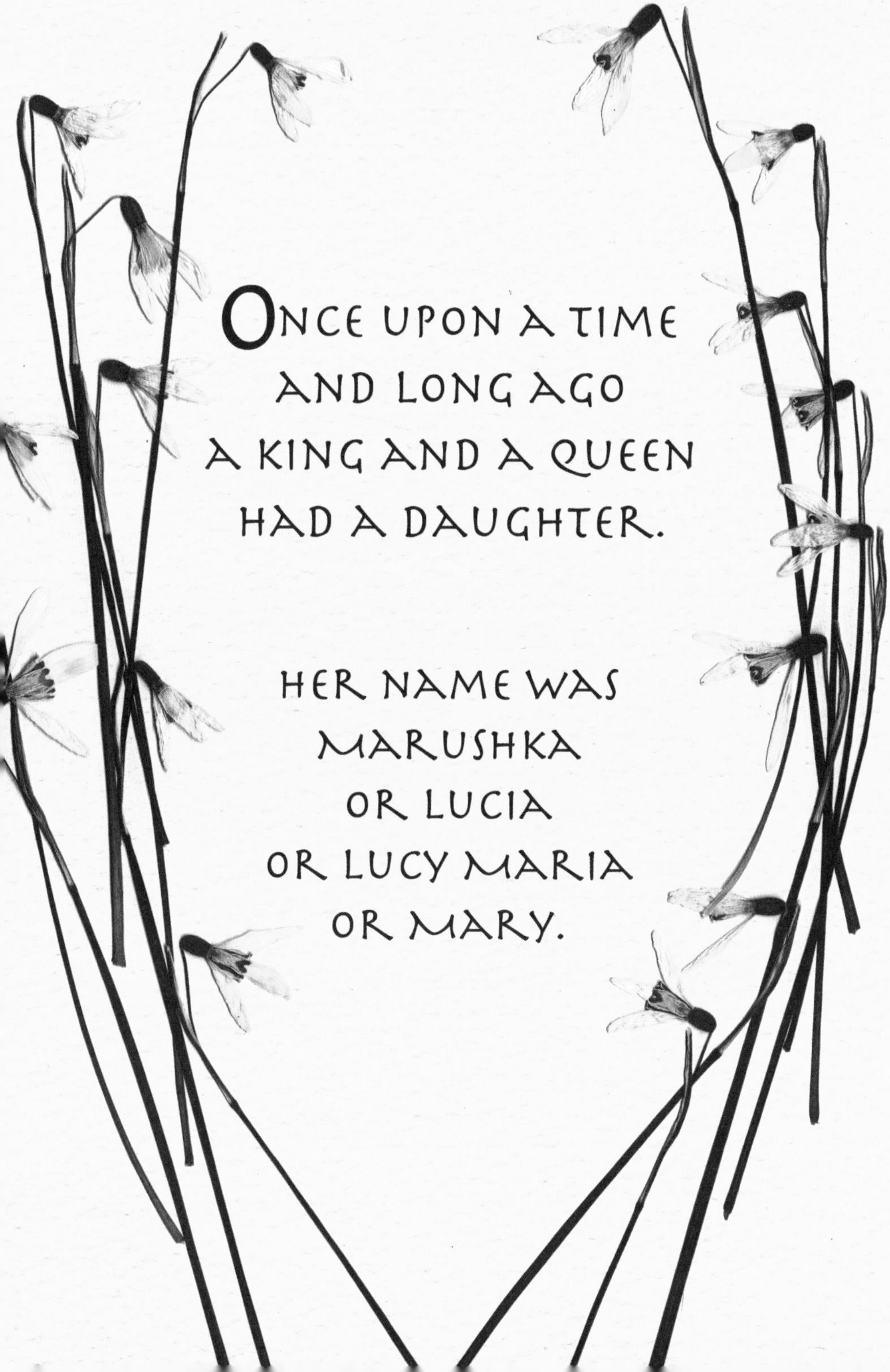

Once upon a time
and long ago
a king and a queen
had a daughter.

Her name was
Marushka
or Lucia
or Lucy Maria
or Mary.

1749. FINSBURY

RC1
13

MINISTRY OF FOOD 1952-1953 RATION BOOK

MoF

AJ 695367

SERIAL No.

(GENERAL)

Surname

Address

MAR 1978

NAME

ATHERTON, Mr. J. S.

X

01576

SOCIAL SECURITY

ACCOUNT NUMBER

611-04-2306

HAS BEEN ESTABLISHED FOR

JAMES S. ATHERTON

SIGNATURE J. S. Atherton

1.08 SOCIAL SECURITY AND TAX PURPOSES—NOT FOR IDENTIFICATION

NATIONAL REGISTRATION IDENTITY CARD

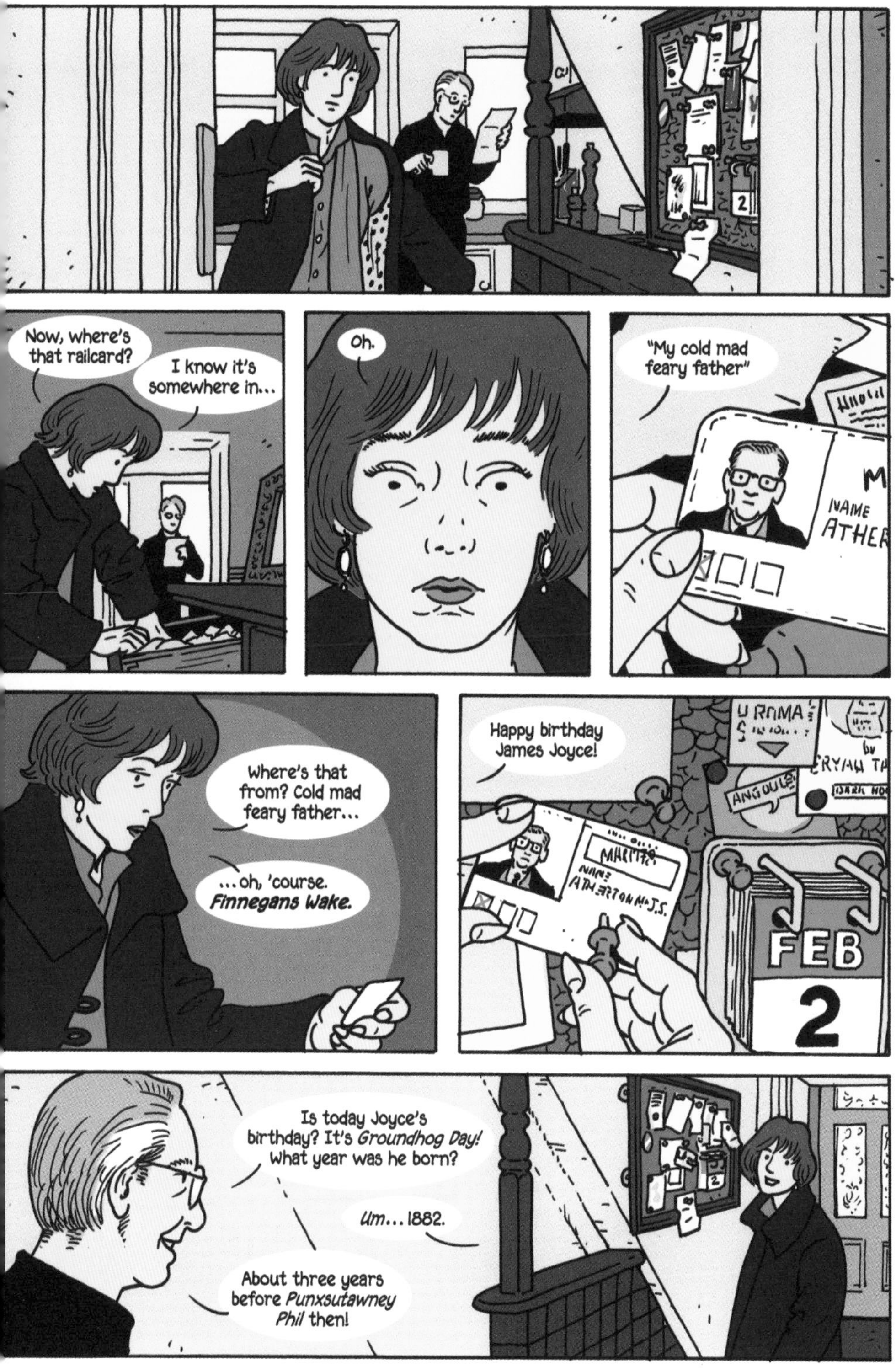
Now, where's that railcard?
I know it's somewhere in...
Oh.
"My cold mad feary father"
Where's that from? Cold mad feary father...
...oh, 'course. *Finnegans Wake.*
Happy birthday James Joyce!
FEB
2
Is today Joyce's birthday? It's *Groundhog Day!* What year was he born?
Um... 1882.
About three years before *Punxsutawney Phil* then!

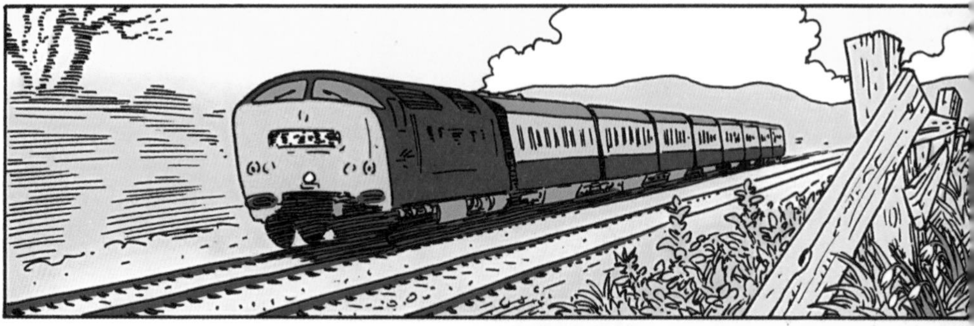

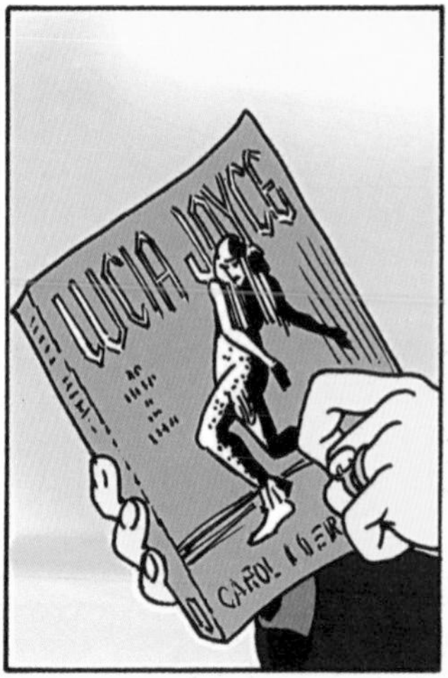
LUCIA JOYCE

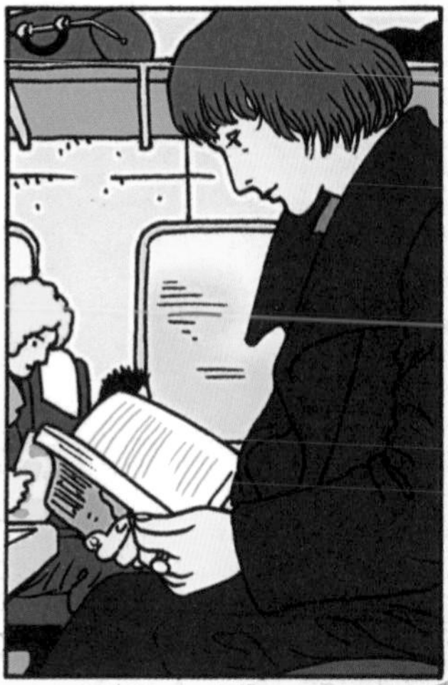

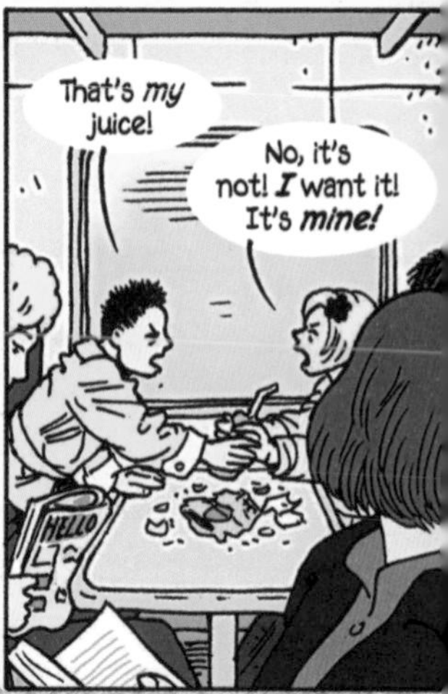
That's *my* juice!
No, it's not! ***I*** want it! It's ***mine!***
HELLO

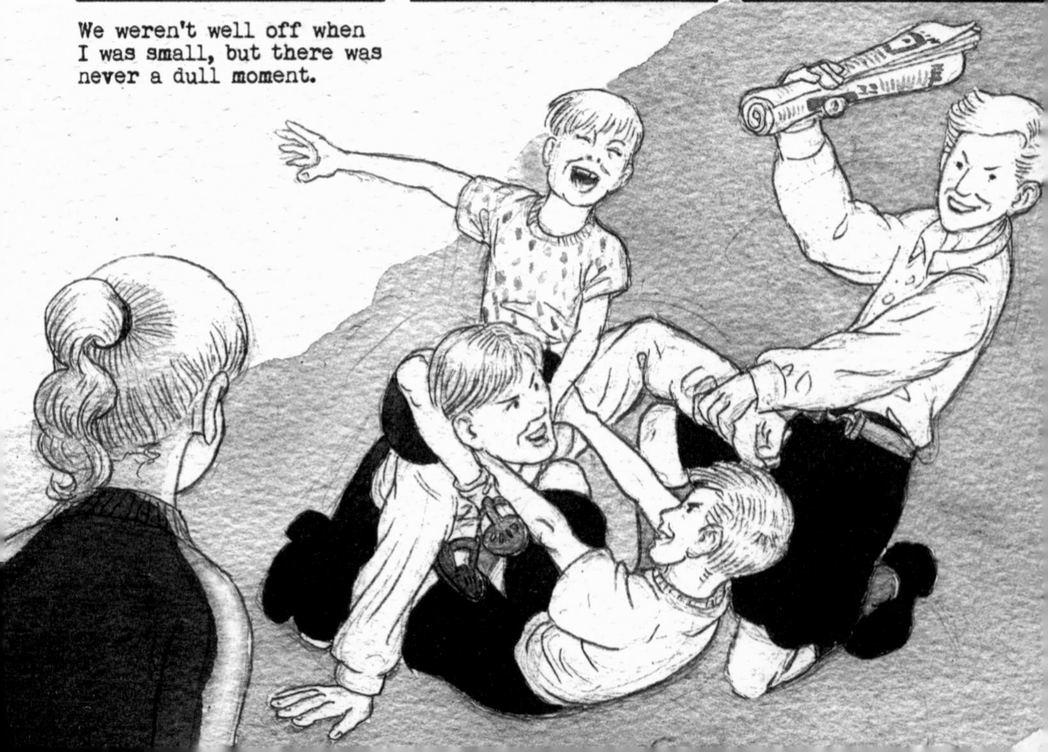
We weren't well off when I was small, but there was never a dull moment.

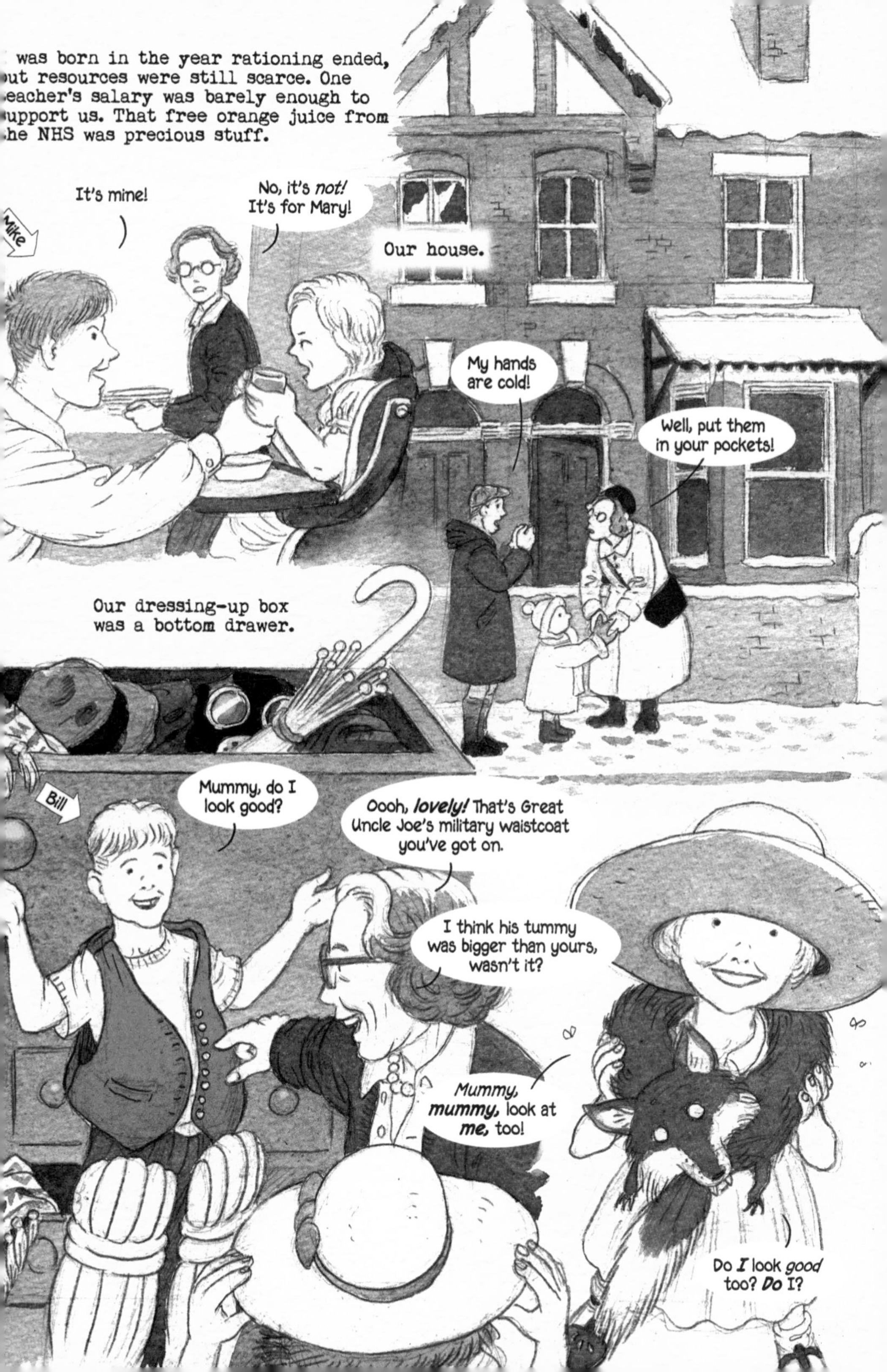
was born in the year rationing ended,
ut resources were still scarce. One
eacher's salary was barely enough to
upport us. That free orange juice from
he NHS was precious stuff.
It's mine!
Mike
No, it's *not!* It's for Mary!
Our house.
My hands are cold!
Well, put them in your pockets!
Our dressing-up box was a bottom drawer.
Bill
Mummy, do I look good?
Oooh, ***lovely!*** That's Great Uncle Joe's military waistcoat you've got on.
I think his tummy was bigger than yours, wasn't it?
Mummy, ***mummy,*** look at ***me,*** too!
Do ***I*** look *good* too? ***Do*** I?

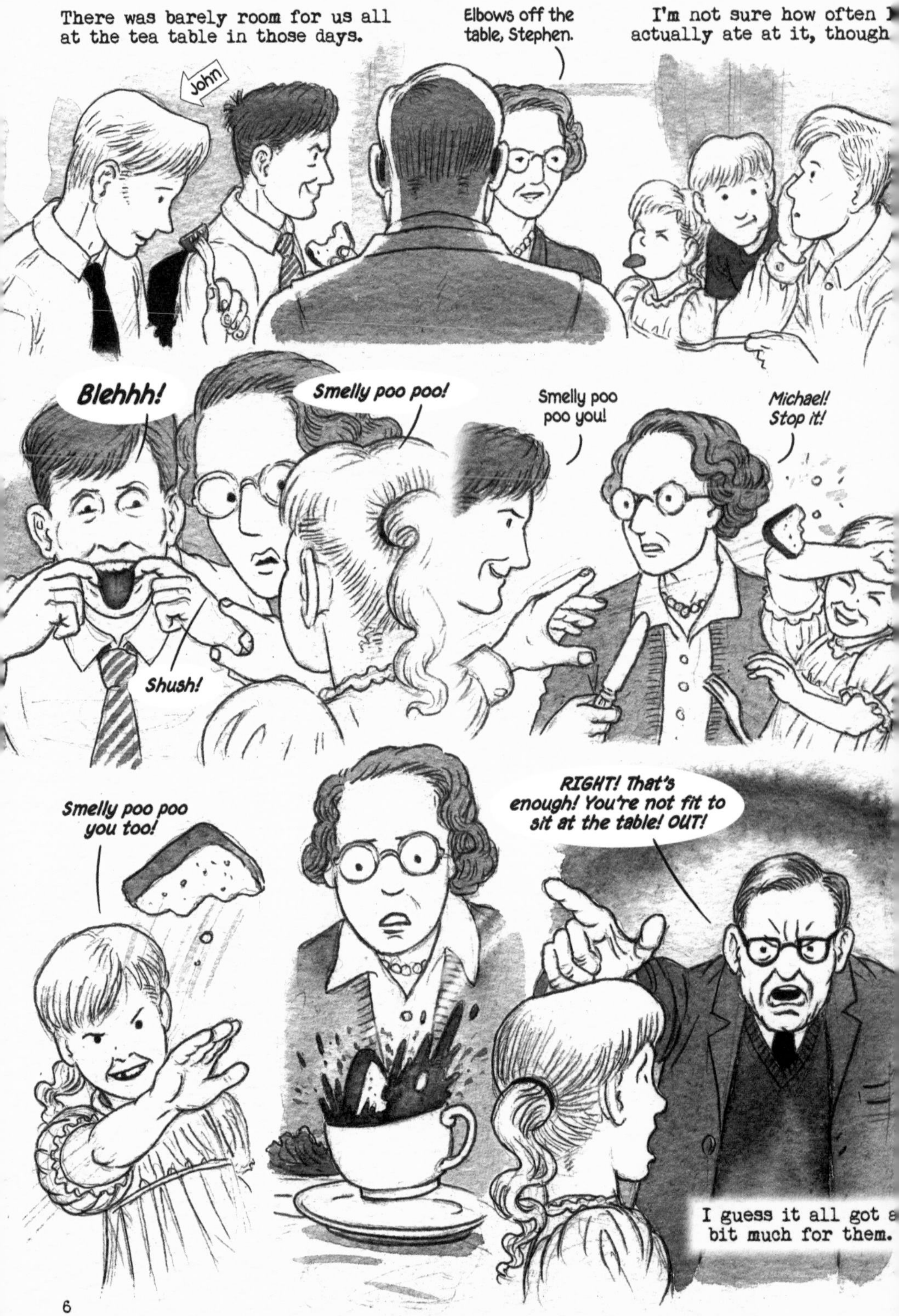

There was barely room for us all at the tea table in those days.
John
Elbows off the table, Stephen.
I'm not sure how often I actually ate at it, though
Blehhh!
Smelly poo poo!
Shush!
Smelly poo poo you!
Michael! Stop it!
Smelly poo poo you too!
RIGHT! That's enough! You're not fit to sit at the table! OUT!
I guess it all got a bit much for them.

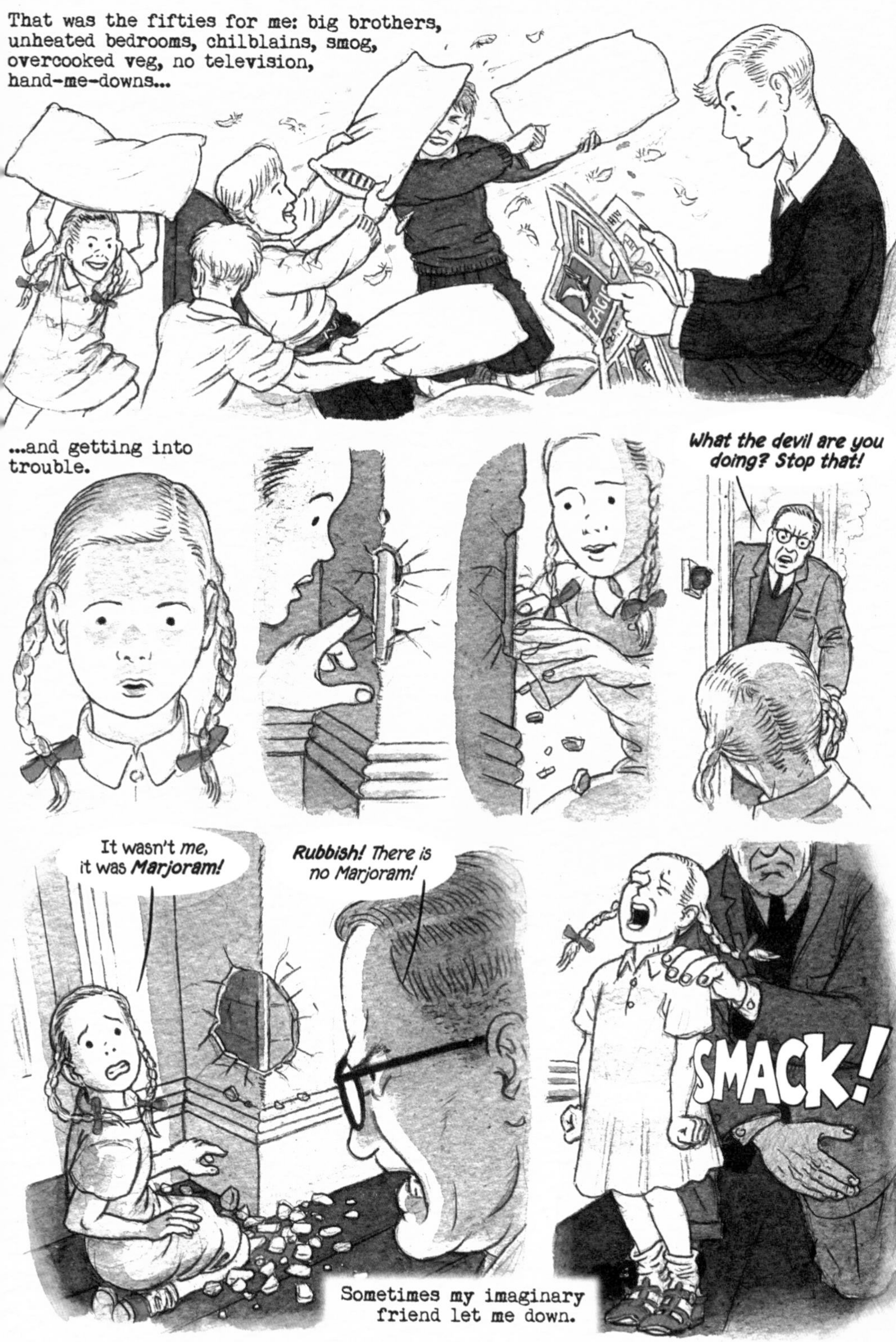
That was the fifties for me: big brothers, unheated bedrooms, chilblains, smog, overcooked veg, no television, hand-me-downs...
...and getting into trouble.
What the devil are you doing? Stop that!
It wasn't *me*, it was ***Marjoram!***
Rubbish! *There is no Marjoram!*
SMACK!
Sometimes my imaginary friend let me down.

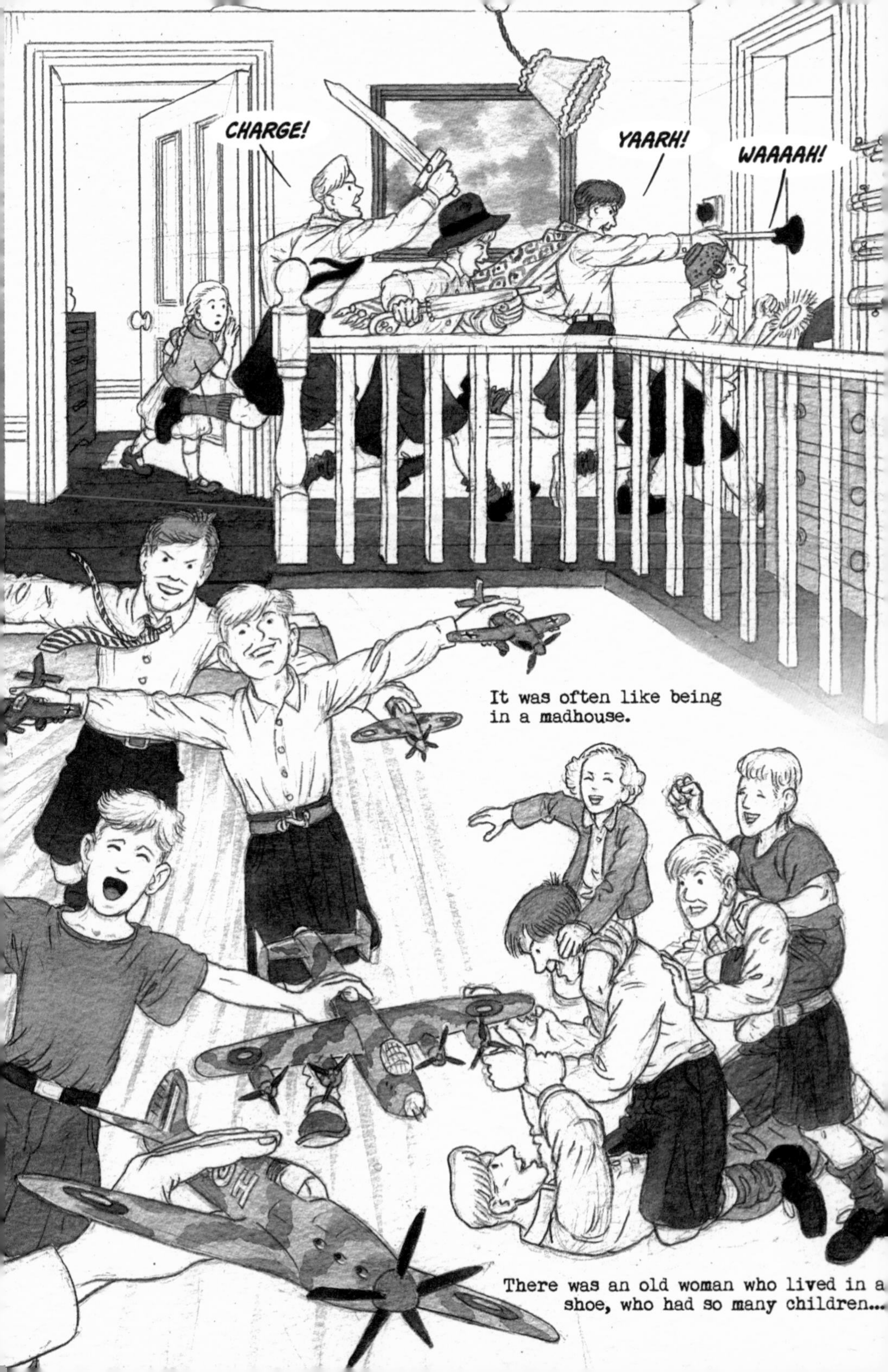
CHARGE!
YAARH!
WAAAAH!
It was often like being in a madhouse.
There was an old woman who lived in a shoe, who had so many children...

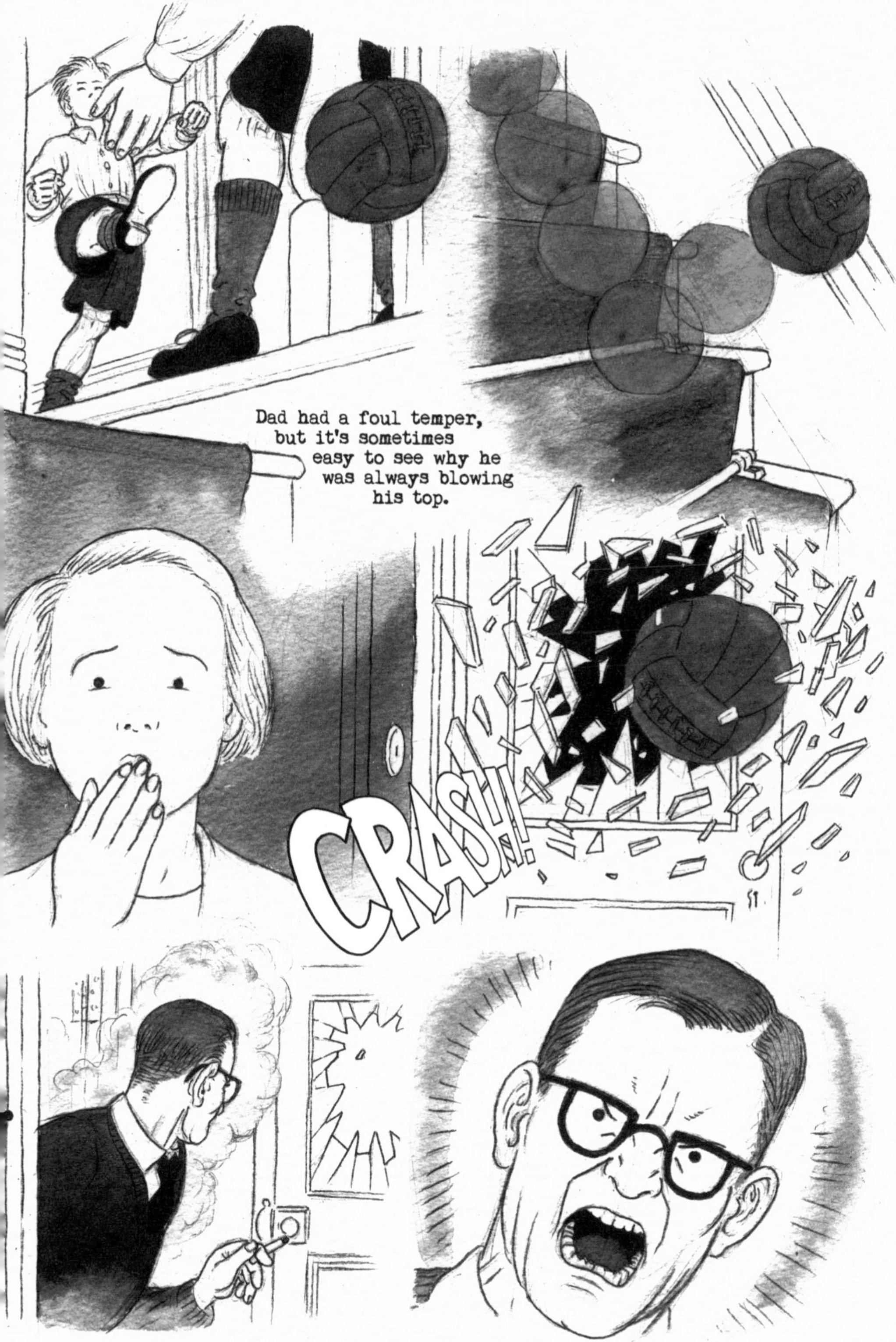

Dad had a foul temper, but it's sometimes easy to see why he was always blowing his top.
CRASH!!

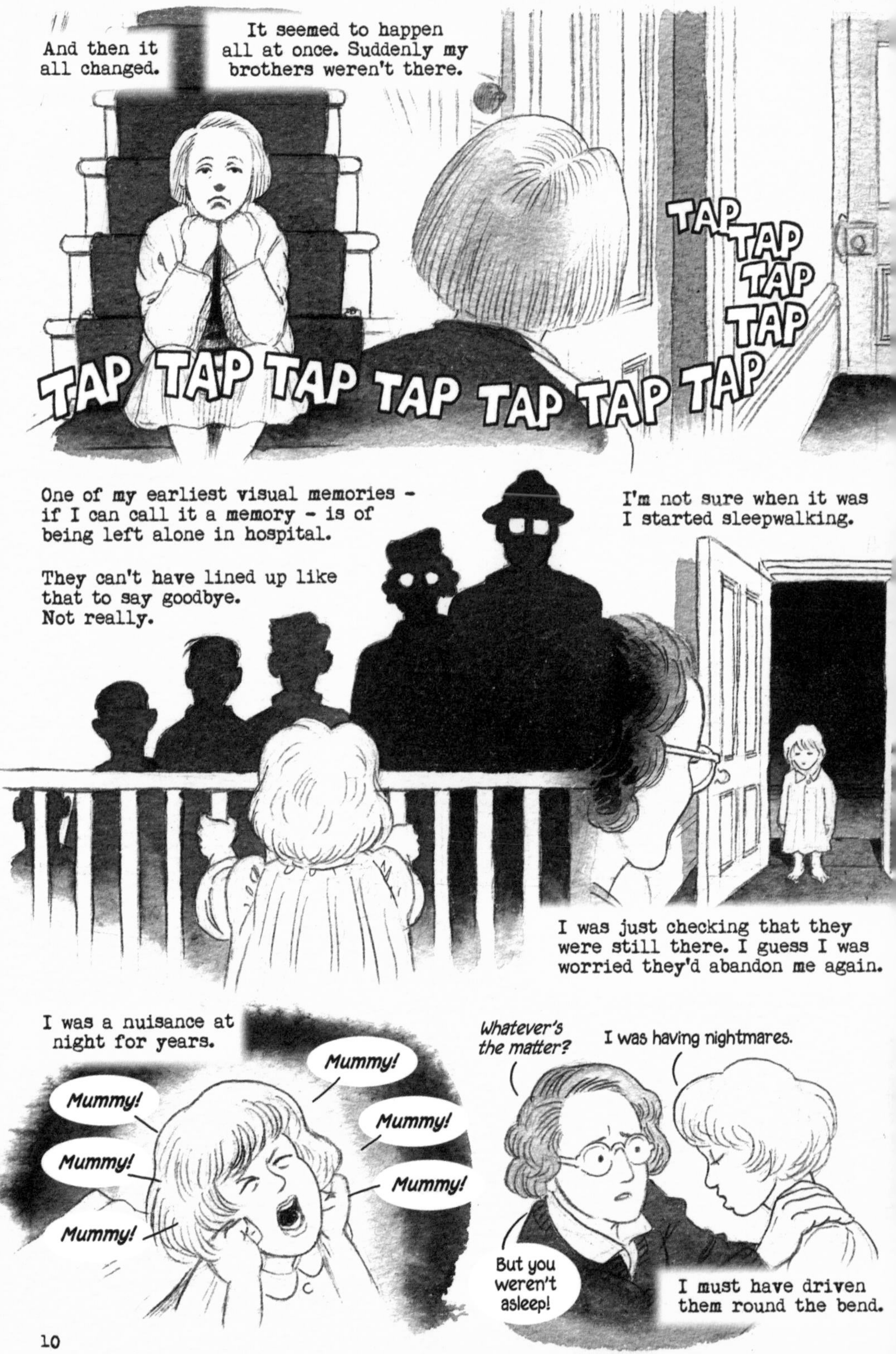
And then it all changed.
It seemed to happen all at once. Suddenly my brothers weren't there.
TAP TAP TAP TAP
TAP TAP TAP TAP TAP TAP TAP
One of my earliest visual memories - if I can call it a memory - is of being left alone in hospital.
They can't have lined up like that to say goodbye. Not really.
I'm not sure when it was I started sleepwalking.
I was just checking that they were still there. I guess I was worried they'd abandon me again.
I was a nuisance at night for years.
Mummy!
Mummy!
Mummy!
Mummy!
Mummy!
Mummy!
Whatever's the matter?
I was having nightmares.
But you weren't asleep!
I must have driven them round the bend.

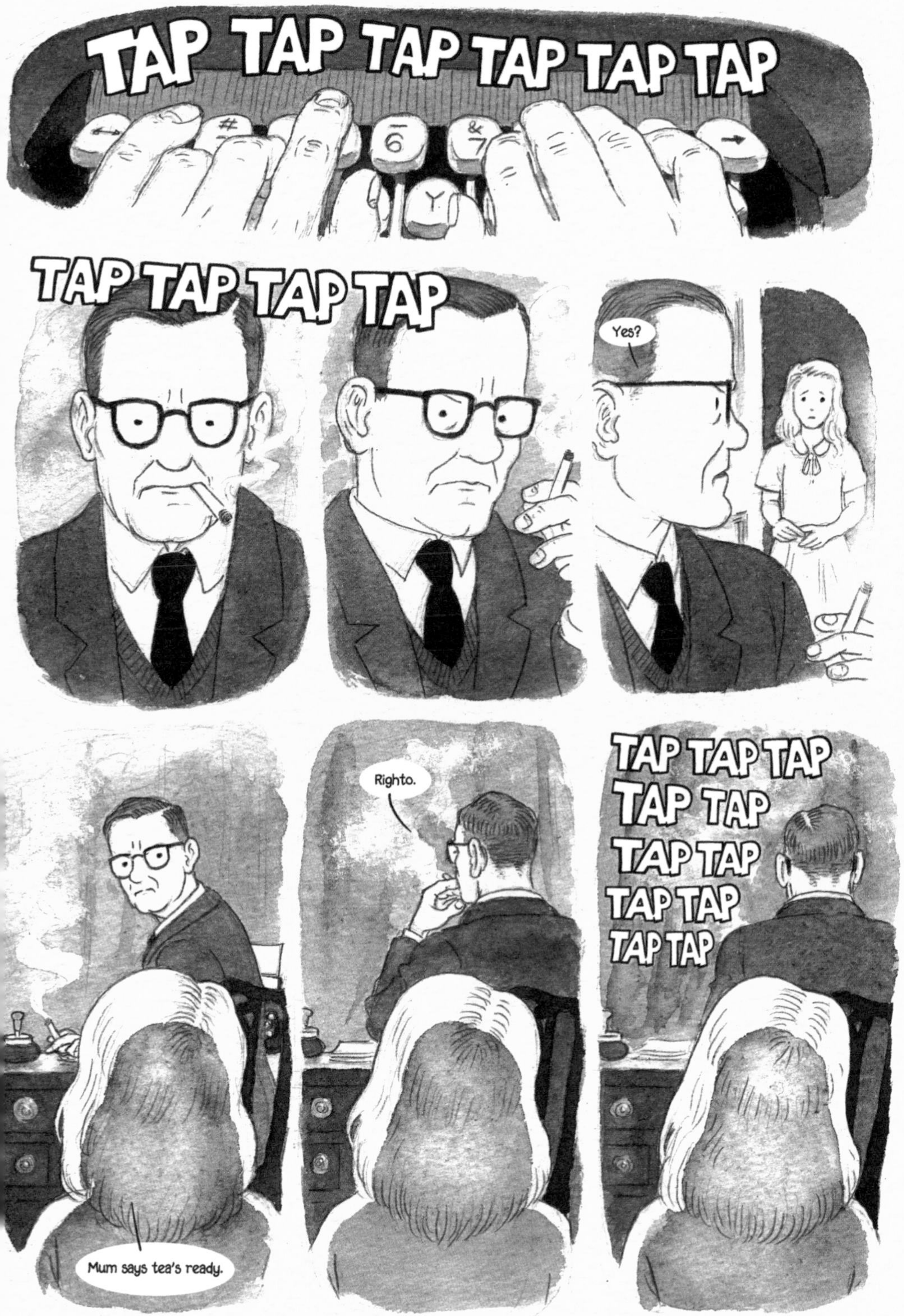
TAP TAP TAP TAP TAP TAP
TAP TAP TAP TAP
Yes?
Mum says tea's ready.
Righto.
TAP TAP TAP
TAP TAP
TAP TAP
TAP TAP
TAP TAP

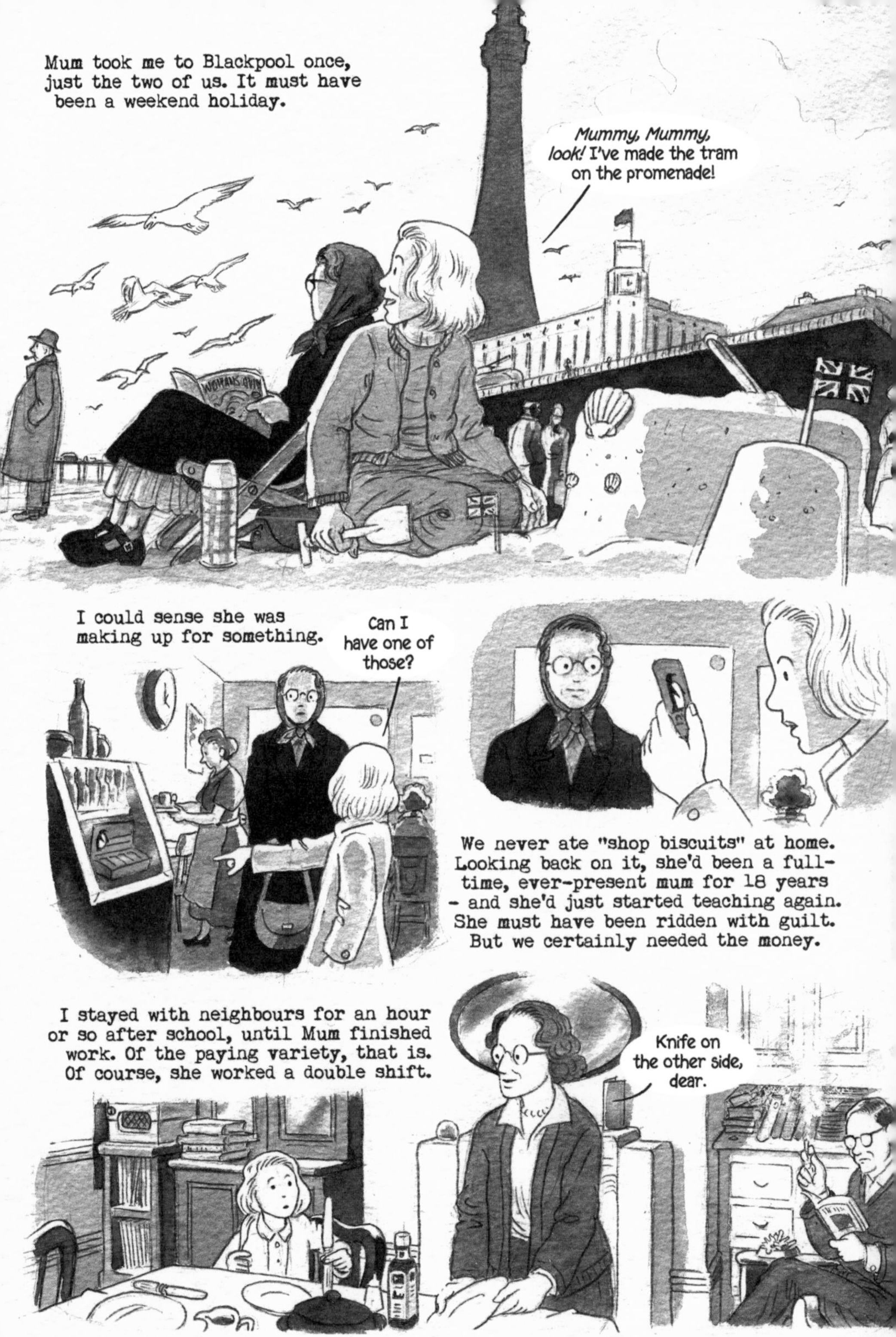
Mum took me to Blackpool once, just the two of us. It must have been a weekend holiday.
Mummy, Mummy, look! I've made the tram on the promenade!
I could sense she was making up for something.
Can I have one of those?
We never ate "shop biscuits" at home. Looking back on it, she'd been a full-time, ever-present mum for 18 years - and she'd just started teaching again. She must have been ridden with guilt. But we certainly needed the money.
I stayed with neighbours for an hour or so after school, until Mum finished work. Of the paying variety, that is. Of course, she worked a double shift.
Knife on the other side, dear.

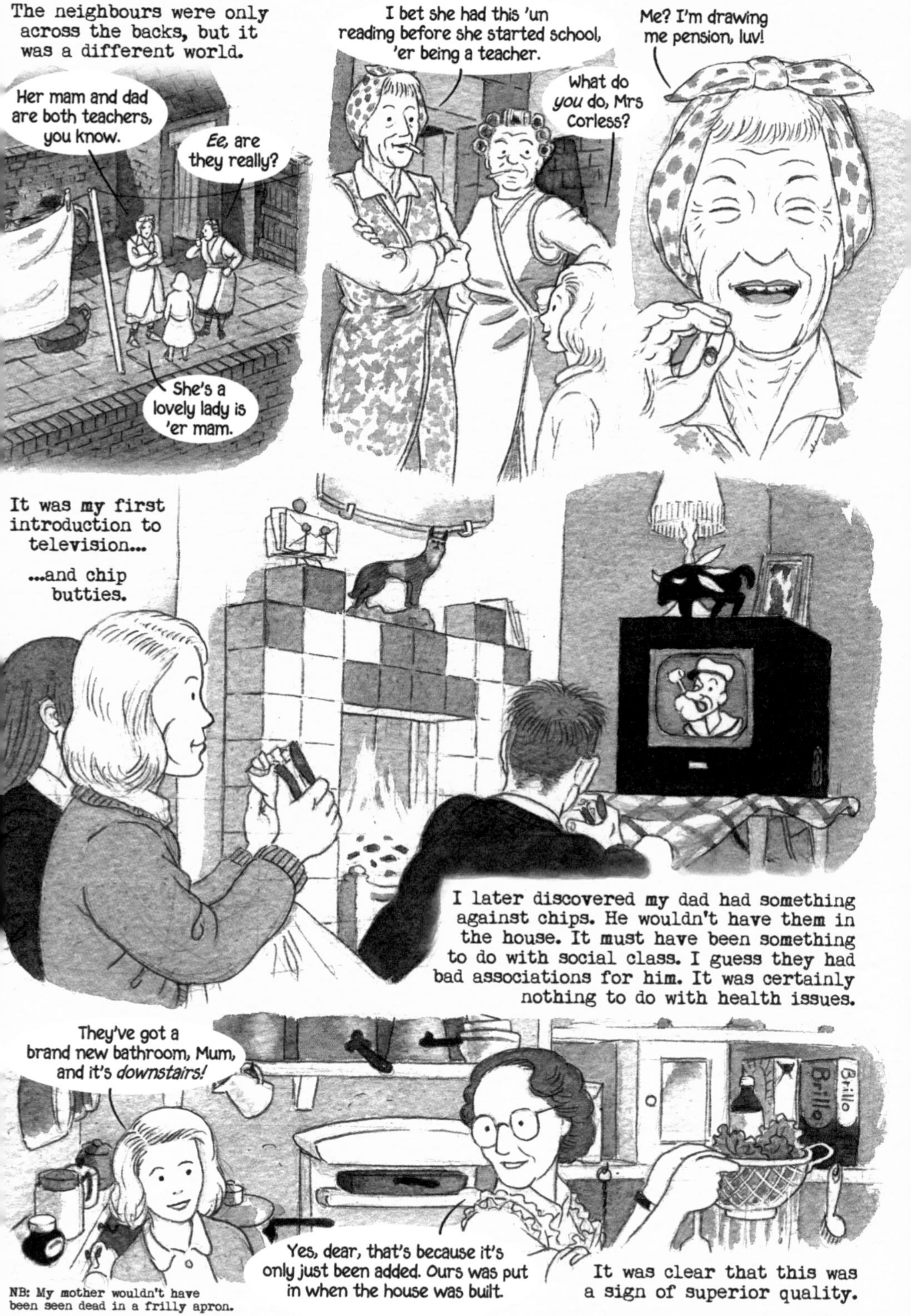

The neighbours were only across the backs, but it was a different world.
Her mam and dad are both teachers, you know.
Ee, are they really?
She's a lovely lady is 'er mam.
I bet she had this 'un reading before she started school, 'er being a teacher.
What do *you* do, Mrs Corless?
Me? I'm drawing me pension, luv!
It was my first introduction to television...
...and chip butties.
I later discovered my dad had something against chips. He wouldn't have them in the house. It must have been something to do with social class. I guess they had bad associations for him. It was certainly nothing to do with health issues.
They've got a brand new bathroom, Mum, and it's *downstairs!*
Brillo
Brillo
Yes, dear, that's because it's only just been added. Ours was put in when the house was built.
It was clear that this was a sign of superior quality.
NB: My mother wouldn't have been seen dead in a frilly apron.

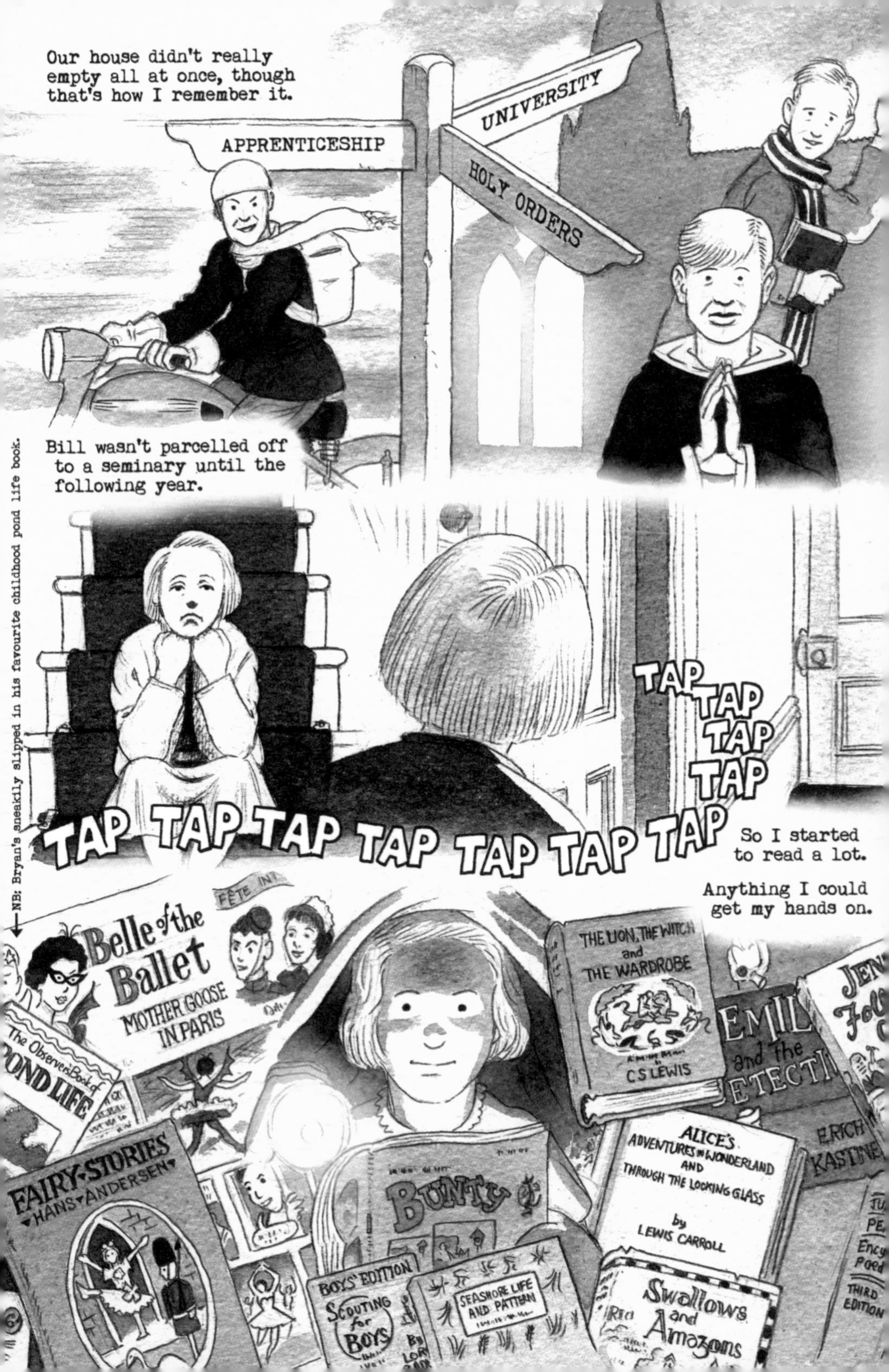

Our house didn't really empty all at once, though that's how I remember it.
APPRENTICESHIP
UNIVERSITY
HOLY ORDERS
Bill wasn't parcelled off to a seminary until the following year.
TAP TAP TAP TAP
TAP TAP TAP TAP TAP TAP TAP
So I started to read a lot.
Anything I could get my hands on.
Belle of the Ballet
MOTHER GOOSE IN PARIS
The Observer's Book of POND LIFE
THE LION, THE WITCH and THE WARDROBE
C S LEWIS
EMIL and the
ERICH KASTNER
FAIRY-STORIES
HANS ANDERSEN
BUNTY
ALICE'S ADVENTURES IN WONDERLAND AND THROUGH THE LOOKING GLASS
by LEWIS CARROLL
BOYS' EDITION
SCOUTING for BOYS
SEASHORE LIFE AND PATTERN
Swallows and Amazons
THIRD EDITION
NB: Bryan's sneakily slipped in his favourite childhood pond life book.

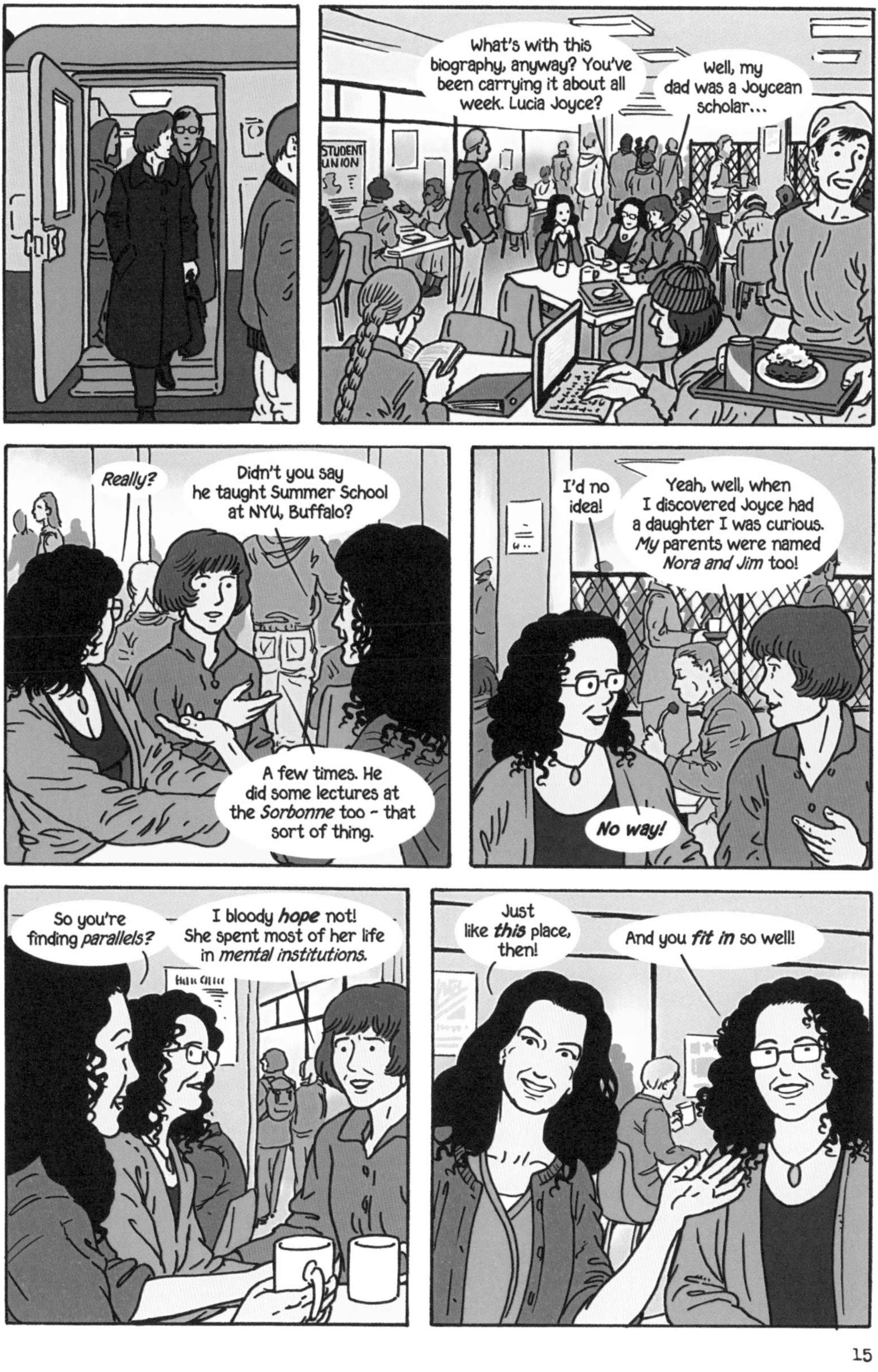
STUDENT UNION
What's with this biography, anyway? You've been carrying it about all week. Lucia Joyce?
Well, my dad was a Joycean scholar…
Really?
Didn't you say he taught Summer School at NYU, Buffalo?
A few times. He did some lectures at the *Sorbonne* too – that sort of thing.
I'd no idea!
Yeah, well, when I discovered Joyce had a daughter I was curious. *My* parents were named *Nora and Jim* too!
No way!
So you're finding *parallels?*
I bloody ***hope*** not! She spent most of her life in *mental institutions.*
Just like ***this*** place, then!
And you ***fit in*** so well!

Parallels with Lucia Joyce? We grew up
in different eras. There were few careers
for girls to aspire to in those days.

Splendid hats, though. Here
she is with her aunt Eva.

Trieste 1910

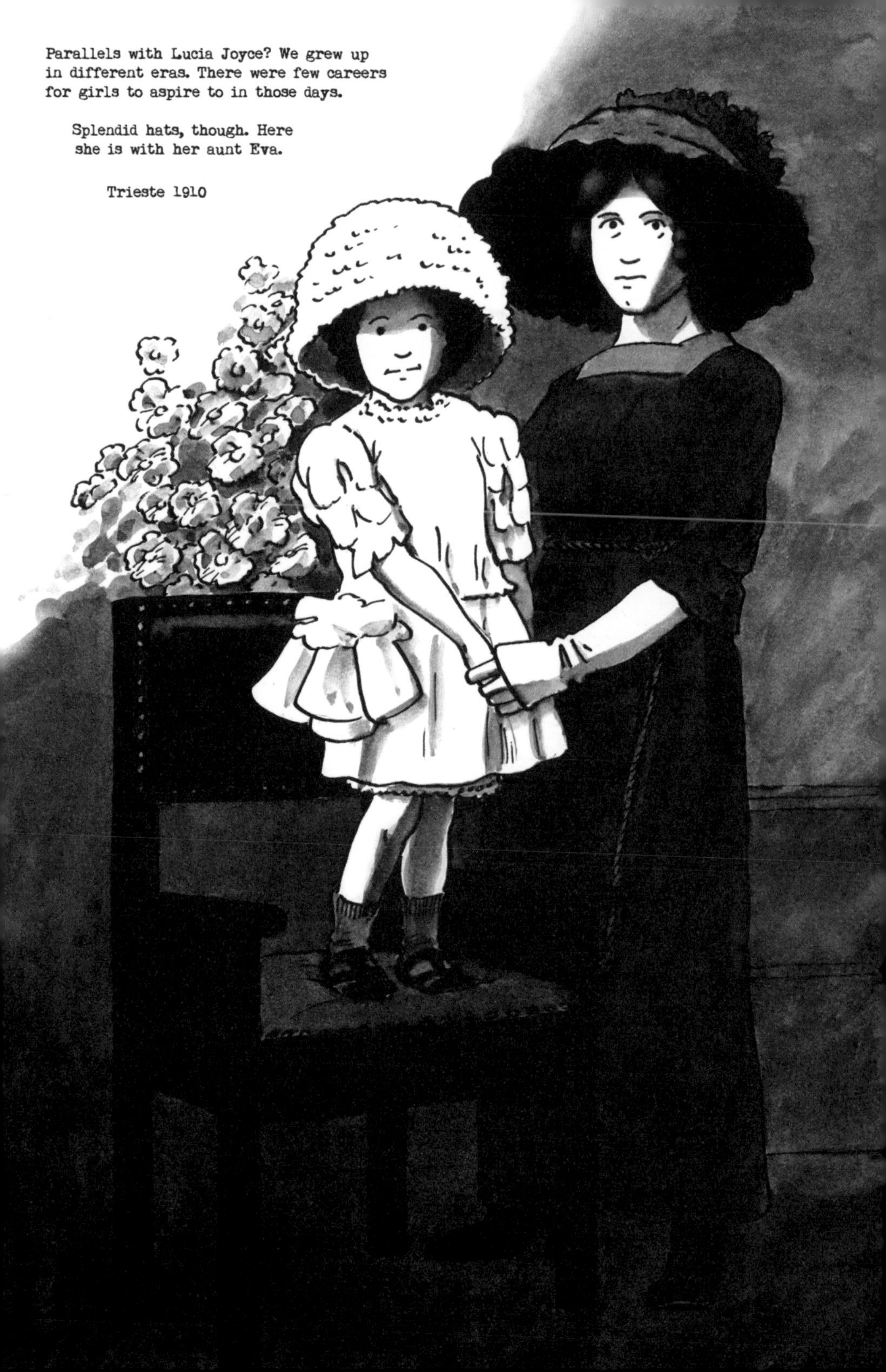

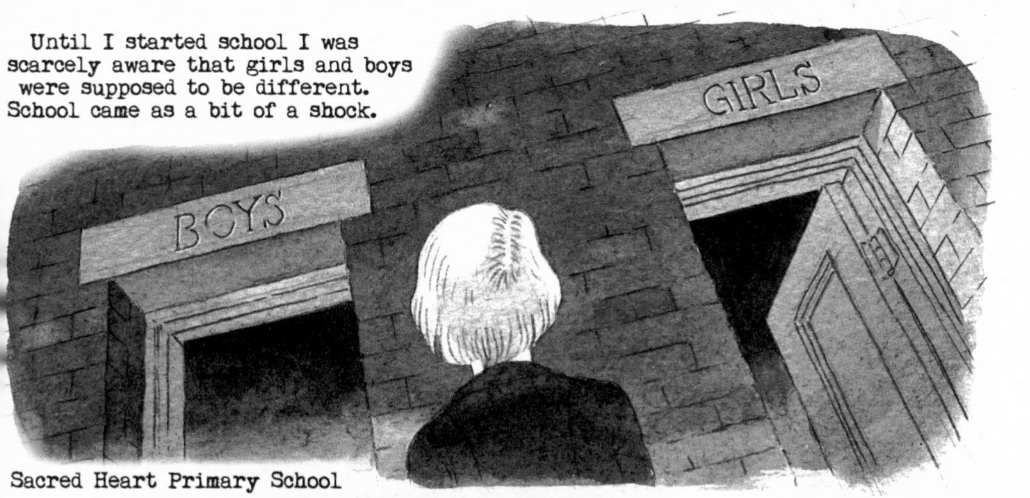
Until I started school I was scarcely aware that girls and boys were supposed to be different. School came as a bit of a shock.
GIRLS
BOYS

Sacred Heart Primary School

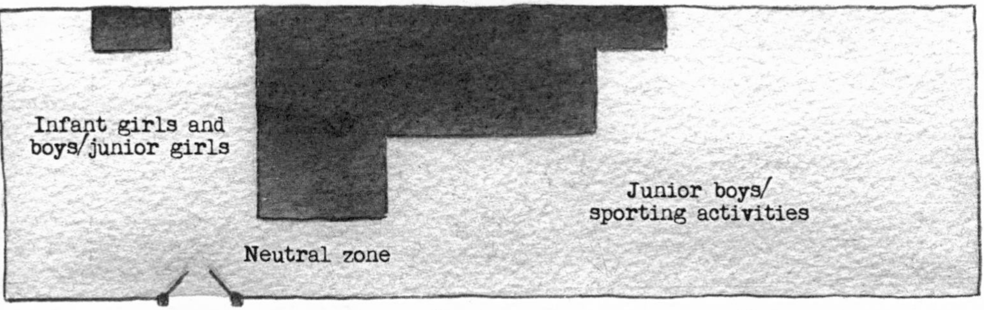
Infant girls and boys/junior girls
Junior boys/ sporting activities
Neutral zone

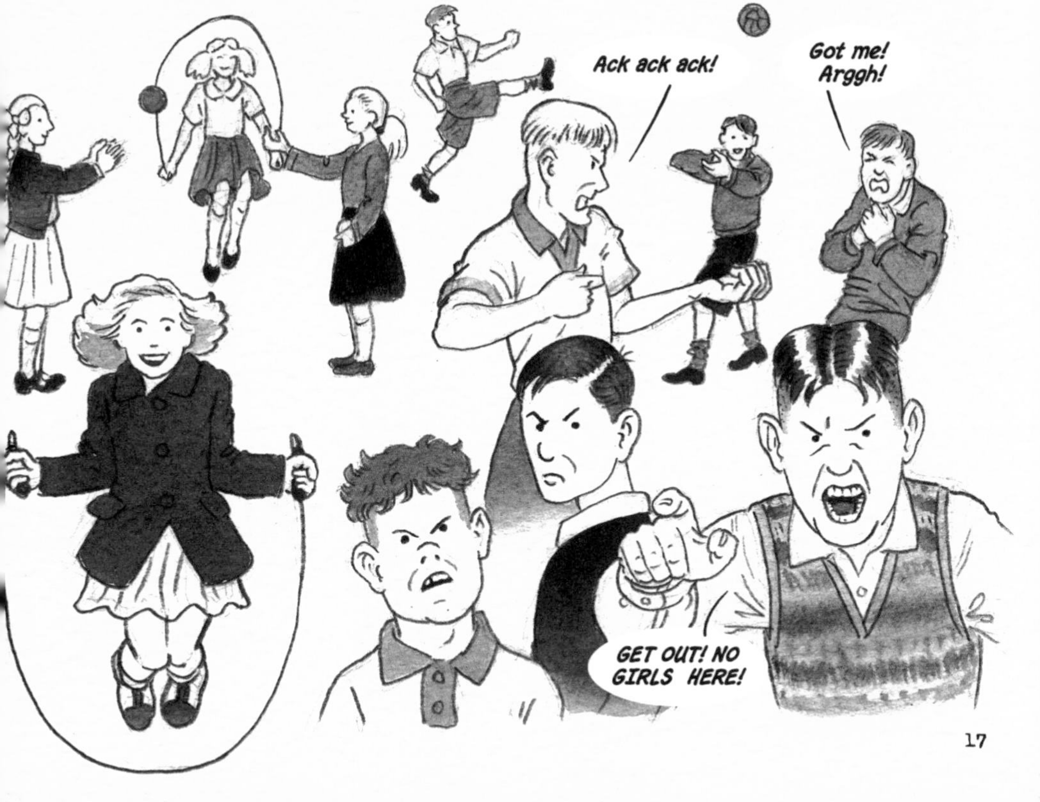
Ack ack ack!
Got me! Arggh!
GET OUT! NO GIRLS HERE!

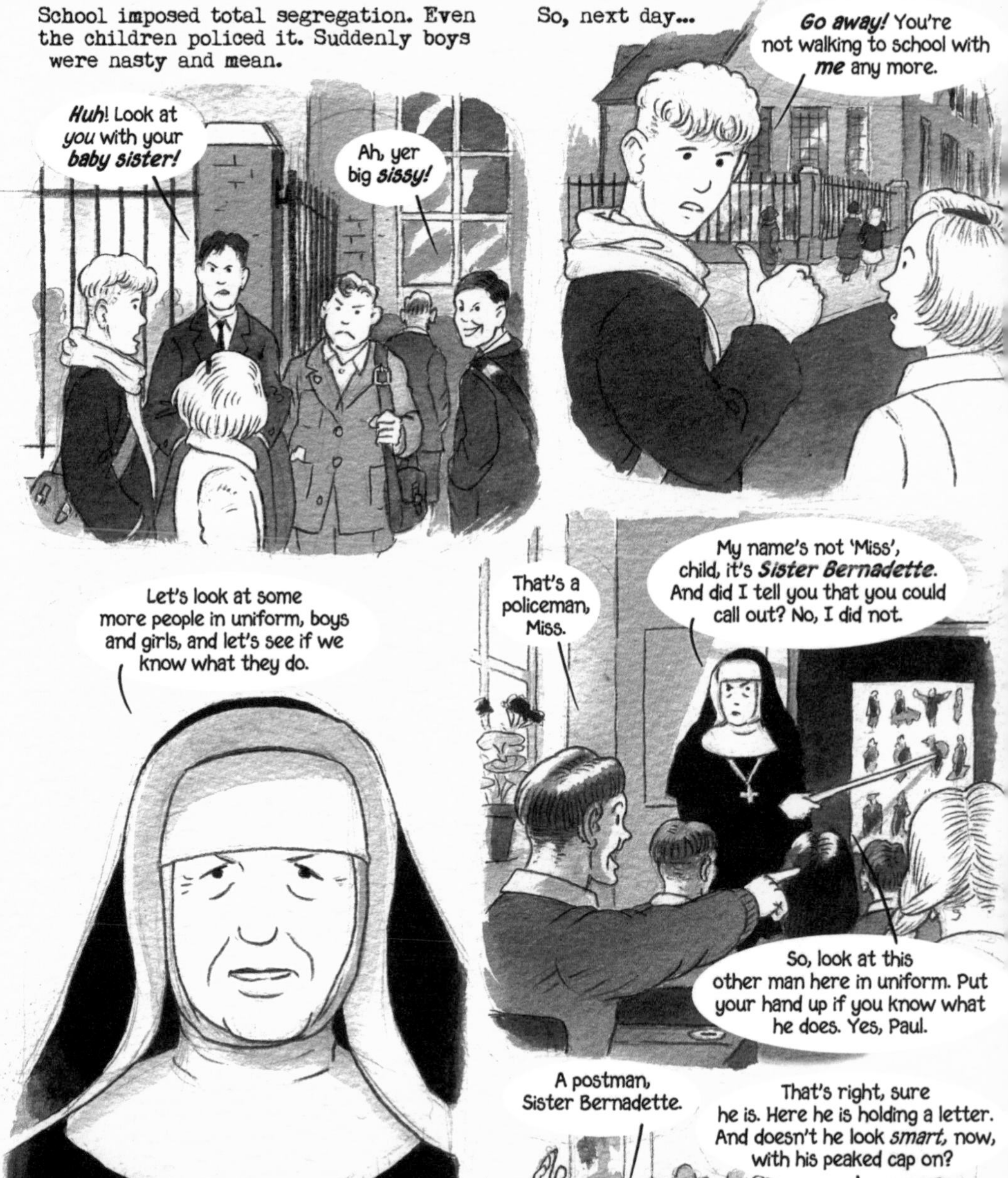
School imposed total segregation. Even the children policed it. Suddenly boys were nasty and mean.
Huh! Look at *you* with your *baby sister!*
Ah, yer big *sissy!*
So, next day...
Go away! You're not walking to school with *me* any more.
Let's look at some more people in uniform, boys and girls, and let's see if we know what they do.
That's a policeman, Miss.
My name's not 'Miss', child, it's *Sister Bernadette*. And did I tell you that you could call out? No, I did not.
So, look at this other man here in uniform. Put your hand up if you know what he does. Yes, Paul.
A postman, Sister Bernadette.
That's right, sure he is. Here he is holding a letter. And doesn't he look *smart,* now, with his peaked cap on?
Now, boys and girls, I wonder what *you* want to be when you grow up? *Douglas?* What about *you?*

NB: Bryan's wrong again. In my school boys were seated on one side of the classroom, the girls on the other. Always.

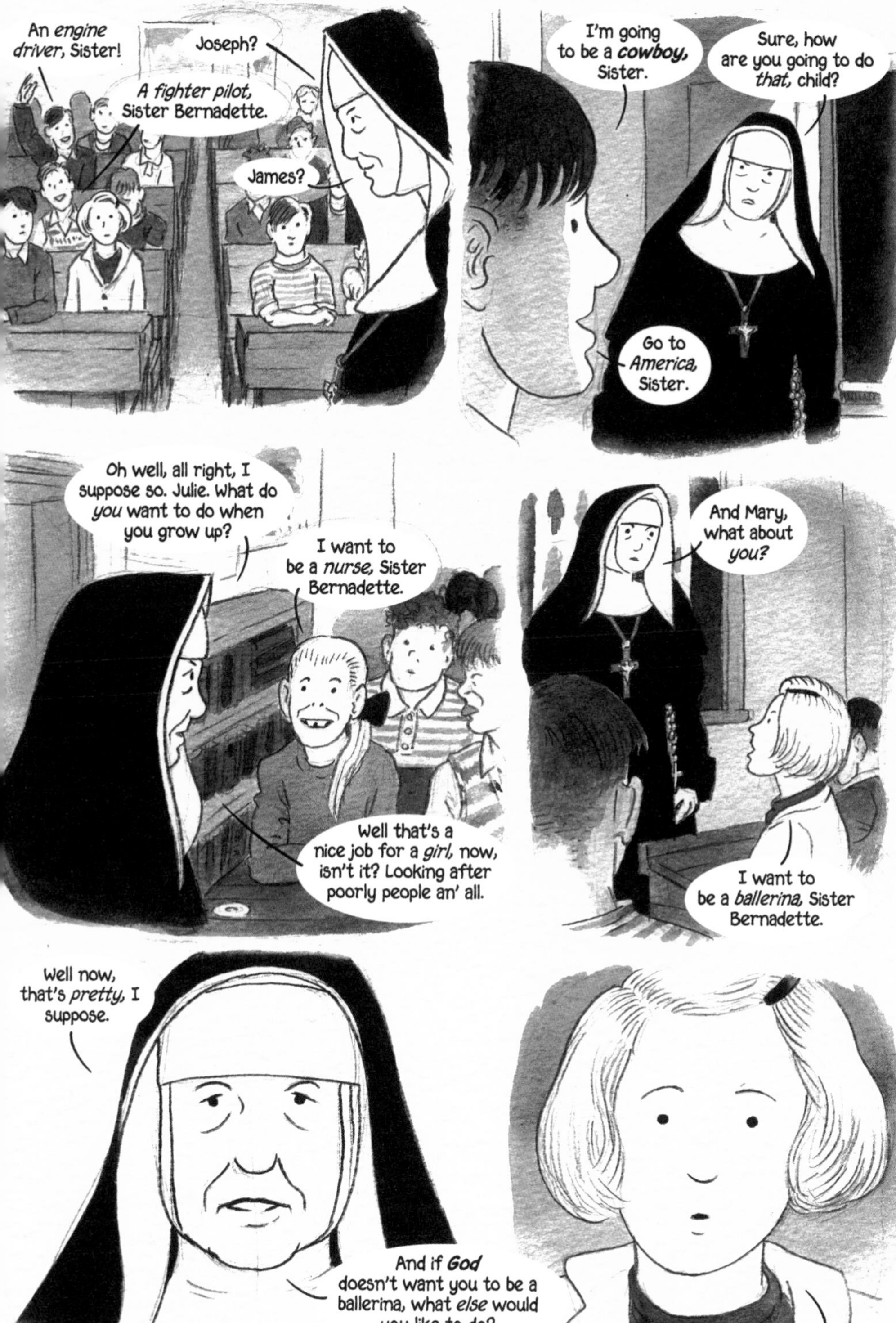
An *engine driver*, Sister!
Joseph?
A fighter pilot, Sister Bernadette.
James?
I'm going to be a ***cowboy***, Sister.
Sure, how are you going to do *that*, child?
Go to *America*, Sister.
Oh well, all right, I suppose so. Julie. What do *you* want to do when you grow up?
I want to be a *nurse*, Sister Bernadette.
Well that's a nice job for a *girl*, now, isn't it? Looking after poorly people an' all.
And Mary, what about *you?*
I want to be a *ballerina*, Sister Bernadette.
Well now, that's *pretty*, I suppose.
And if ***God*** doesn't want you to be a ballerina, what *else* would you like to do?
Draw a pension, Sister.

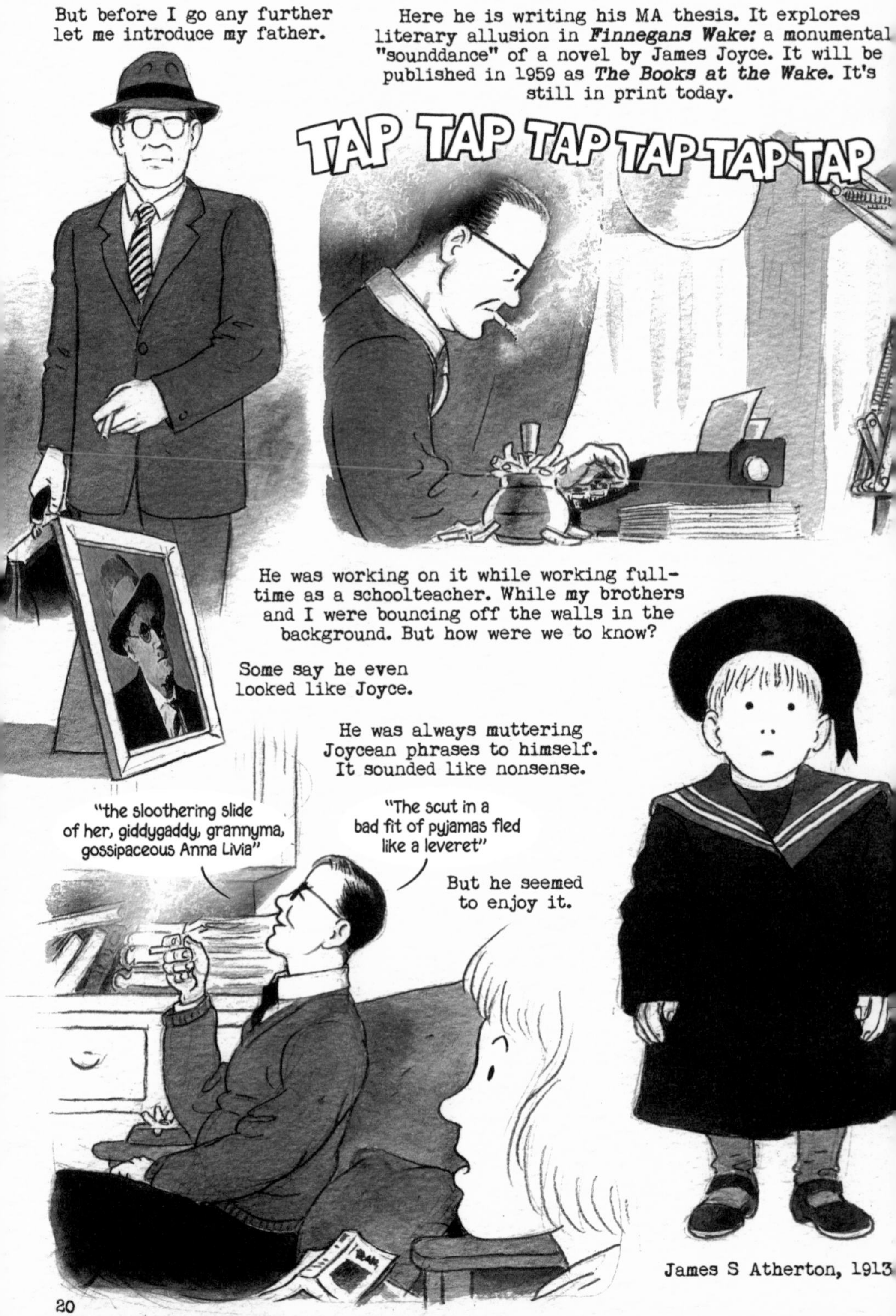
But before I go any further let me introduce my father.
Here he is writing his MA thesis. It explores literary allusion in *Finnegans Wake:* a monumental "sounddance" of a novel by James Joyce. It will be published in 1959 as *The Books at the Wake.* It's still in print today.
TAP TAP TAP TAP TAP TAP
He was working on it while working full-time as a schoolteacher. While my brothers and I were bouncing off the walls in the background. But how were we to know?
Some say he even looked like Joyce.
He was always muttering Joycean phrases to himself. It sounded like nonsense.
"the sloothering slide of her, giddygaddy, grannyma, gossipaceous Anna Livia"
"The scut in a bad fit of pyjamas fled like a leveret"
But he seemed to enjoy it.
James S Atherton, 1913

He grew up over the family shop. Him and three sisters.

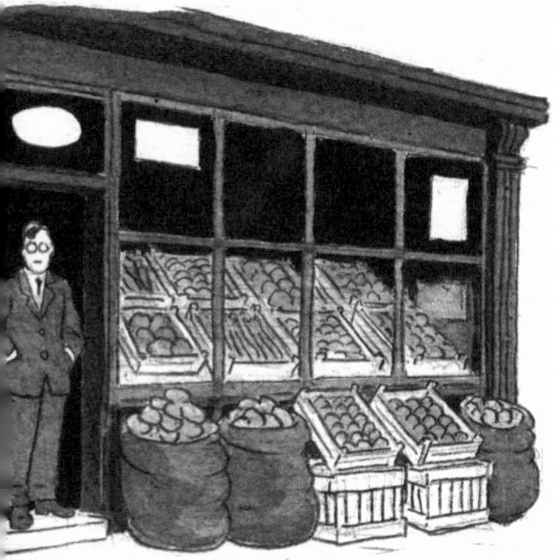

Darlington Street, Wigan.

George Orwell took rooms close by, briefly, when he was researching *The Road to Wigan Pier* in the 1930s.

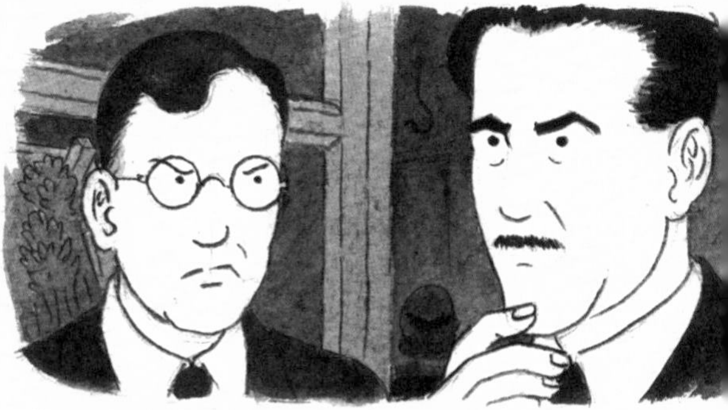

Dad took an instant dislike to the man. He claimed that Orwell had moved to another street in order to research the living conditions of the working-class poor...

...because their street wasn't squalid enough. Hm.

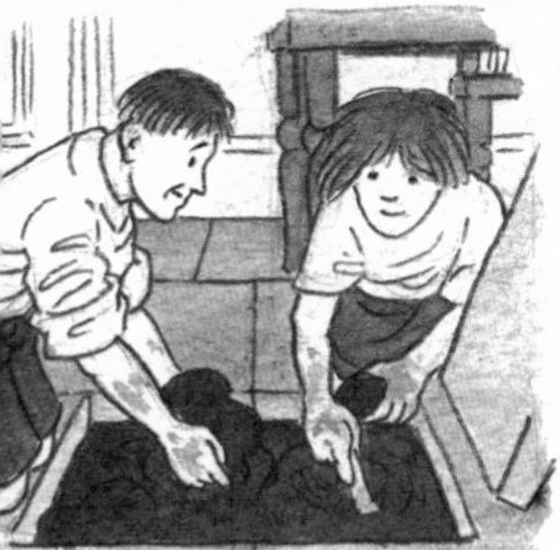

This was the part of town where kids still played mud pies indoors in the 1950s.

Later, the shop belonged to his eldest sister and her husband - my Auntie Nellie and Uncle Ted.

I sometimes helped in the shop but it was creepy. The cellar was damp and dark. I dreaded going there for lettuces.

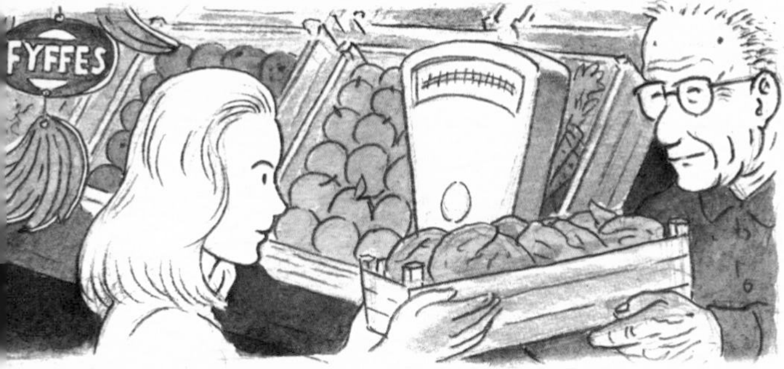
FYFFES

The kitchen was always warm.

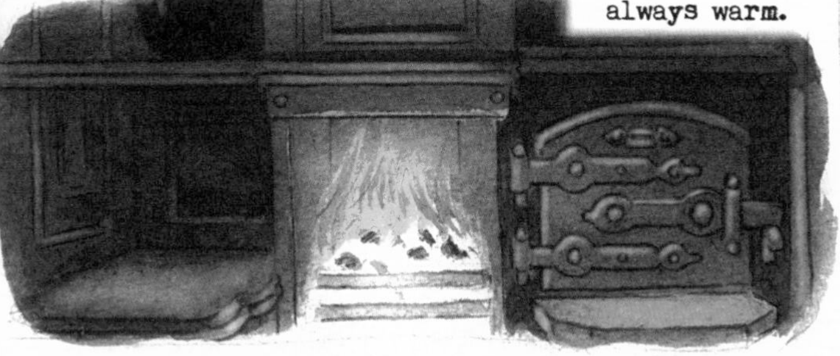

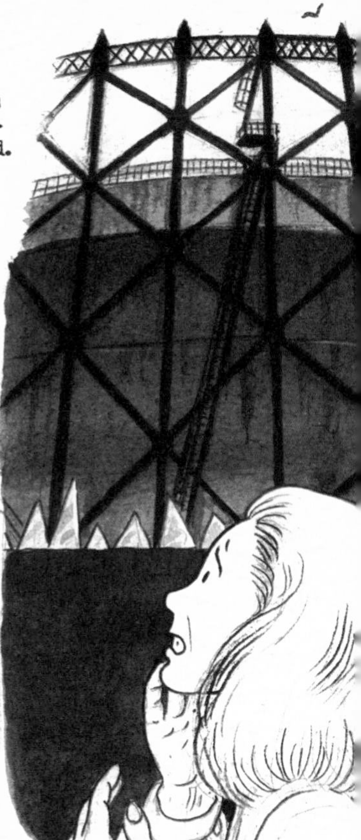

Creepy? On one side was the gas works, on the other the abbatoir.

The street was transformed when our procession went down it on the annual "Walking Day" - the traditional Lancashire church parade.

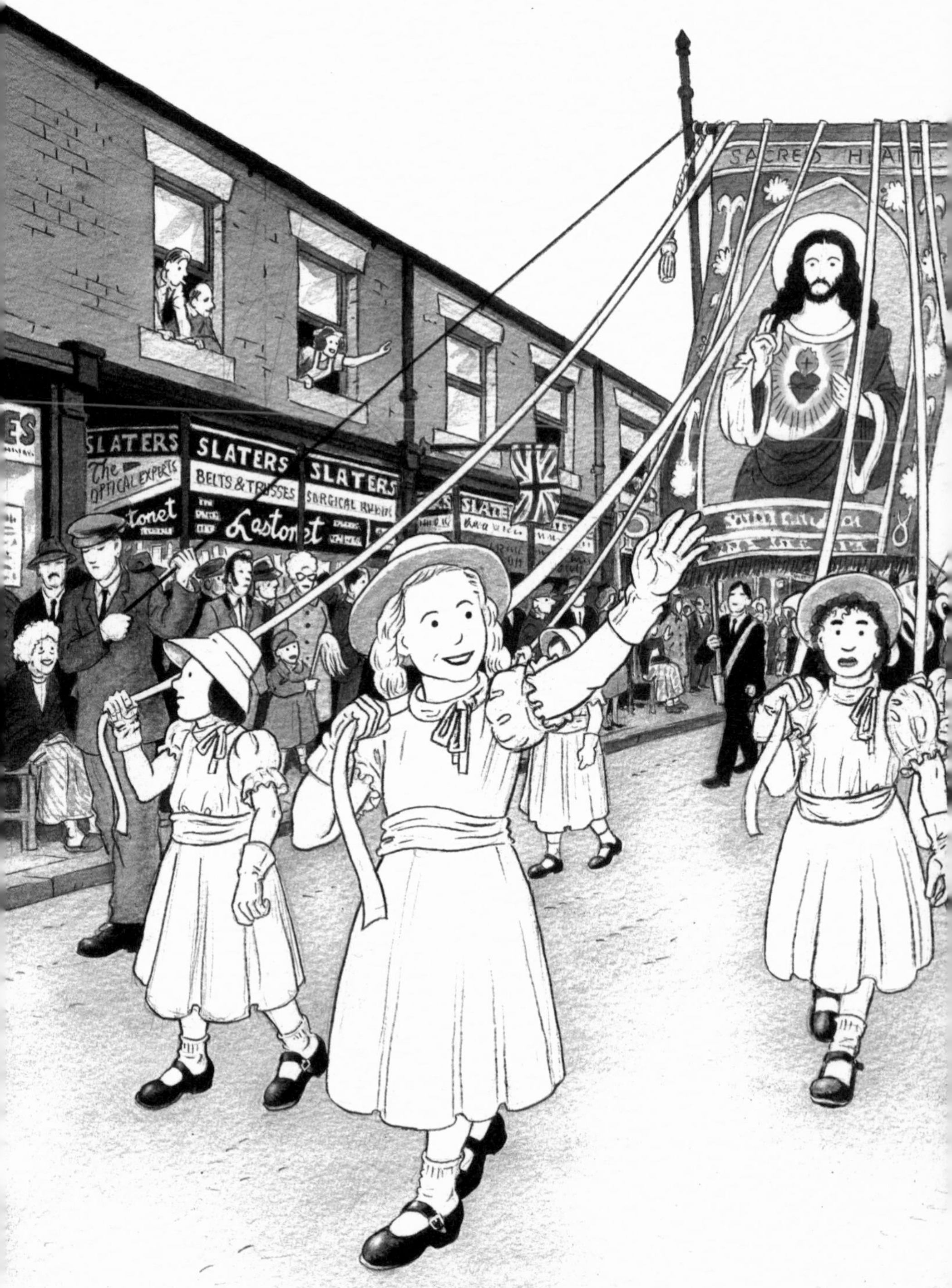
SACRED HEART
SLATERS
The OPTICAL EXPERTS
SLATERS
BELTS & TRUSSES
SLATERS

Books at the Wake was followed by further studies of Irish literature, mostly on Joyce. Dad became known internationally as an eminent Joycean scholar.

When the publishers of the *Encyclopaedia Britannica* decided that the writer merited inclusion, it was my father they approached for the entry.

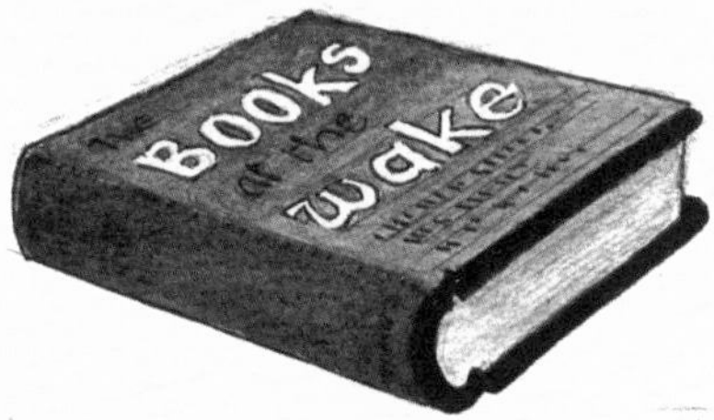

The Books at the Wake

"James Joyce's abilities as a novelist and his subtle yet frank portrayal of human nature coupled with his mastery of language and brilliant development of new literary methods have made him one of the most commanding influences on the writers of our time. Although originally banned in most countries..."

It's still used today, though the fulsome praise of his original opening paragraph has been edited out of later editions.

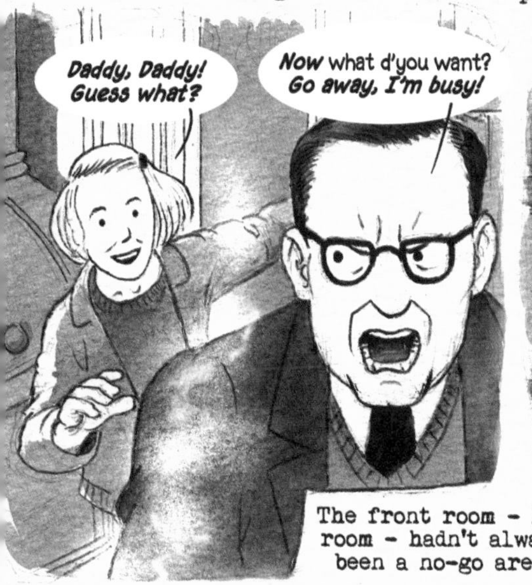

Daddy, Daddy! Guess what?
Now what d'you want? Go away, I'm busy!
The front room - *his* room - hadn't always been a no-go area.

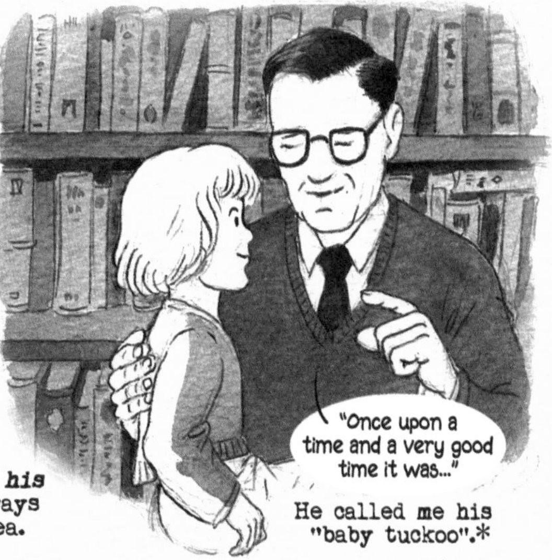

"Once upon a time and a very good time it was..."
He called me his "baby tuckoo".*

Under his desk was good for hide and seek.

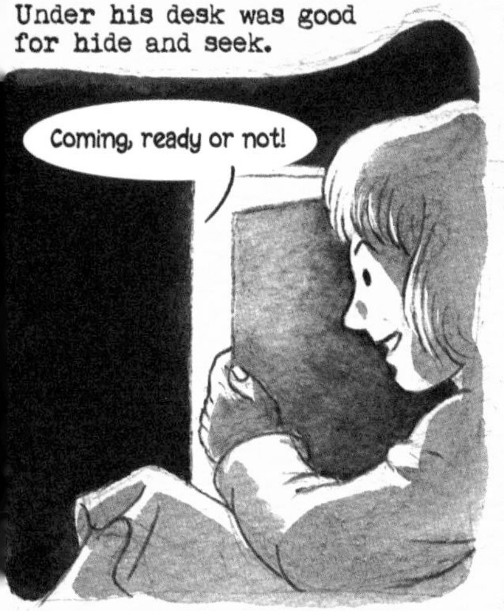

Coming, ready or not!

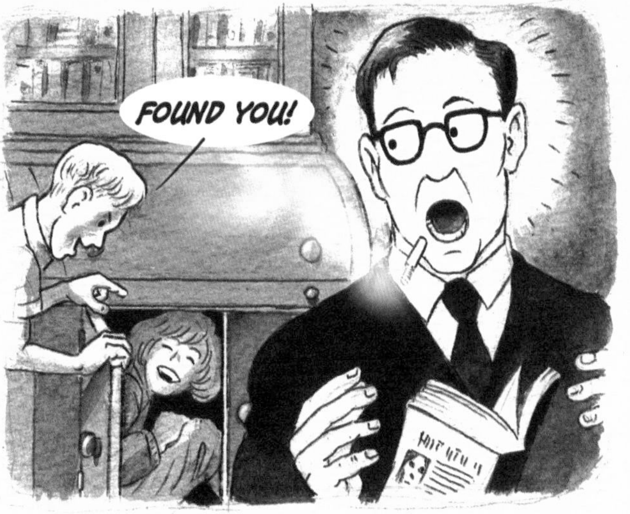

FOUND YOU!

* Joyce's *Portrait of the Artist as a Young Man* opens like this: "Once upon a time and a very good time it was there was a moocow coming down along the road and this moocow that was coming down along the road met a nicens little boy named baby tuckoo."

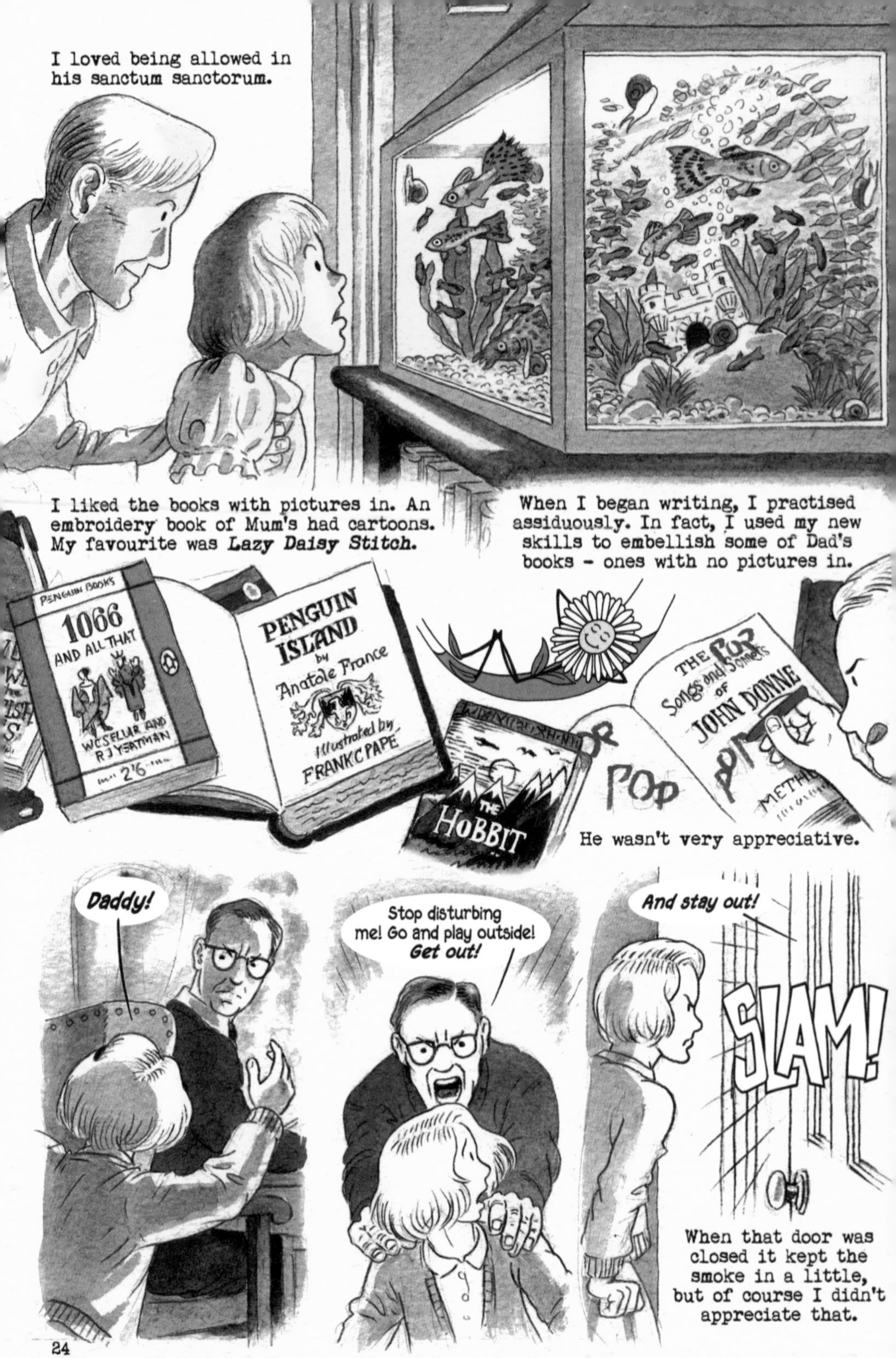

I loved being allowed in his sanctum sanctorum.
I liked the books with pictures in. An embroidery book of Mum's had cartoons. My favourite was *Lazy Daisy Stitch.*
PENGUIN BOOKS
1066 AND ALL THAT
W.C. SELLAR AND R.J. YEATMAN
2'6
PENGUIN ISLAND by Anatole France Illustrated by FRANK C PAPE
THE HOBBIT
When I began writing, I practised assiduously. In fact, I used my new skills to embellish some of Dad's books - ones with no pictures in.
THE Songs and Sonnets OF JOHN DONNE
POP
He wasn't very appreciative.
Daddy!
Stop disturbing me! Go and play outside! ***Get out!***
And stay out!
SLAM!
When that door was closed it kept the smoke in a little, but of course I didn't appreciate that.

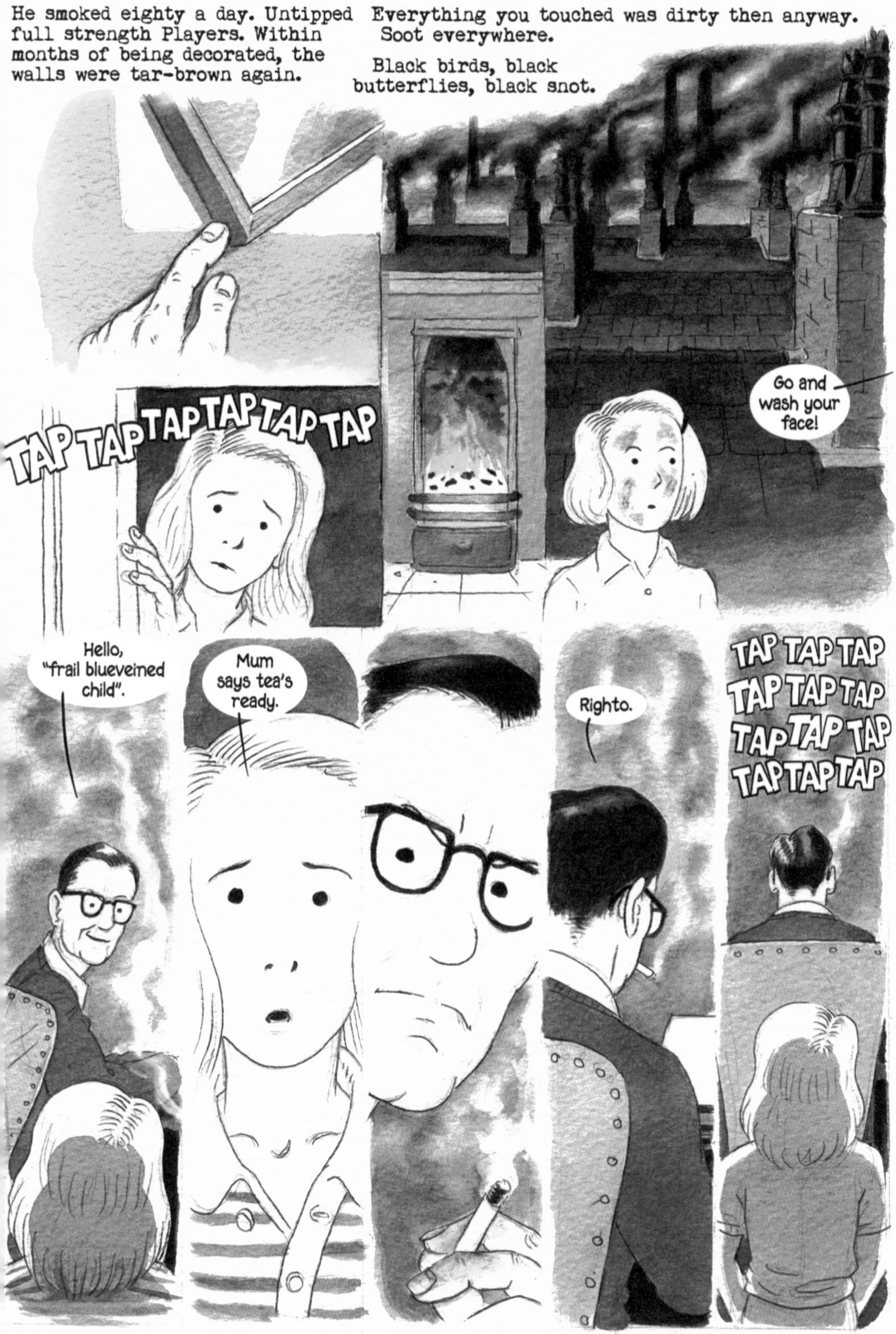

He smoked eighty a day. Untipped full strength Players. Within months of being decorated, the walls were tar-brown again.
Everything you touched was dirty then anyway. Soot everywhere.
Black birds, black butterflies, black snot.
TAP TAP TAP TAP TAP TAP
Go and wash your face!
Hello, "frail blueveined child".
Mum says tea's ready.
Righto.
TAP TAP TAP TAP TAP TAP TAP TAP TAP TAP TAP TAP

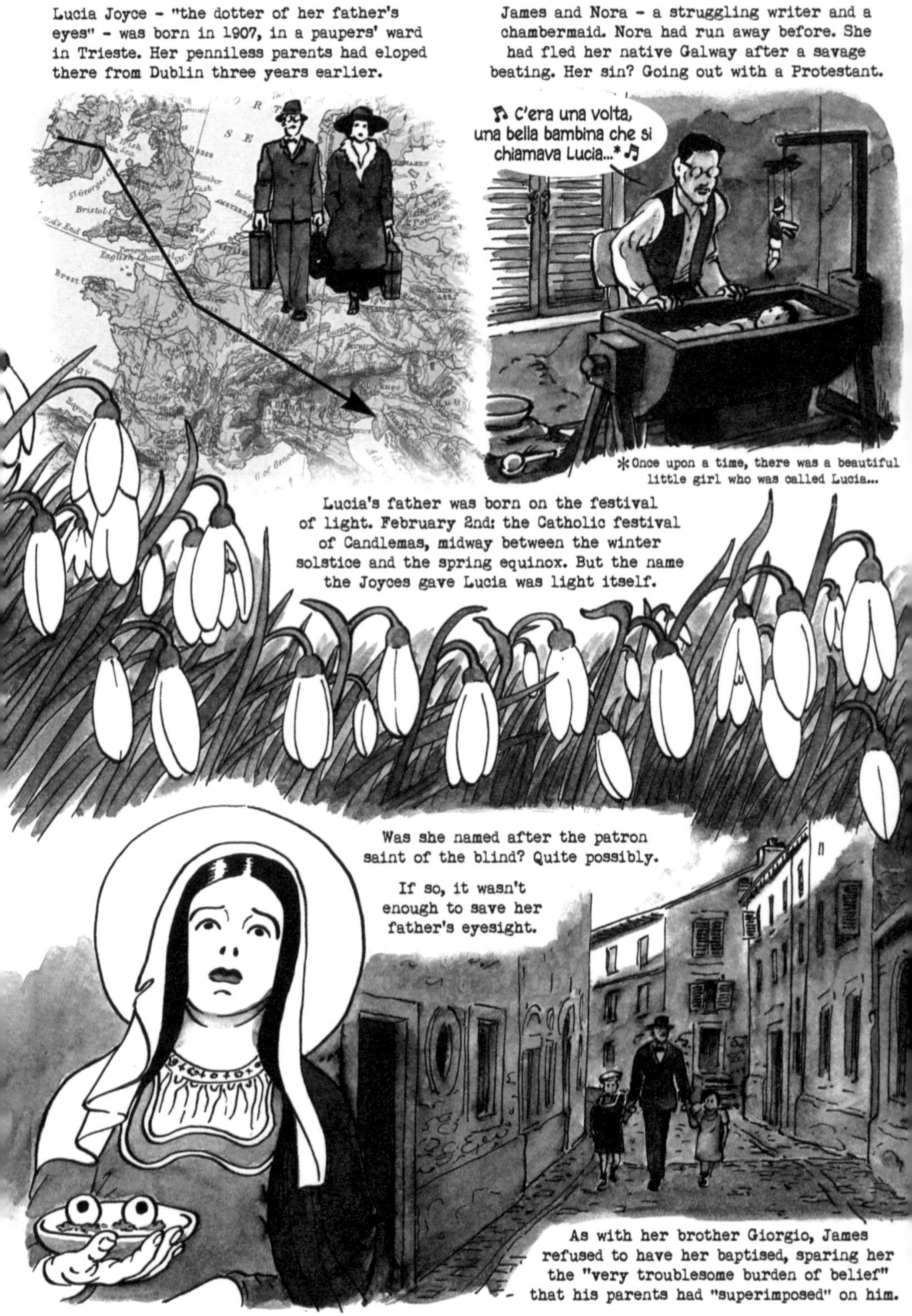
Lucia Joyce - "the dotter of her father's eyes" - was born in 1907, in a paupers' ward in Trieste. Her penniless parents had eloped there from Dublin three years earlier.
James and Nora - a struggling writer and a chambermaid. Nora had run away before. She had fled her native Galway after a savage beating. Her sin? Going out with a Protestant.
♫ C'era una volta, una bella bambina che si chiamava Lucia...* ♫
*Once upon a time, there was a beautiful little girl who was called Lucia...
Lucia's father was born on the festival of light. February 2nd: the Catholic festival of Candlemas, midway between the winter solstice and the spring equinox. But the name the Joyces gave Lucia was light itself.
Was she named after the patron saint of the blind? Quite possibly.
If so, it wasn't enough to save her father's eyesight.
As with her brother Giorgio, James refused to have her baptised, sparing her the "very troublesome burden of belief" that his parents had "superimposed" on him.

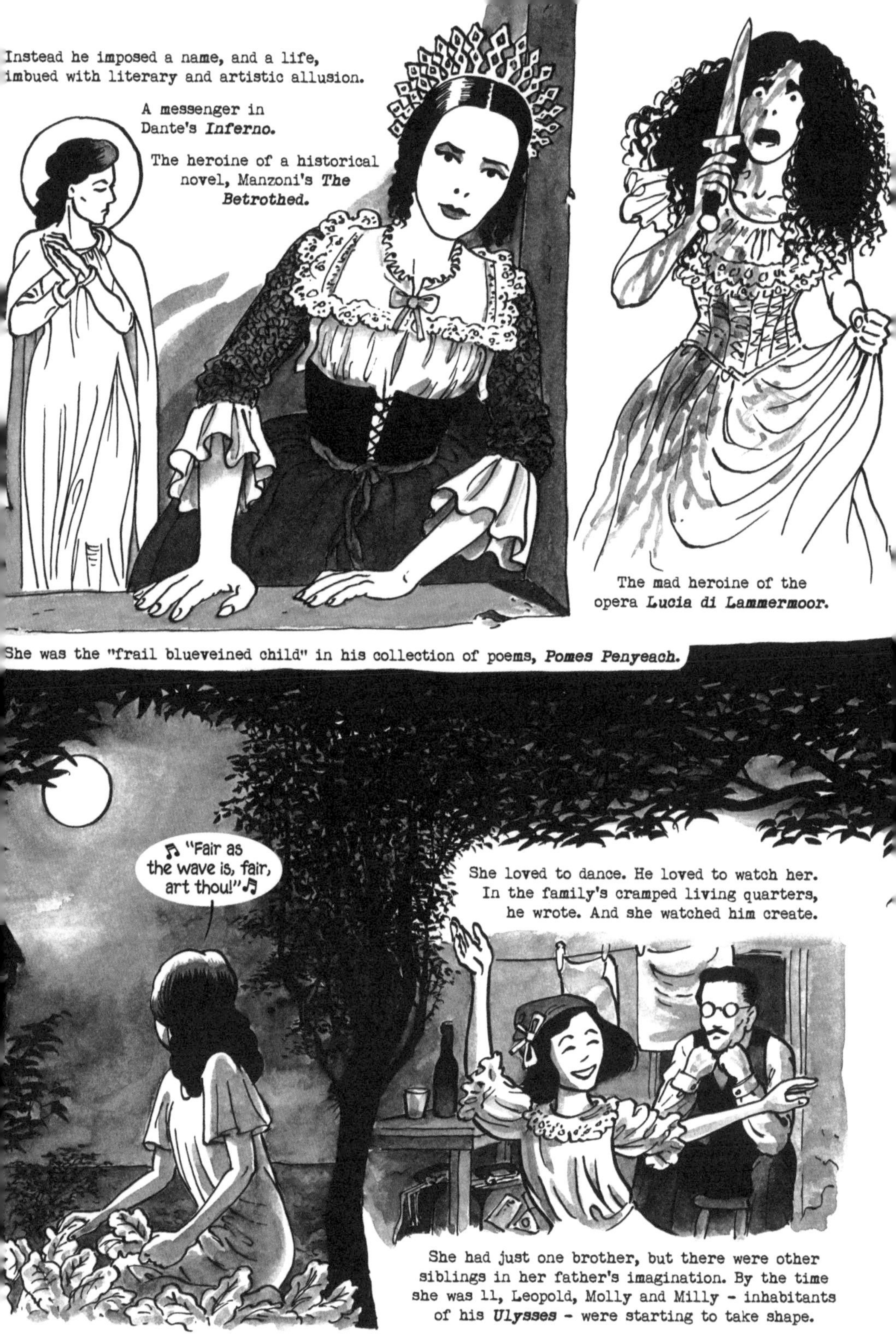
Instead he imposed a name, and a life, imbued with literary and artistic allusion.
A messenger in Dante's *Inferno.*
The heroine of a historical novel, Manzoni's *The Betrothed.*
The mad heroine of the opera *Lucia di Lammermoor.*
She was the "frail blueveined child" in his collection of poems, *Pomes Penyeach.*
♫ "Fair as the wave is, fair, art thou!" ♫
She loved to dance. He loved to watch her. In the family's cramped living quarters, he wrote. And she watched him create.
She had just one brother, but there were other siblings in her father's imagination. By the time she was 11, Leopold, Molly and Milly - inhabitants of his *Ulysses* - were starting to take shape.

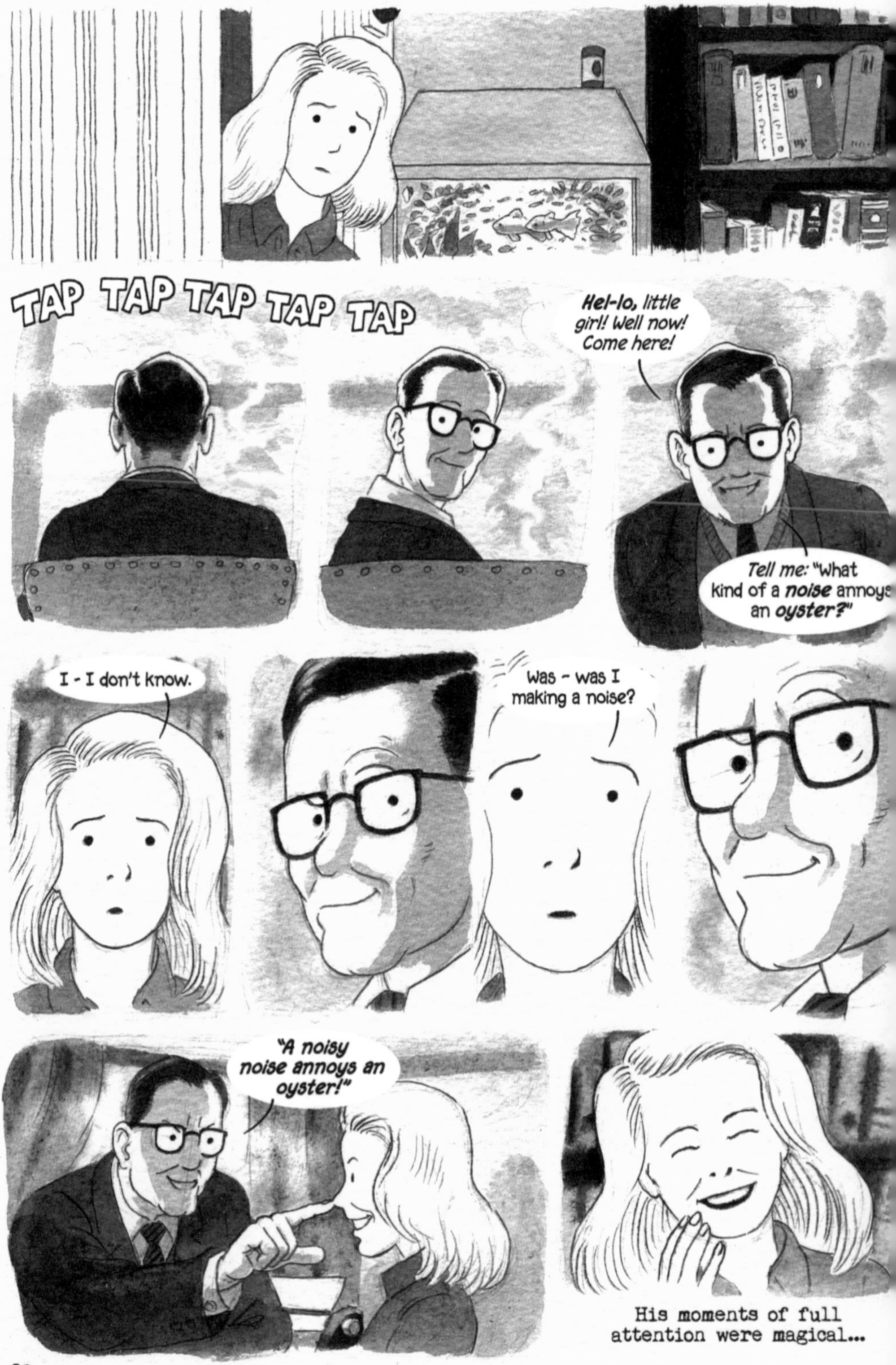
TAP TAP TAP TAP TAP
Hel-lo, little girl! Well now! Come here!
Tell me: "What kind of a noise annoys an oyster?"
I - I don't know.
Was - was I making a noise?
"A noisy noise annoys an oyster!"
His moments of full attention were magical...

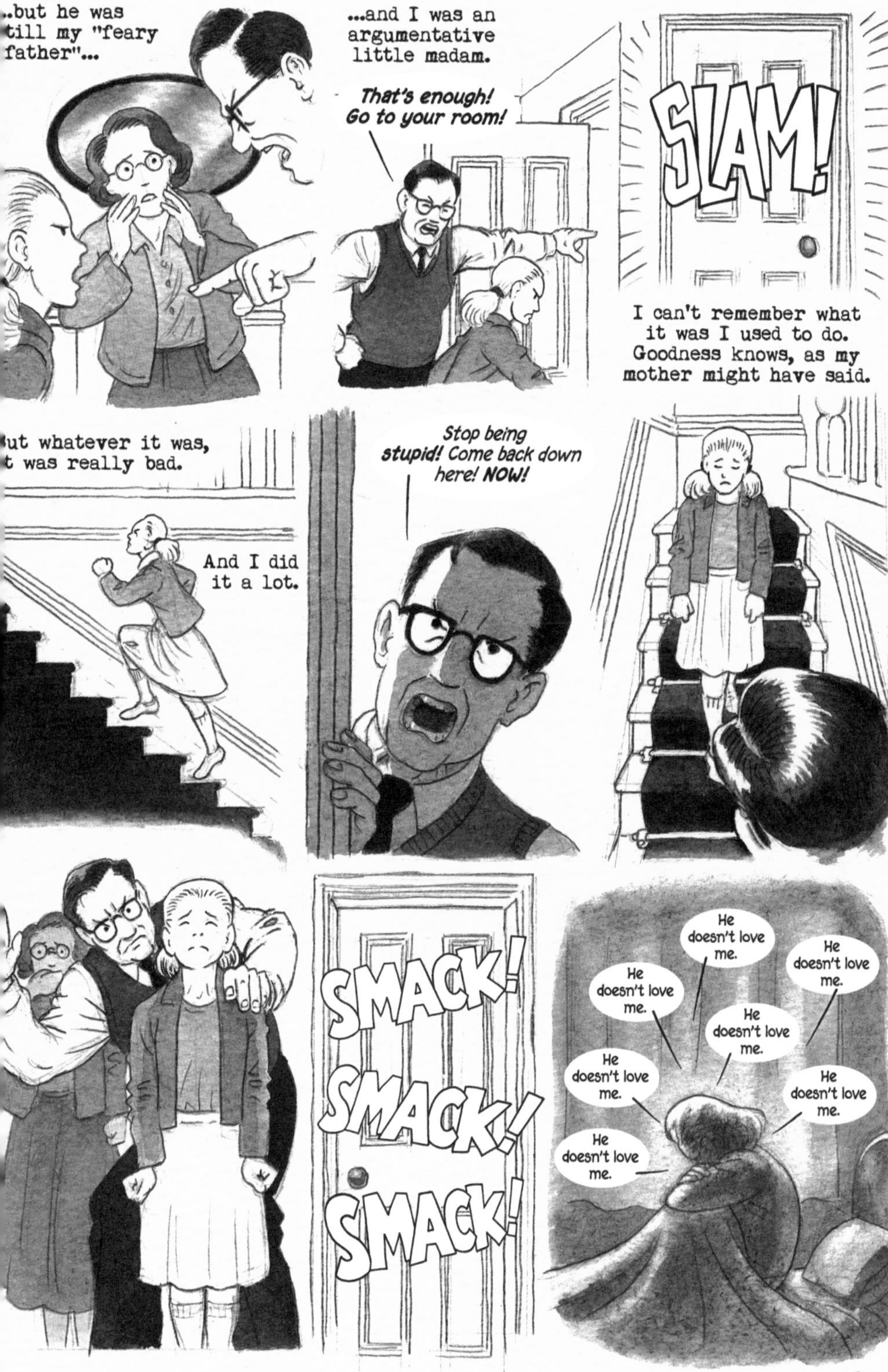
..but he was
till my "feary
father"...
...and I was an
argumentative
little madam.
That's enough!
Go to your room!
SLAM!
I can't remember what
it was I used to do.
Goodness knows, as my
mother might have said.
ut whatever it was,
t was really bad.
And I did
it a lot.
Stop being
stupid! Come back down
here! NOW!
SMACK!
SMACK!
SMACK!
He
doesn't love
me.
He
doesn't love
me.
He
doesn't love
me.
He
doesn't love
me.
He
doesn't love
me.
He
doesn't love
me.
He
doesn't love
me.

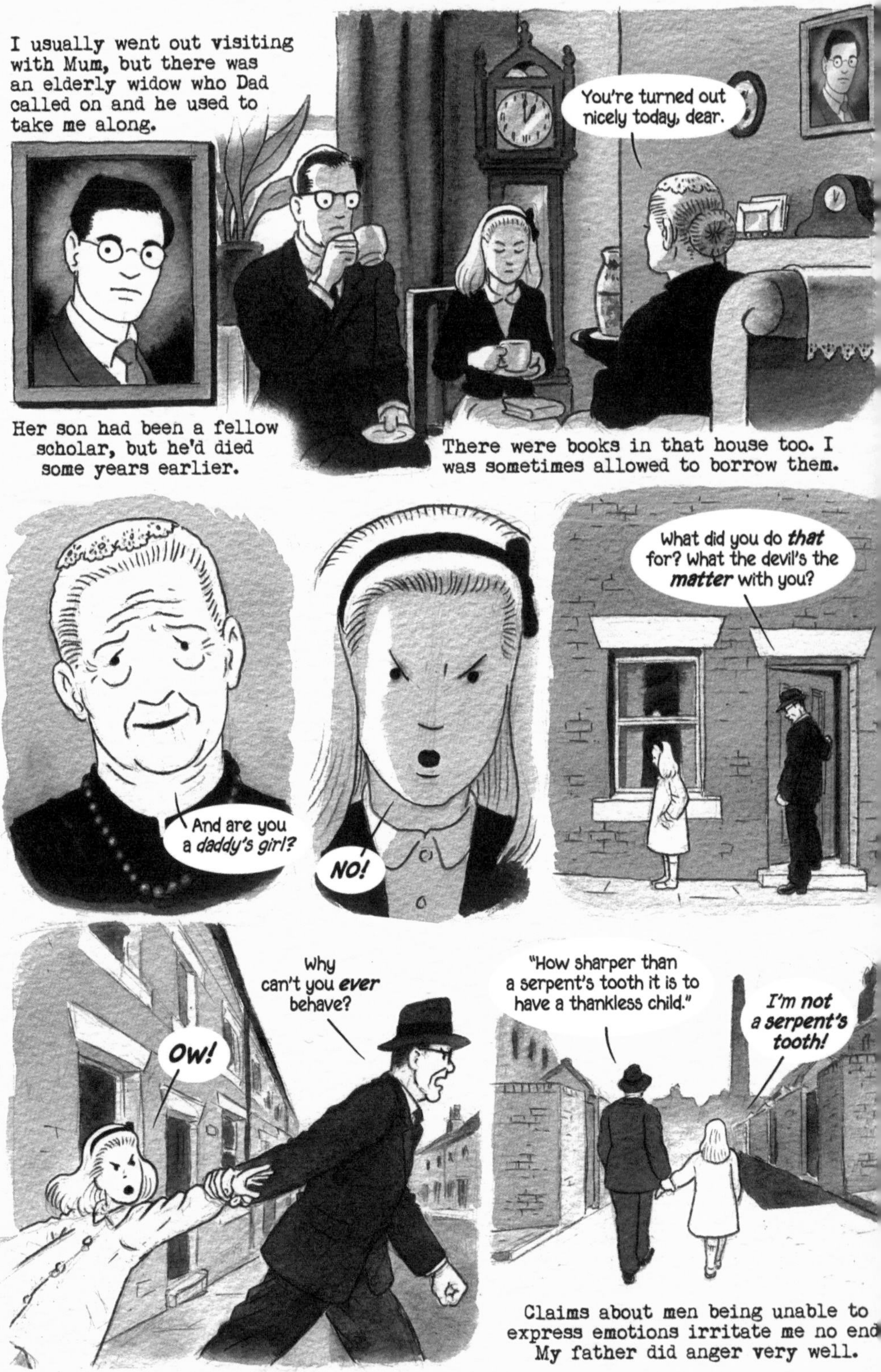
I usually went out visiting with Mum, but there was an elderly widow who Dad called on and he used to take me along.
You're turned out nicely today, dear.
Her son had been a fellow scholar, but he'd died some years earlier.
There were books in that house too. I was sometimes allowed to borrow them.
And are you a *daddy's girl?*
NO!
What did you do *that* for? What the devil's the *matter* with you?
OW!
Why can't you *ever* behave?
"How sharper than a serpent's tooth it is to have a thankless child."
I'm not a serpent's tooth!
Claims about men being unable to express emotions irritate me no end
My father did anger very well.

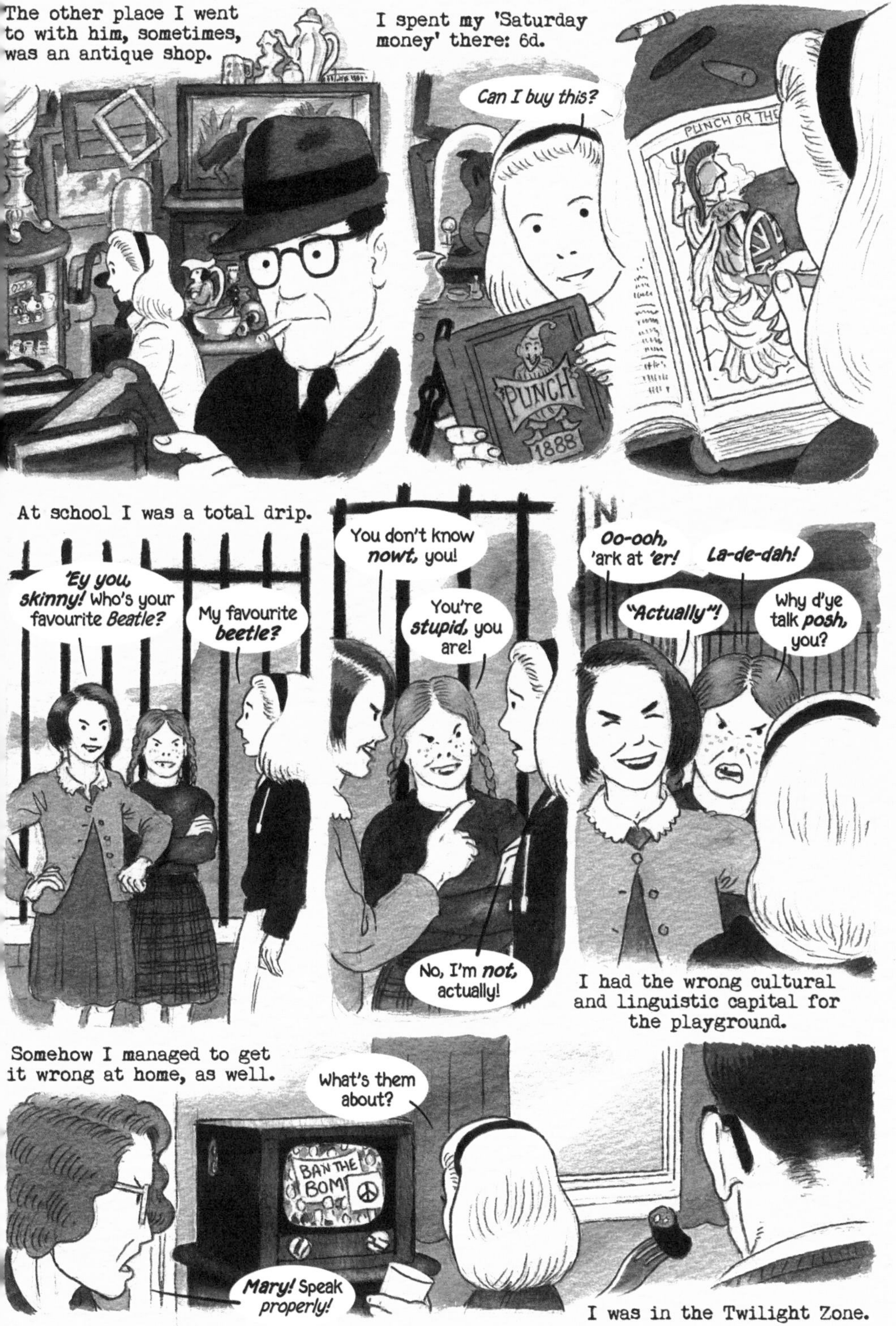
The other place I went to with him, sometimes, was an antique shop.
I spent my 'Saturday money' there: 6d.
Can I buy this?
PUNCH
1888
PUNCH OR THE
At school I was a total drip.
'Ey you, skinny! Who's your favourite Beatle?
My favourite beetle?
You don't know nowt, you!
You're stupid, you are!
No, I'm not, actually!
Oo-ooh, 'ark at 'er!
La-de-dah!
"Actually"!
Why d'ye talk posh, you?
I had the wrong cultural and linguistic capital for the playground.
Somehow I managed to get it wrong at home, as well.
What's them about?
BAN THE BOM
Mary! Speak properly!
I was in the Twilight Zone.

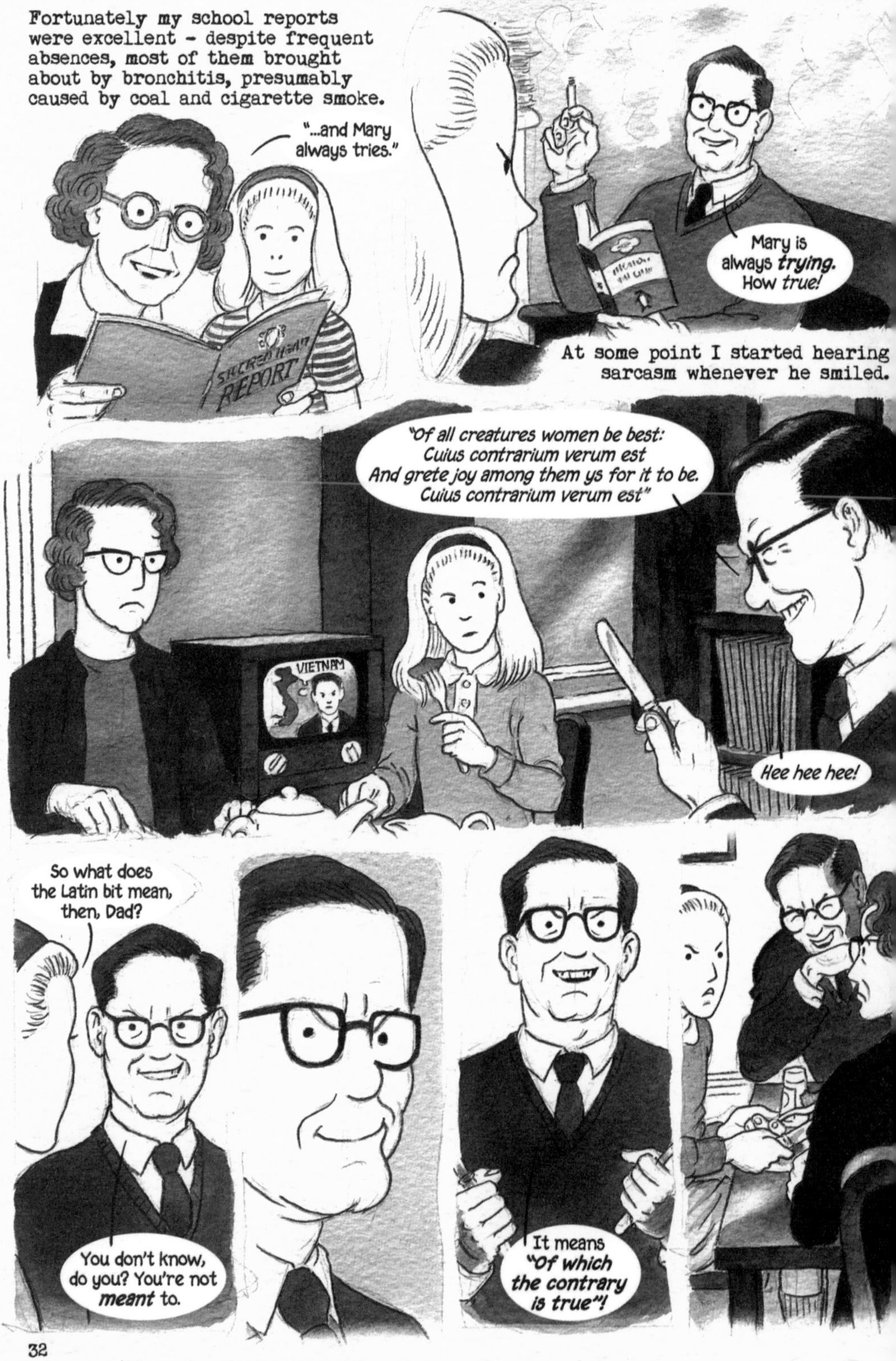
Fortunately my school reports were excellent - despite frequent absences, most of them brought about by bronchitis, presumably caused by coal and cigarette smoke.
"...and Mary always tries."
Mary is always *trying.* How *true!*
At some point I started hearing sarcasm whenever he smiled.
"Of all creatures women be best: Cuius contrarium verum est And grete joy among them ys for it to be. Cuius contrarium verum est"
VIETNAM
Hee hee hee!
So what does the Latin bit mean, then, Dad?
You don't know, do you? You're not *meant* to.
It means ***"Of which the contrary is true"!***

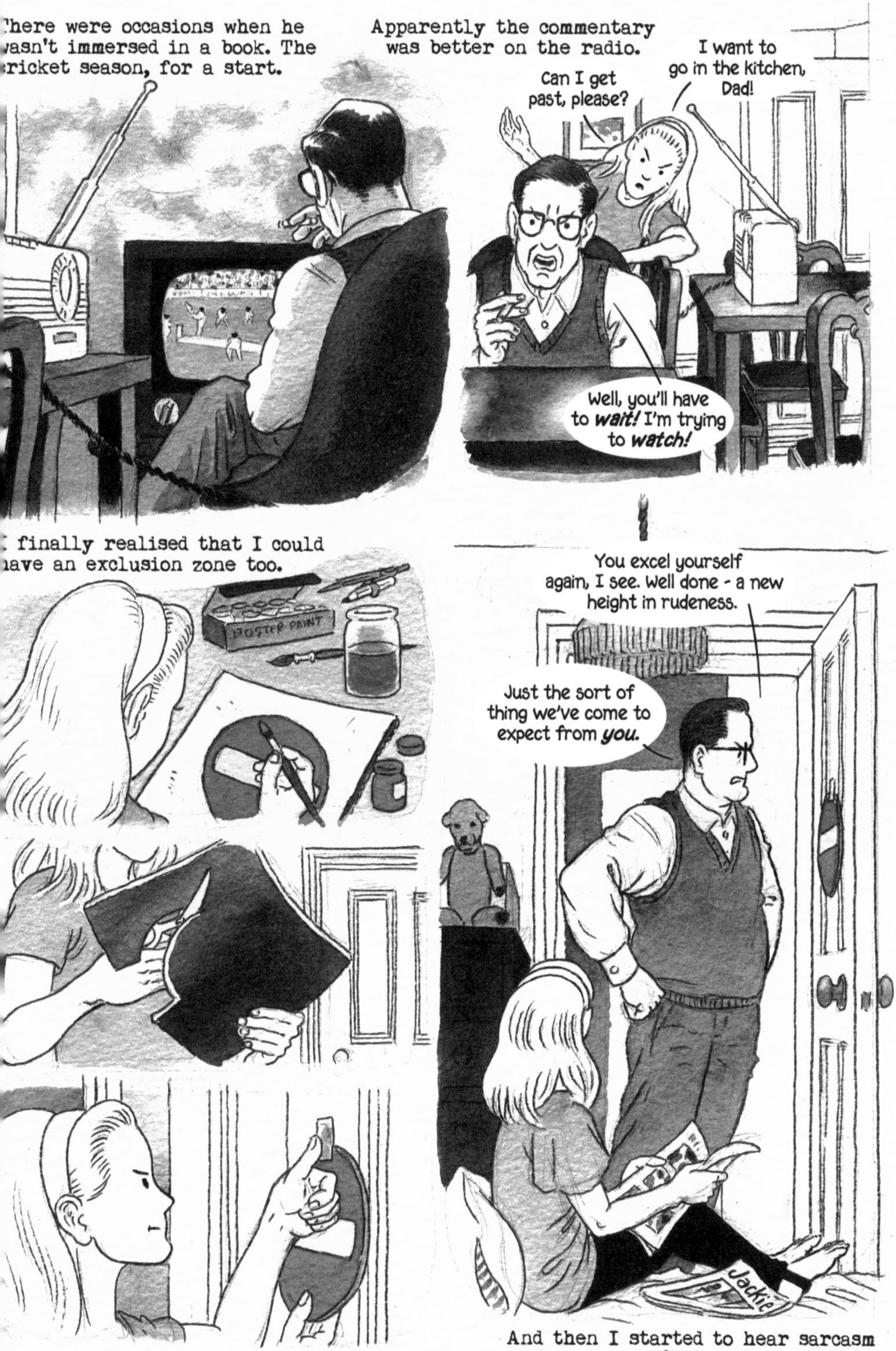
There were occasions when he wasn't immersed in a book. The cricket season, for a start.
Apparently the commentary was better on the radio.
Can I get past, please?
I want to go in the kitchen, Dad!
Well, you'll have to ***wait!*** I'm trying to ***watch!***
I finally realised that I could have an exclusion zone too.
POSTER PAINT
You excel yourself again, I see. Well done - a new height in rudeness.
Just the sort of thing we've come to expect from ***you.***
Jackie
And then I started to hear sarcasm when he wasn't smiling as well.

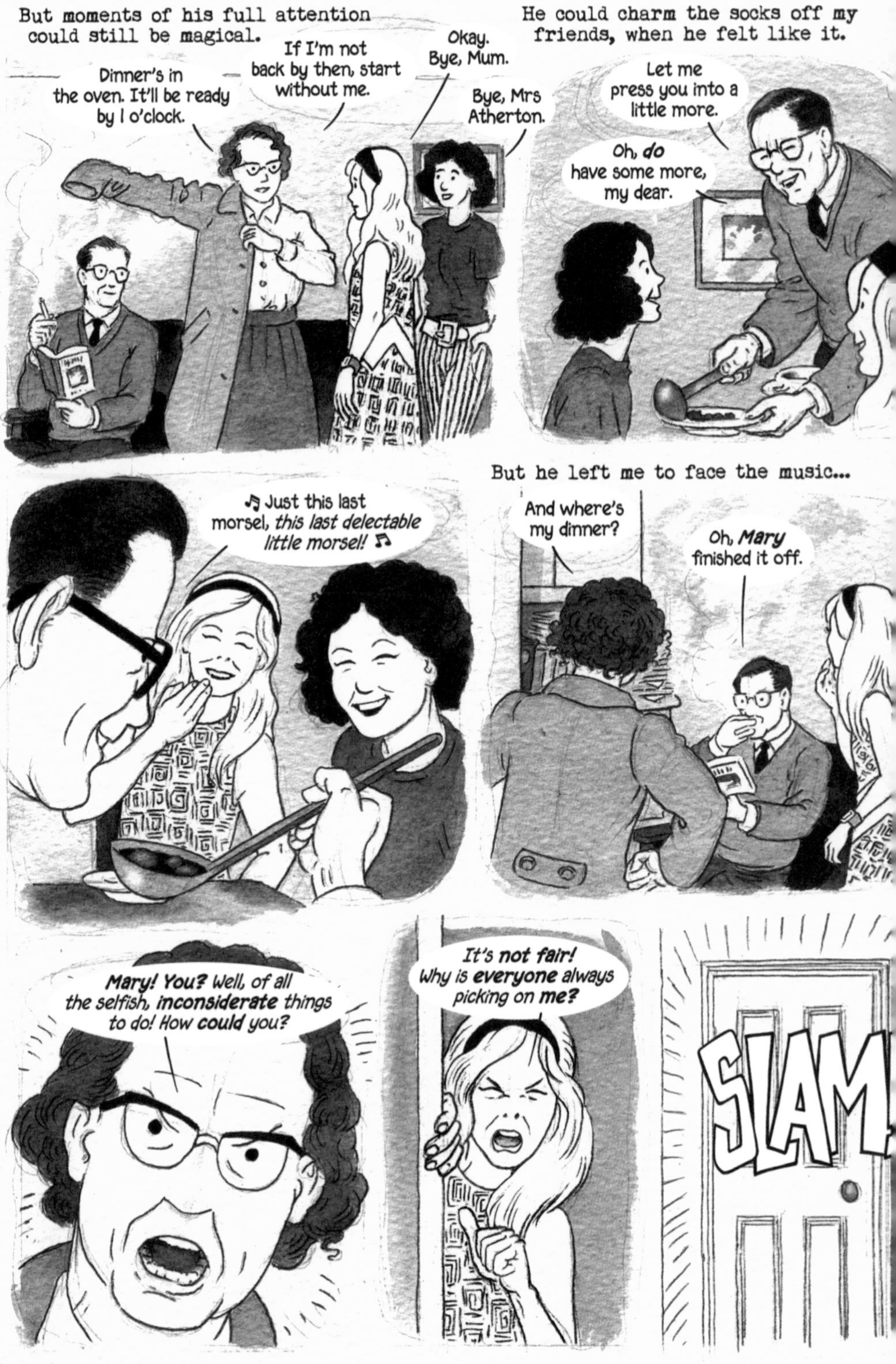
But moments of his full attention could still be magical.
Dinner's in the oven. It'll be ready by 1 o'clock.
If I'm not back by then, start without me.
Okay. Bye, Mum.
Bye, Mrs Atherton.
He could charm the socks off my friends, when he felt like it.
Let me press you into a little more.
Oh, *do* have some more, my dear.
♫ Just this last morsel, *this last delectable little morsel!* ♫
But he left me to face the music...
And where's my dinner?
Oh, ***Mary*** finished it off.
Mary! You? Well, of all the selfish, ***inconsiderate*** things to do! How ***could*** you?
*It's **not fair!** Why is **everyone** always picking on **me?***
SLAM!

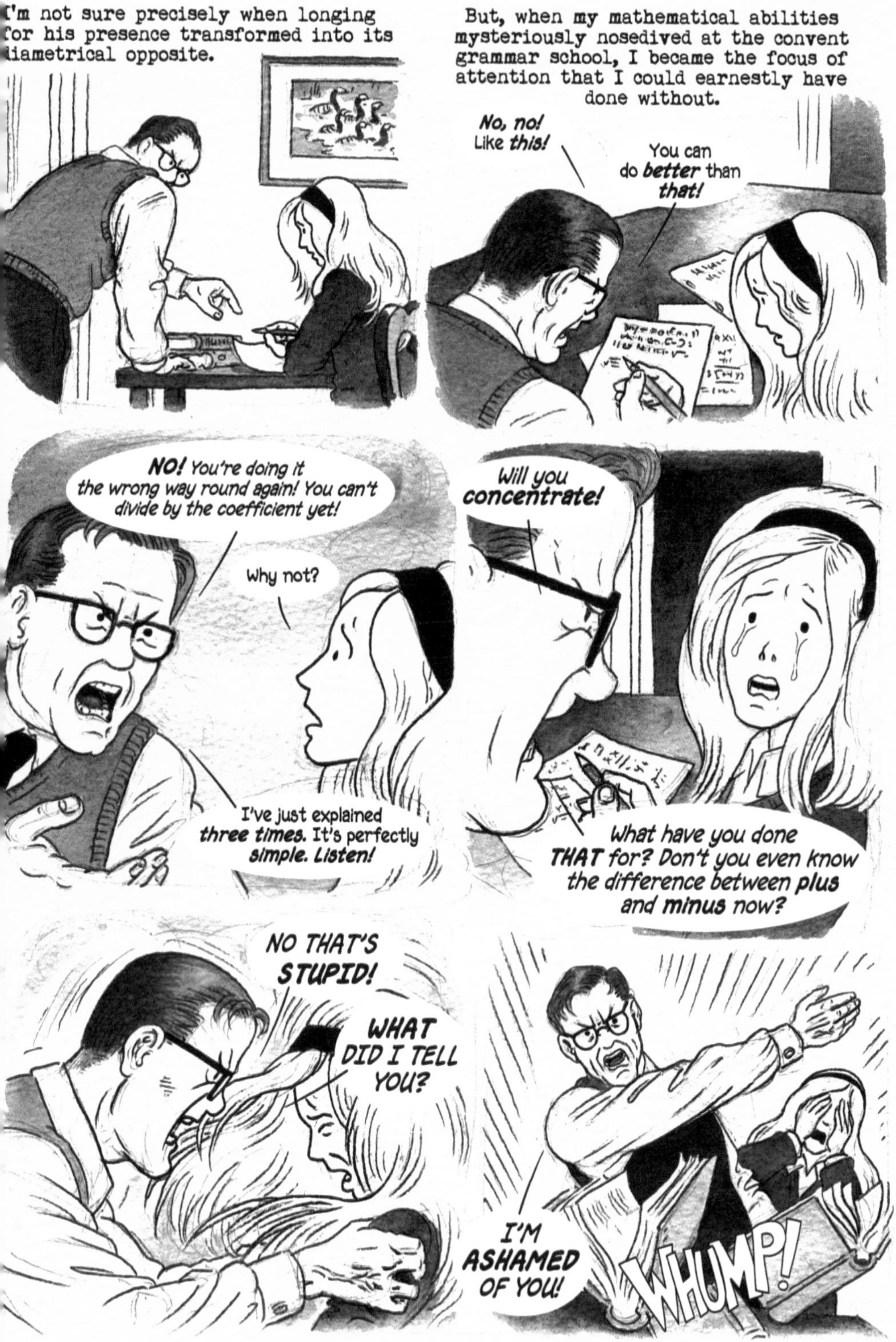
I'm not sure precisely when longing for his presence transformed into its diametrical opposite.
But, when my mathematical abilities mysteriously nosedived at the convent grammar school, I became the focus of attention that I could earnestly have done without.
No, no! Like this!
You can do better than that!
NO! You're doing it the wrong way round again! You can't divide by the coefficient yet!
Why not?
I've just explained three times. It's perfectly simple. Listen!
Will you concentrate!
What have you done THAT for? Don't you even know the difference between plus and minus now?
NO THAT'S STUPID!
WHAT DID I TELL YOU?
I'M ASHAMED OF YOU!
WHUMP!

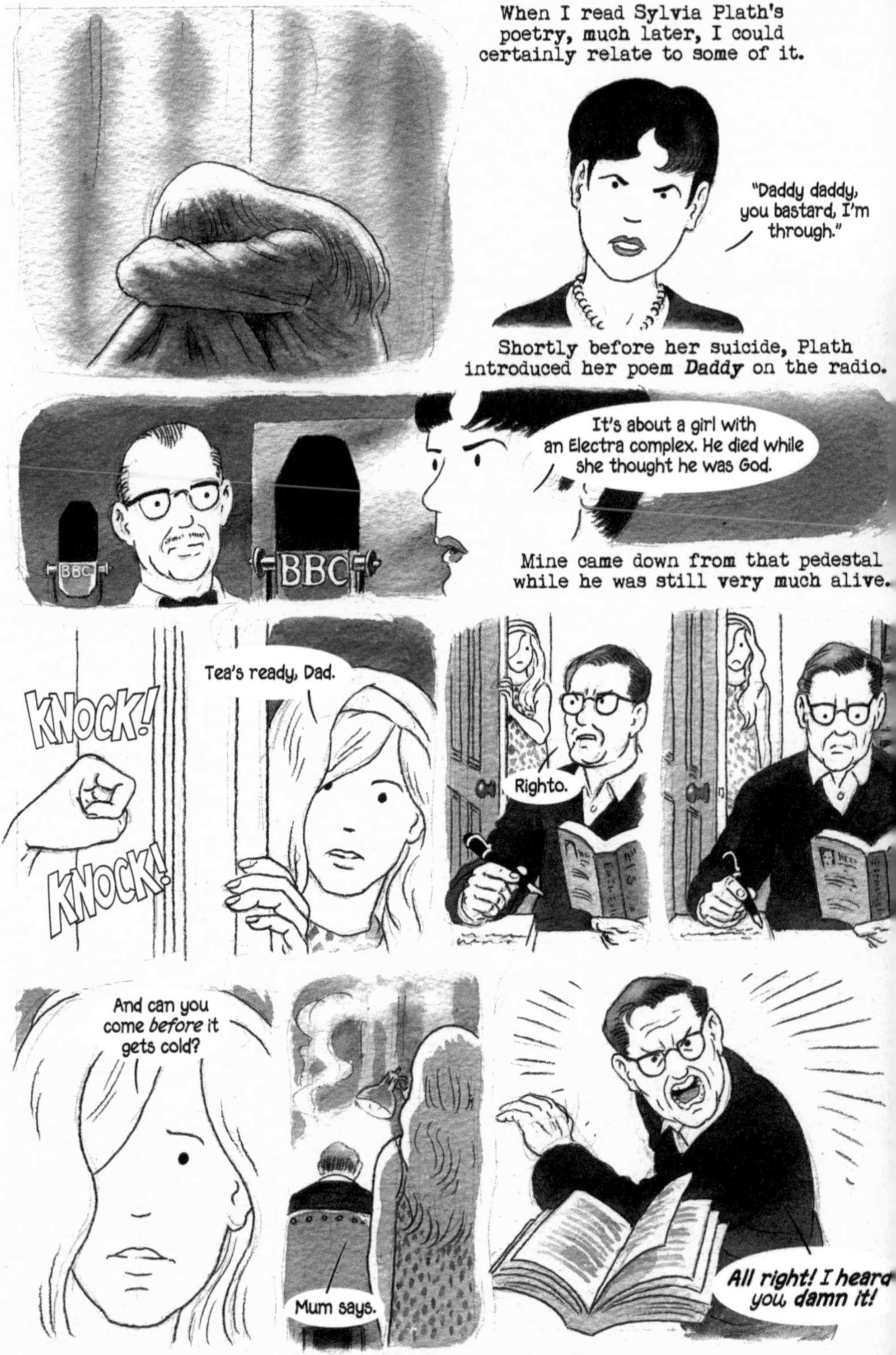
When I read Sylvia Plath's poetry, much later, I could certainly relate to some of it.
"Daddy daddy, you bastard, I'm through."
Shortly before her suicide, Plath introduced her poem *Daddy* on the radio.
BBC
BBC
It's about a girl with an Electra complex. He died while she thought he was God.
Mine came down from that pedestal while he was still very much alive.
KNOCK!
KNOCK!
Tea's ready, Dad.
Righto.
And can you come *before* it gets cold?
Mum says.
All right! I heard you, damn it!

In Trieste, life was difficult. The Joyces lived like displaced persons, moving from one furnished flat to another, and they often went hungry.

James worked as an English teacher, but he could always spend more than he earned.

His teaching methods, like most things about him, were unconventional. As he said, "Children should be educated by love, not punishment." It was his own upbringing he was reflecting on, as depicted in his coming-of-age novel; but the sentiment was sincere enough.

The novel would eventually be published in 1916 as *A Portrait of the Artist as a Young Man*.

When war broke out in 1914, Italian-speaking Austria was no longer a safe place for foreign nationals. James's brother, Stanislaus, had already been interned. They chose Zurich, thinking that it would be possible to find employment there. Another land, another language.

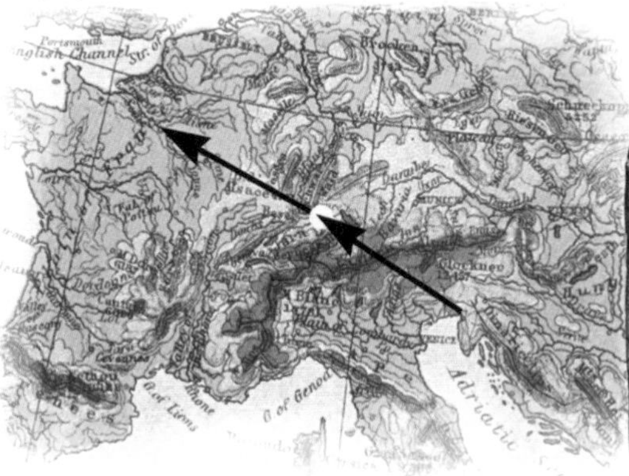

After the war, they went to Paris - on Ezra Pound's recommendation.

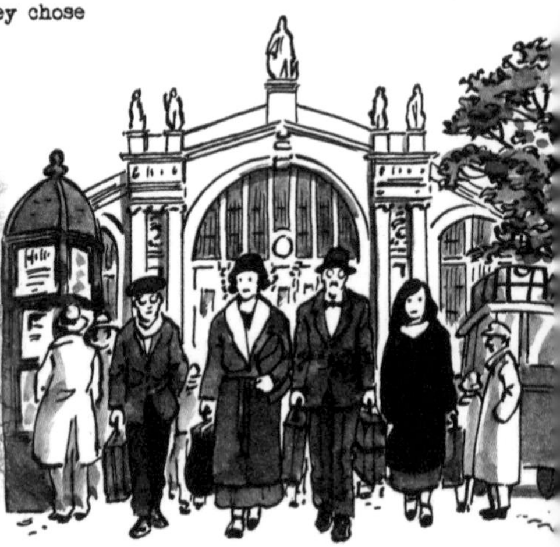

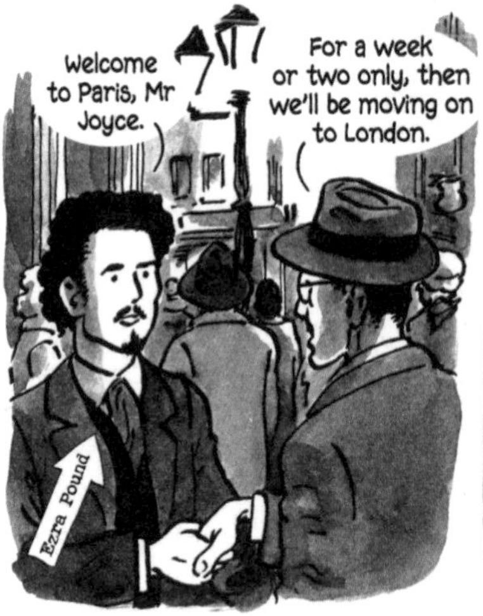
Welcome to Paris, Mr Joyce.
For a week or two only, then we'll be moving on to London.
Ezra Pound

Another land, another language.

9 rue de l'Université, 192

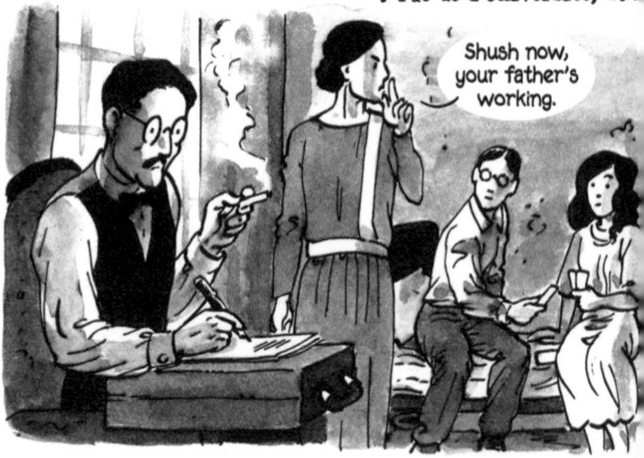
Shush now, your father's working.

Weeks became years. From hotel room to furnished flat to hotel again.

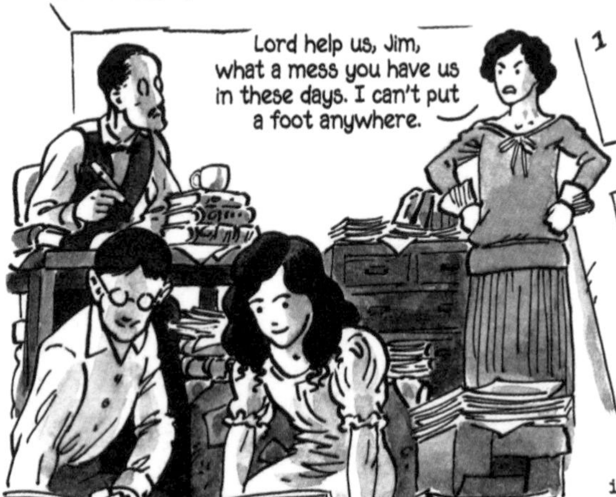
Lord help us, Jim, what a mess you have us in these days. I can't put a foot anywhere.

5 rue de l'Assomption, 1921

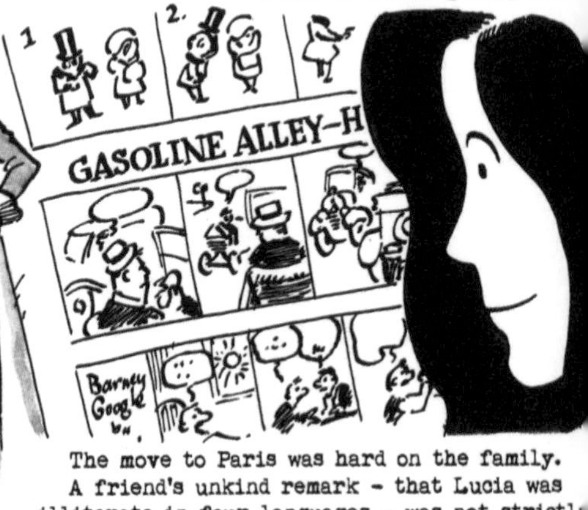
GASOLINE ALLEY-H
Barney Google

The move to Paris was hard on the family. A friend's unkind remark - that Lucia was illiterate in four languages - was not strictl speaking true. But they were all struggling.

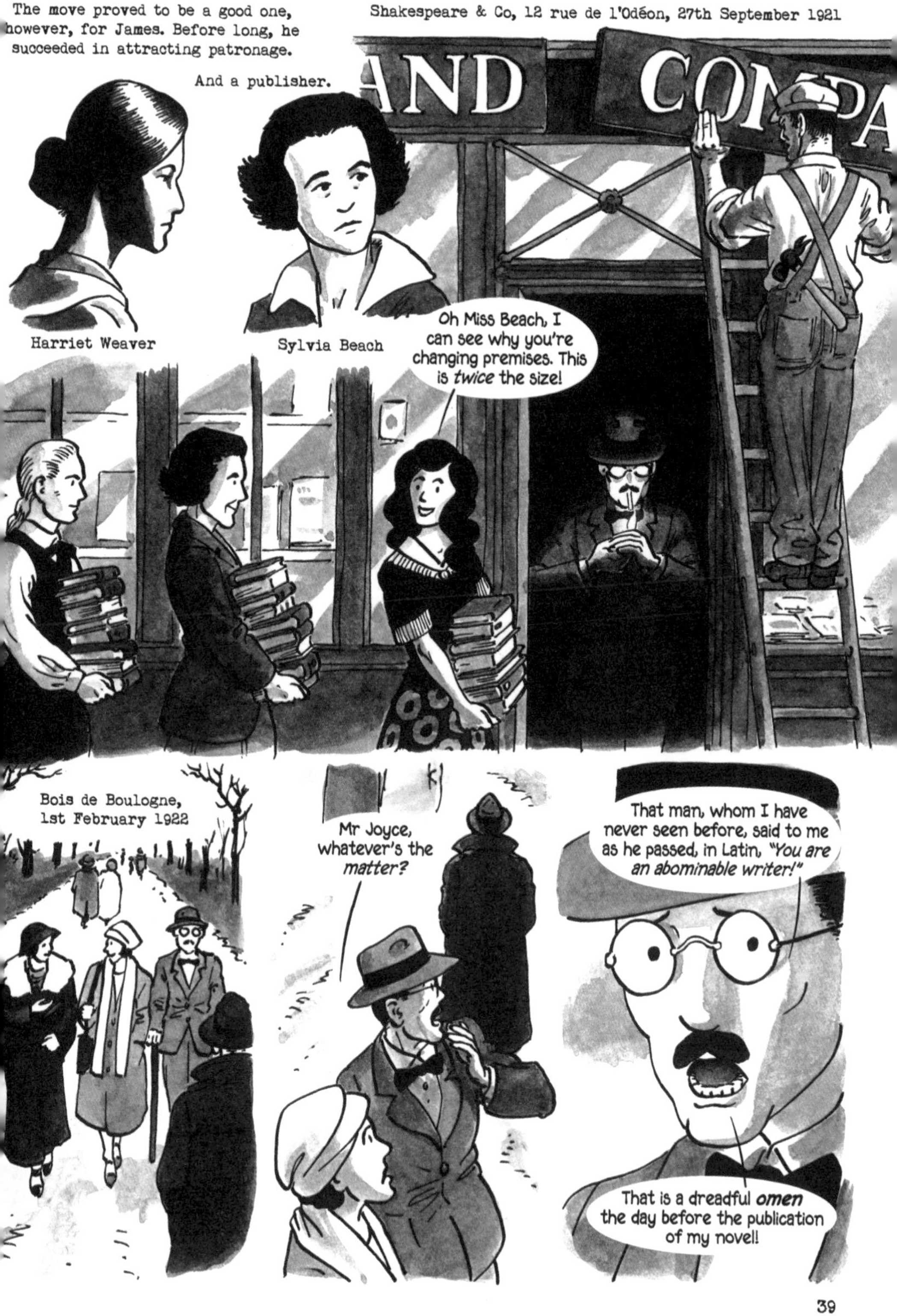

The move proved to be a good one, however, for James. Before long, he succeeded in attracting patronage.
And a publisher.
Harriet Weaver
Sylvia Beach
Shakespeare & Co, 12 rue de l'Odéon, 27th September 1921
AND COMPA
Oh Miss Beach, I can see why you're changing premises. This is *twice* the size!
Bois de Boulogne, 1st February 1922
Mr Joyce, whatever's the *matter?*
That man, whom I have never seen before, said to me as he passed, in Latin, *"You are an abominable writer!"*
That is a dreadful **omen** the day before the publication of my novel!

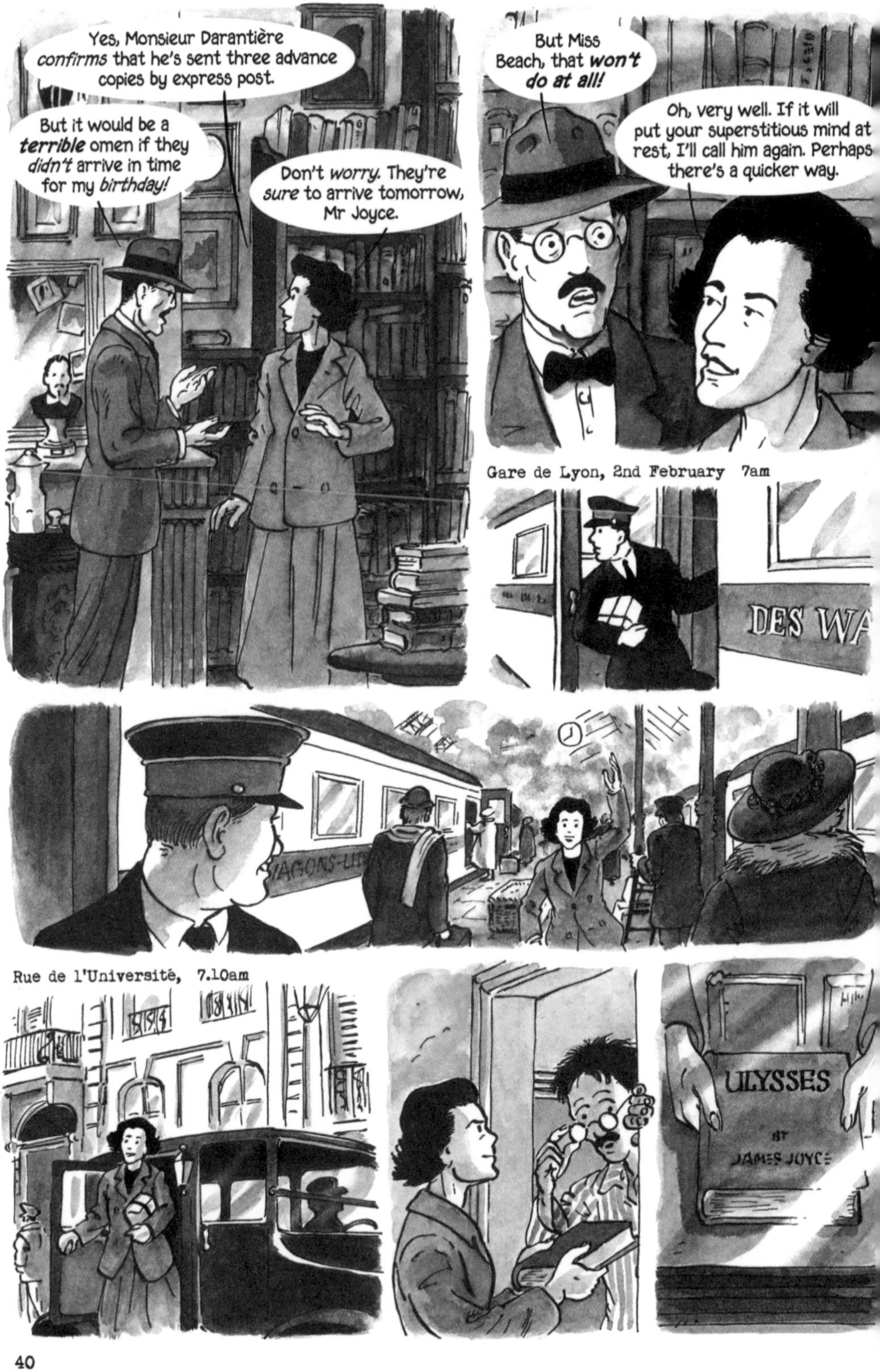
Yes, Monsieur Darantière confirms that he's sent three advance copies by express post.
But it would be a terrible omen if they didn't arrive in time for my birthday!
Don't worry. They're sure to arrive tomorrow, Mr Joyce.
But Miss Beach, that won't do at all!
Oh, very well. If it will put your superstitious mind at rest, I'll call him again. Perhaps there's a quicker way.
Gare de Lyon, 2nd February 7am
DES WA
WAGONS-LIT
Rue de l'Université, 7.10am
ULYSSES
BY
JAMES JOYCE

Ferrari's Italian Restaurant, 2 February 1922

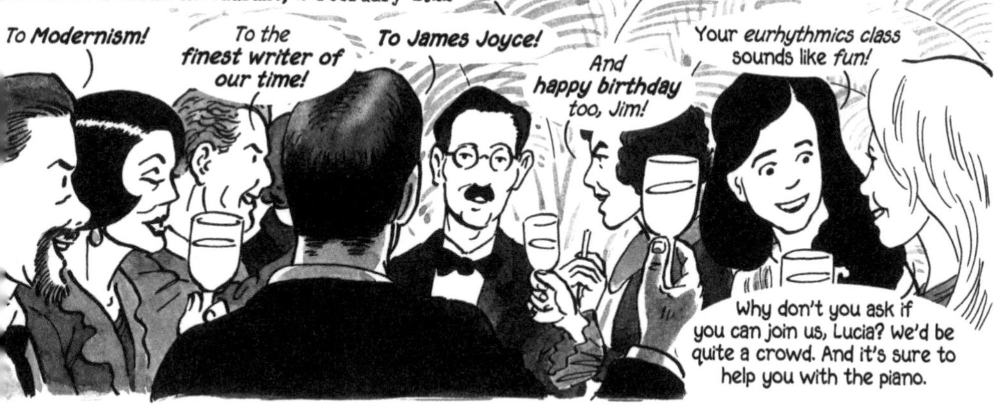
To Modernism!
To the finest writer of our time!
To James Joyce!
And happy birthday too, Jim!
Your eurhythmics class sounds like fun!
Why don't you ask if you can join us, Lucia? We'd be quite a crowd. And it's sure to help you with the piano.

The dancing daughters learned rhythm and gesture, movement and voice. Eurhythmics.

For Lucia it was a liberation.

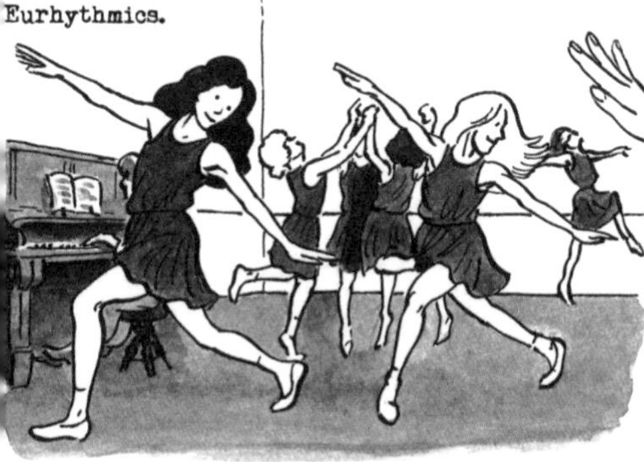

Jaques-Dalcroze Institut, 28 rue de l'Annonciation

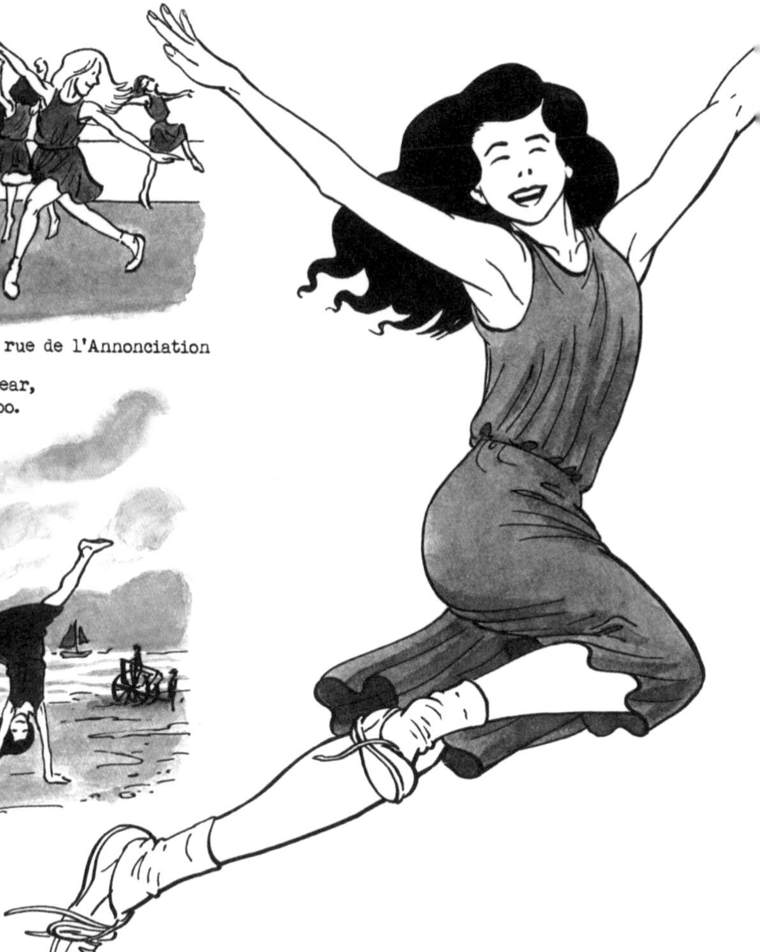

At summer camp later that year, she discovered gymnastics too.

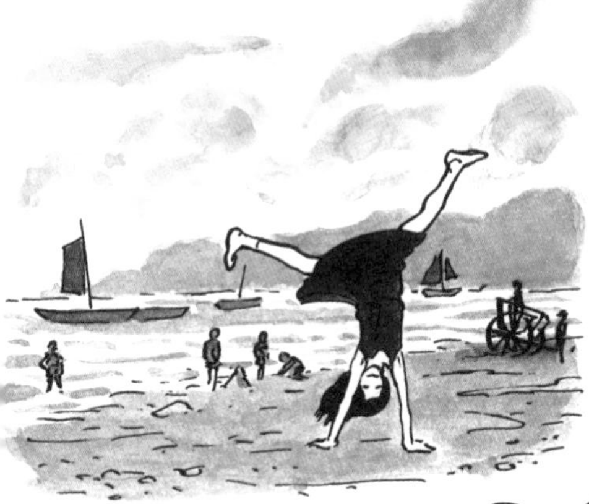

The family was soon immersed in the Parisian cultural life of *les années folles.*

They attended the theatre and the opera.

Father and daughter went to the cinema.

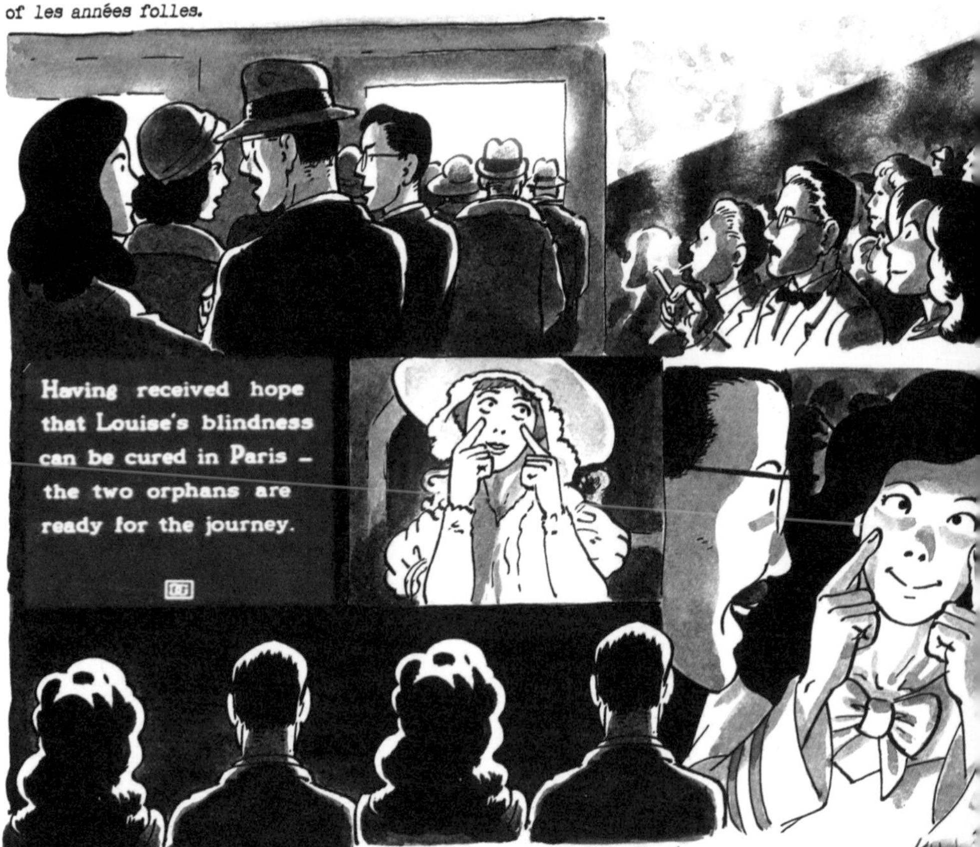
Having received hope that Louise's blindness can be cured in Paris – the two orphans are ready for the journey.

(Lillian Gish in *Orphans of the Storm*)

And they worshipped Chaplin.

26 avenue Charles Floquet, Christmas 1922

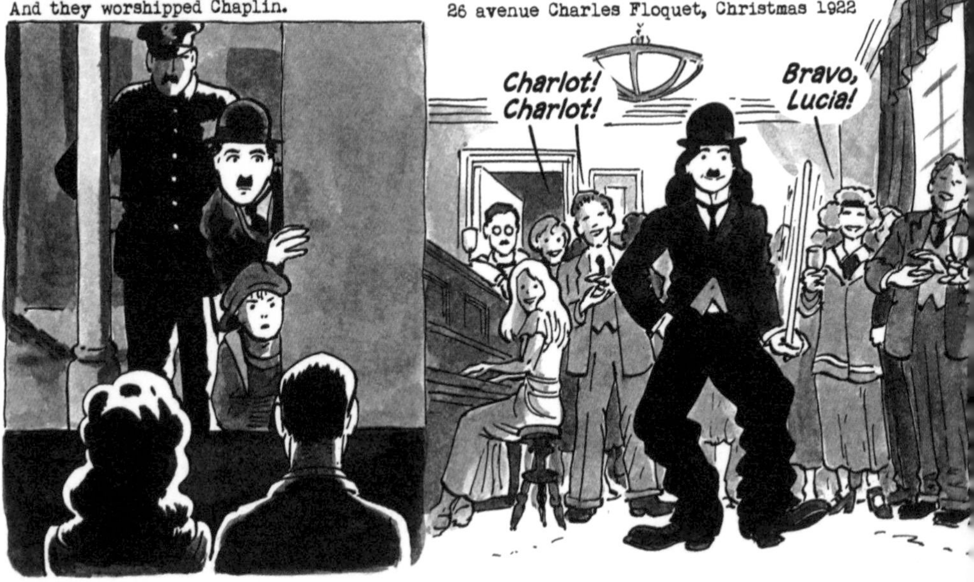
Charlot! Charlot!
Bravo, Lucia!

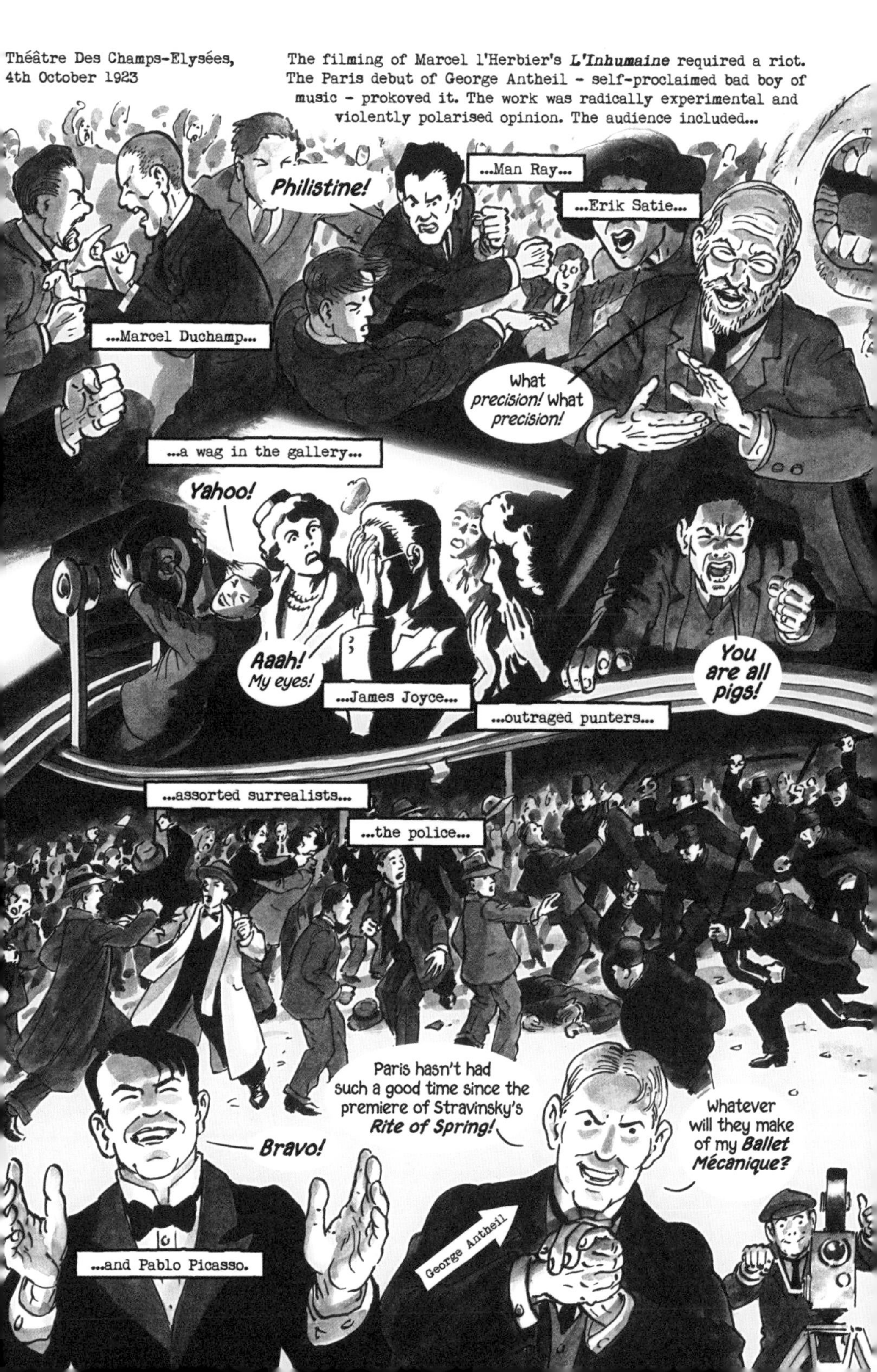
Théâtre Des Champs-Elysées,
4th October 1923
The filming of Marcel l'Herbier's *L'Inhumaine* required a riot. The Paris debut of George Antheil - self-proclaimed bad boy of music - prokoved it. The work was radically experimental and violently polarised opinion. The audience included...
...Man Ray...
Philistine!
...Erik Satie...
...Marcel Duchamp...
What *precision!* What *precision!*
...a wag in the gallery...
Yahoo!
Aaah! My eyes!
...James Joyce...
...outraged punters...
You are all pigs!
...assorted surrealists...
...the police...
Bravo!
Paris hasn't had such a good time since the premiere of Stravinsky's *Rite of Spring!*
Whatever will they make of my *Ballet Mécanique?*
...and Pablo Picasso.
George Antheil

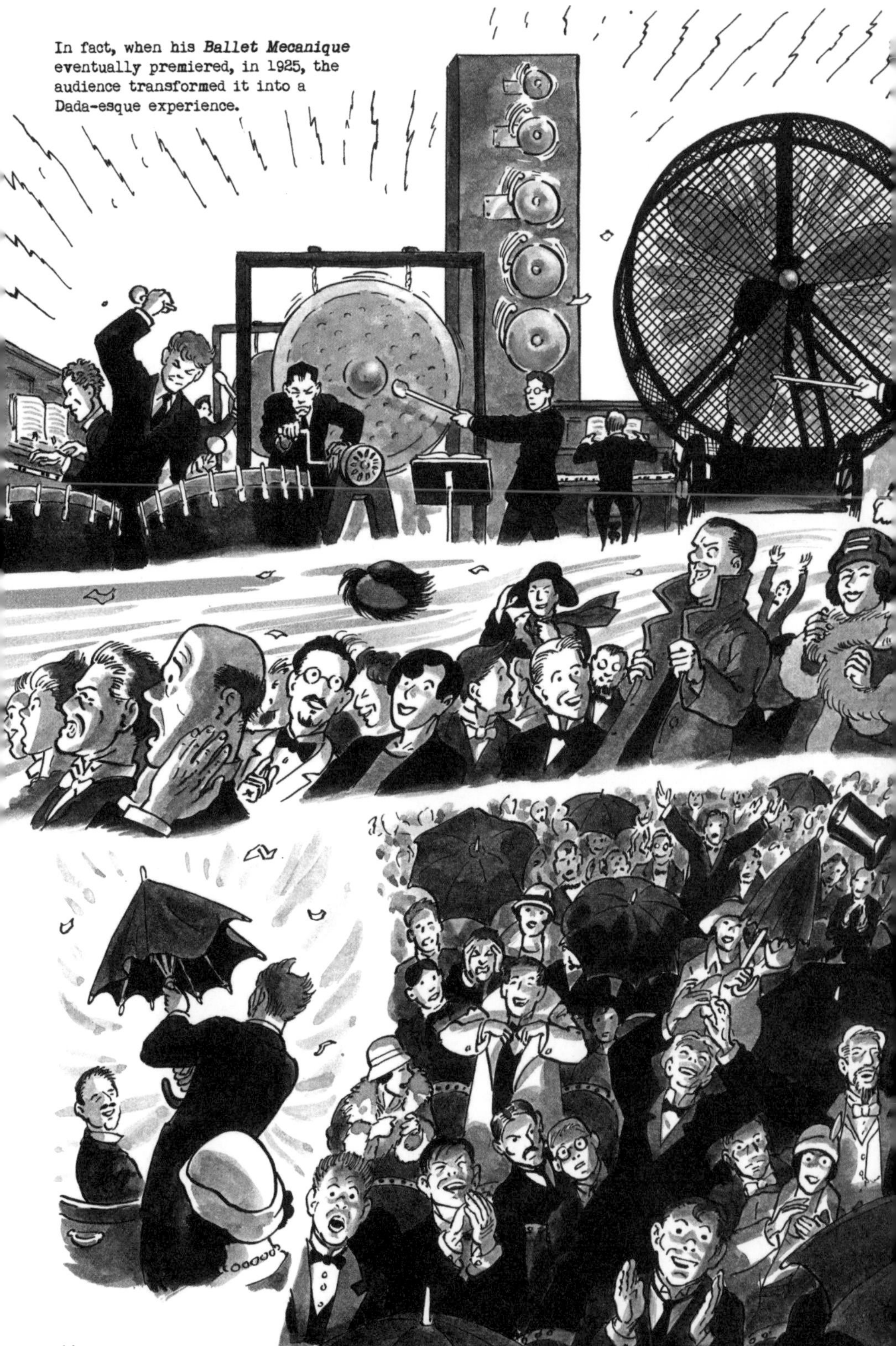
In fact, when his *Ballet Mecanique* eventually premiered, in 1925, the audience transformed it into a Dada-esque experience.

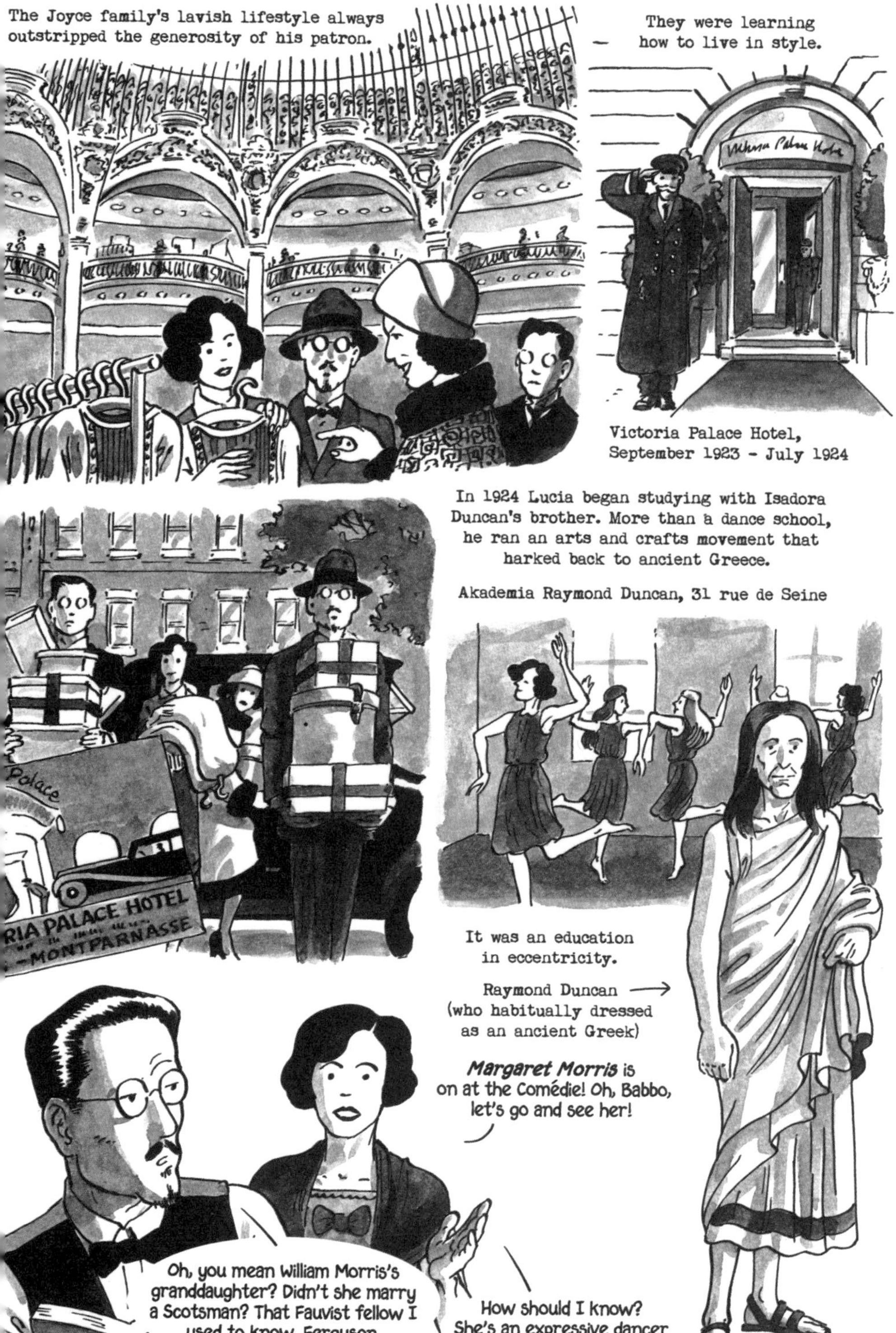

The Joyce family's lavish lifestyle always outstripped the generosity of his patron.
They were learning how to live in style.
Victoria Palace Hotel, September 1923 - July 1924
Palace
RIA PALACE HOTEL
MONTPARNASSE
In 1924 Lucia began studying with Isadora Duncan's brother. More than a dance school, he ran an arts and crafts movement that harked back to ancient Greece.
Akademia Raymond Duncan, 31 rue de Seine
It was an education in eccentricity.
Raymond Duncan (who habitually dressed as an ancient Greek)
Margaret Morris is on at the Comédie! Oh, Babbo, let's go and see her!
Oh, you mean William Morris's granddaughter? Didn't she marry a Scotsman? That Fauvist fellow I used to know, Ferguson.
How should I know? She's an expressive dancer - she's famous!

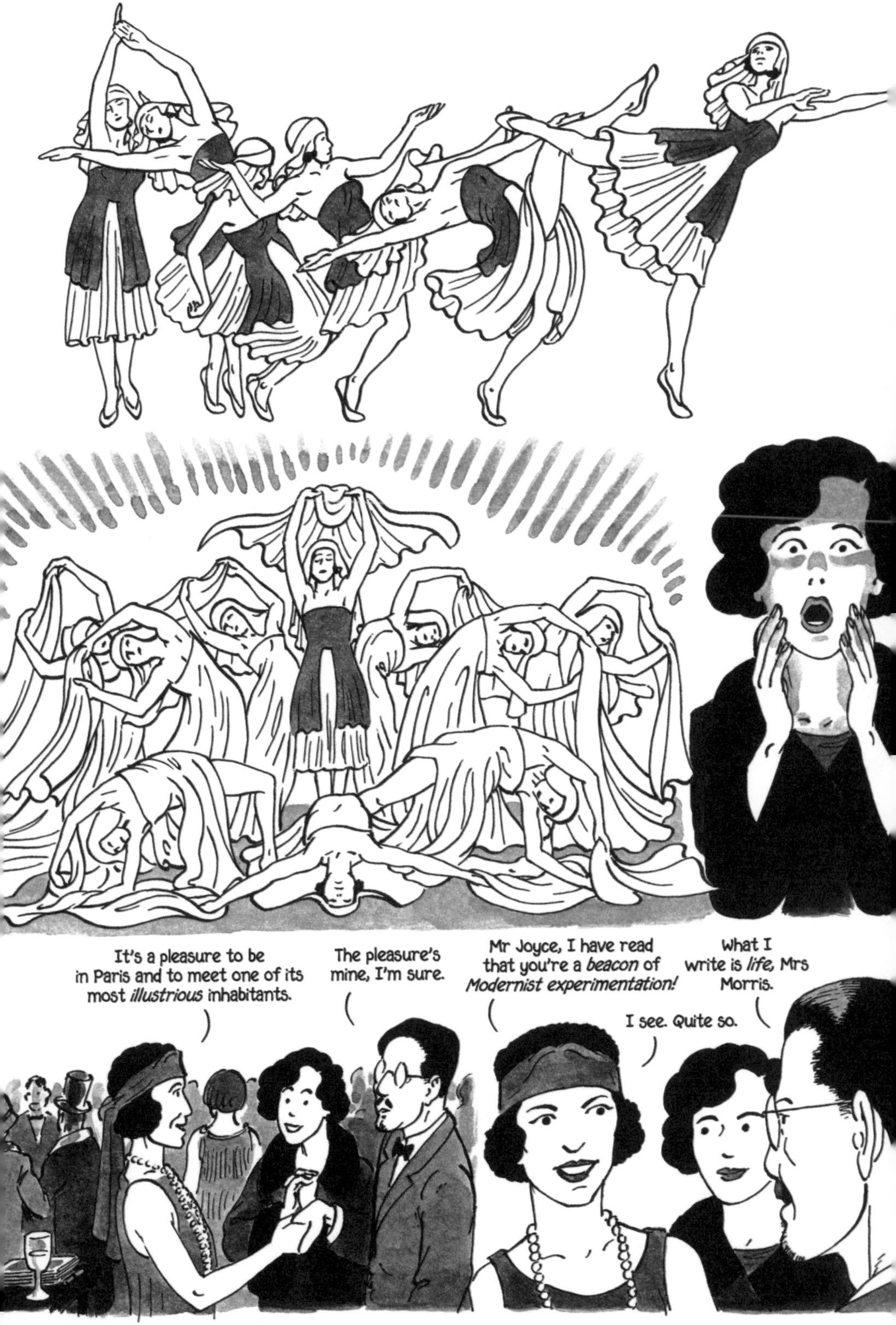

It's a pleasure to be in Paris and to meet one of its most *illustrious* inhabitants.
The pleasure's mine, I'm sure.
Mr Joyce, I have read that you're a *beacon* of *Modernist experimentation!*
What I write is *life,* Mrs Morris.
I see. Quite so.

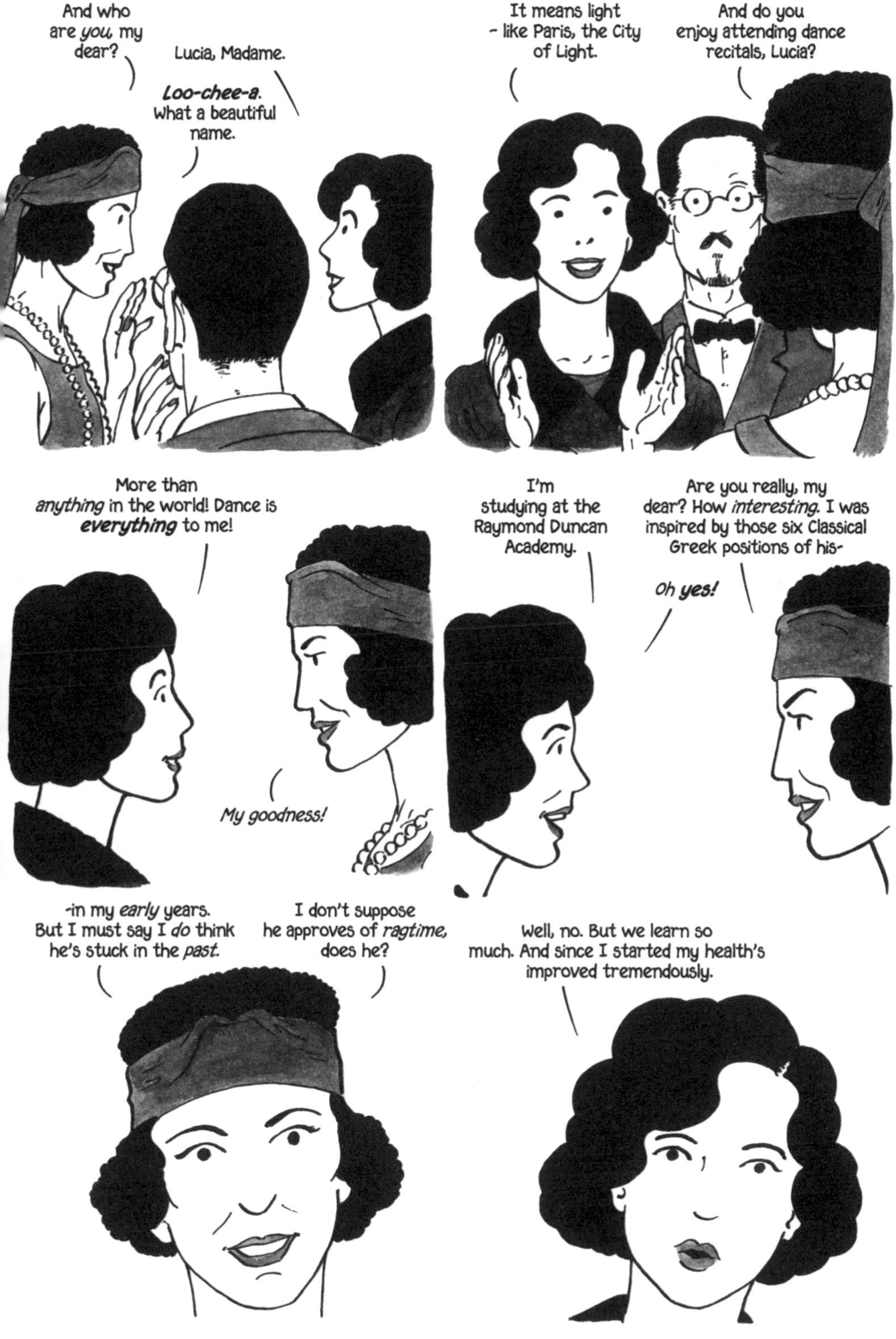

And who are *you*, my dear?
Lucia, Madame.
Loo-chee-a. What a beautiful name.
It means light - like Paris, the City of Light.
And do you enjoy attending dance recitals, Lucia?
More than *anything* in the world! Dance is ***everything*** to me!
My goodness!
I'm studying at the Raymond Duncan Academy.
Are you really, my dear? How *interesting*. I was inspired by those six Classical Greek positions of his-
*Oh **yes!***
-in my *early* years. But I must say I *do* think he's stuck in the *past*.
I don't suppose he approves of *ragtime*, does he?
Well, no. But we learn so much. And since I started my health's improved tremendously.

I'm sure it has, Lucia. Any good physical exercise has tremendous *health benefits*.

As a matter of fact, I've just done a demonstration on the remedial benefits of dance for some surgeons in London.

Their enthusiasm was so *encouraging* that I'm intending to study the medical side.

*You **are?***

Yes, they've impressed on me the need for a professional qualification.

Well, my dear, I'm sure your *father* would like to be going. I'm delighted to meet you.

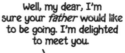

I'm planning to open a school here in Paris. It will have a comprehensive syllabus and I sincerely hope you will consider attending.

MARGARET MORRIS

Take this to remind you.

I won't *need reminding*, Madame Morris!

48

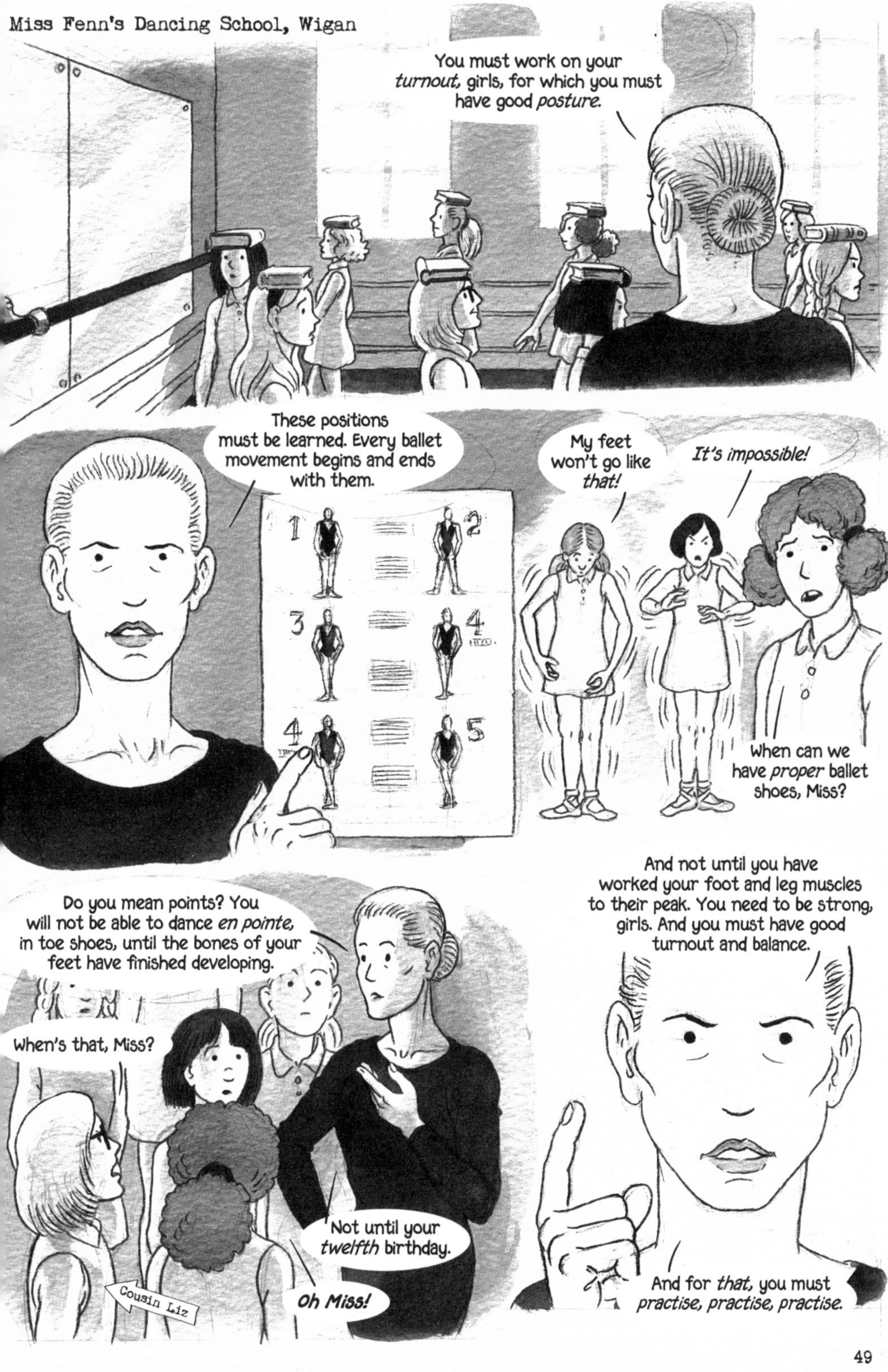

Miss Fenn's Dancing School, Wigan
You must work on your *turnout,* girls, for which you must have good *posture.*
These positions must be learned. Every ballet movement begins and ends with them.
My feet won't go like *that!*
It's impossible!
When can we have *proper* ballet shoes, Miss?
Do you mean points? You will not be able to dance *en pointe,* in toe shoes, until the bones of your feet have finished developing.
When's that, Miss?
Not until your *twelfth* birthday.
Oh Miss!
Cousin Liz
And not until you have worked your foot and leg muscles to their peak. You need to be strong, girls. And you must have good turnout and balance.
And for *that,* you must *practise, practise, practise.*

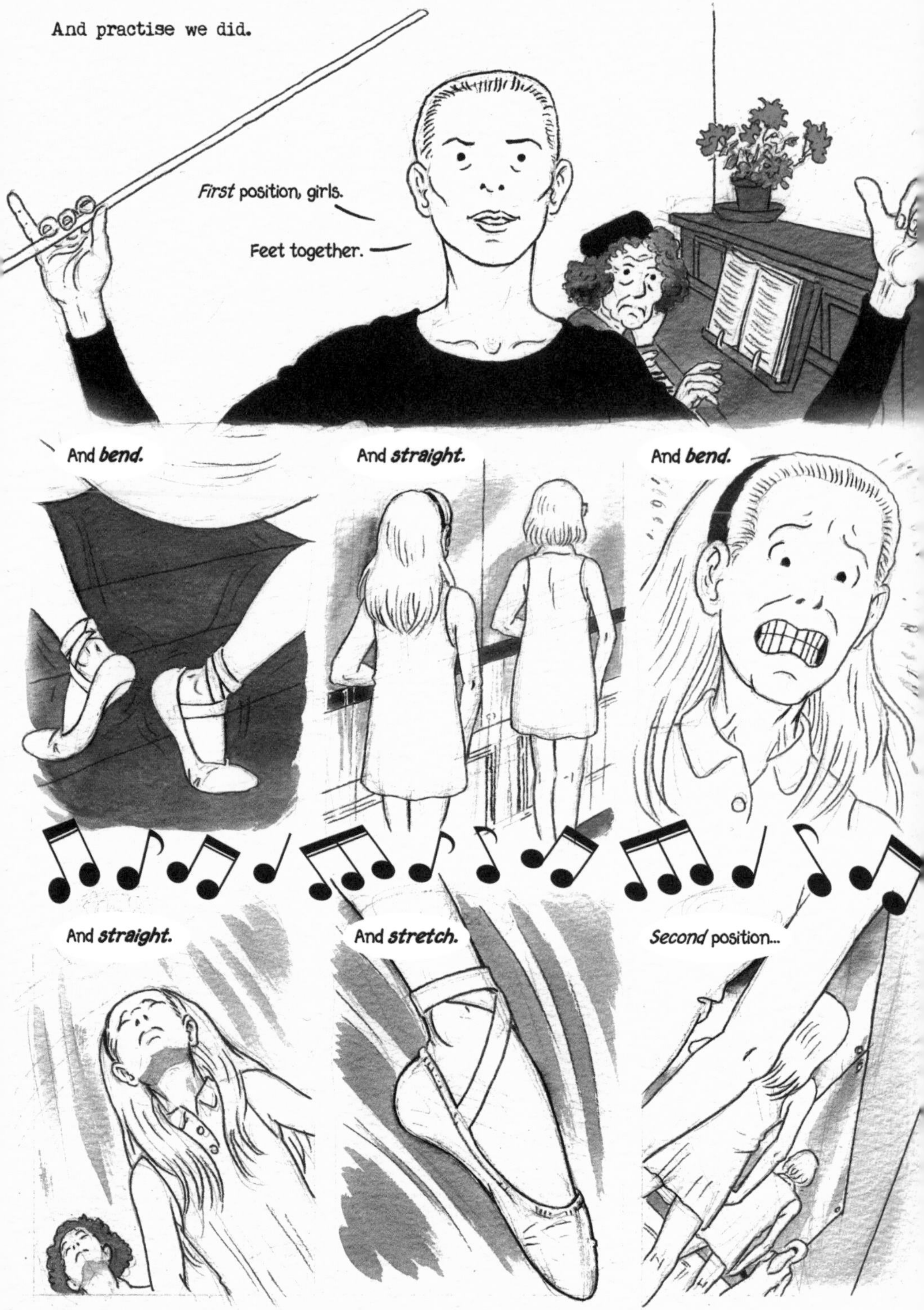
And practise we did.
First position, girls.
Feet together.
And **bend.**
And **straight.**
And **bend.**
And **straight.**
And **stretch.**
Second position...

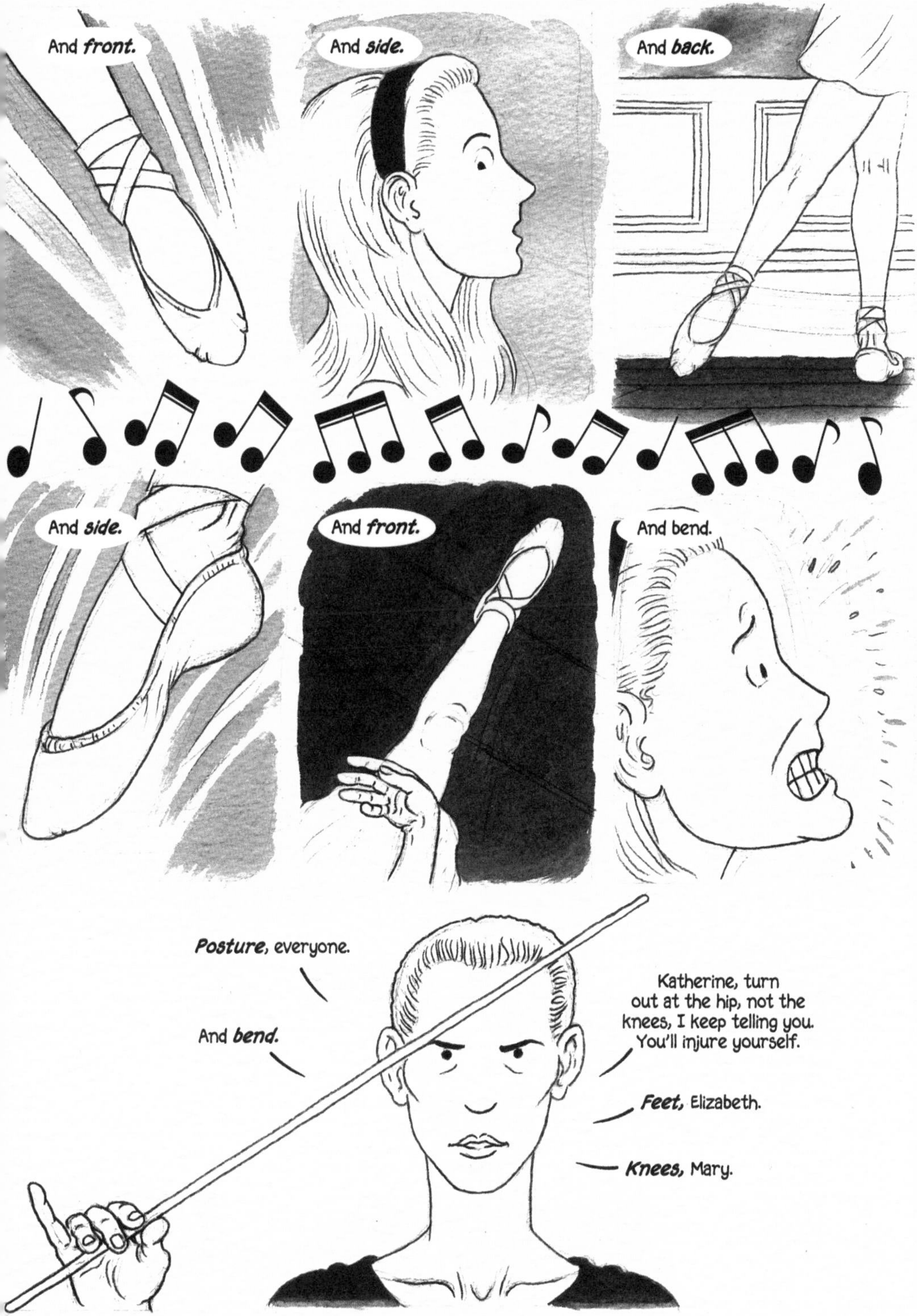
And front.
And side.
And back.
And side.
And front.
And bend.
Posture, everyone.
And bend.
Katherine, turn out at the hip, not the knees, I keep telling you. You'll injure yourself.
Feet, Elizabeth.
Knees, Mary.

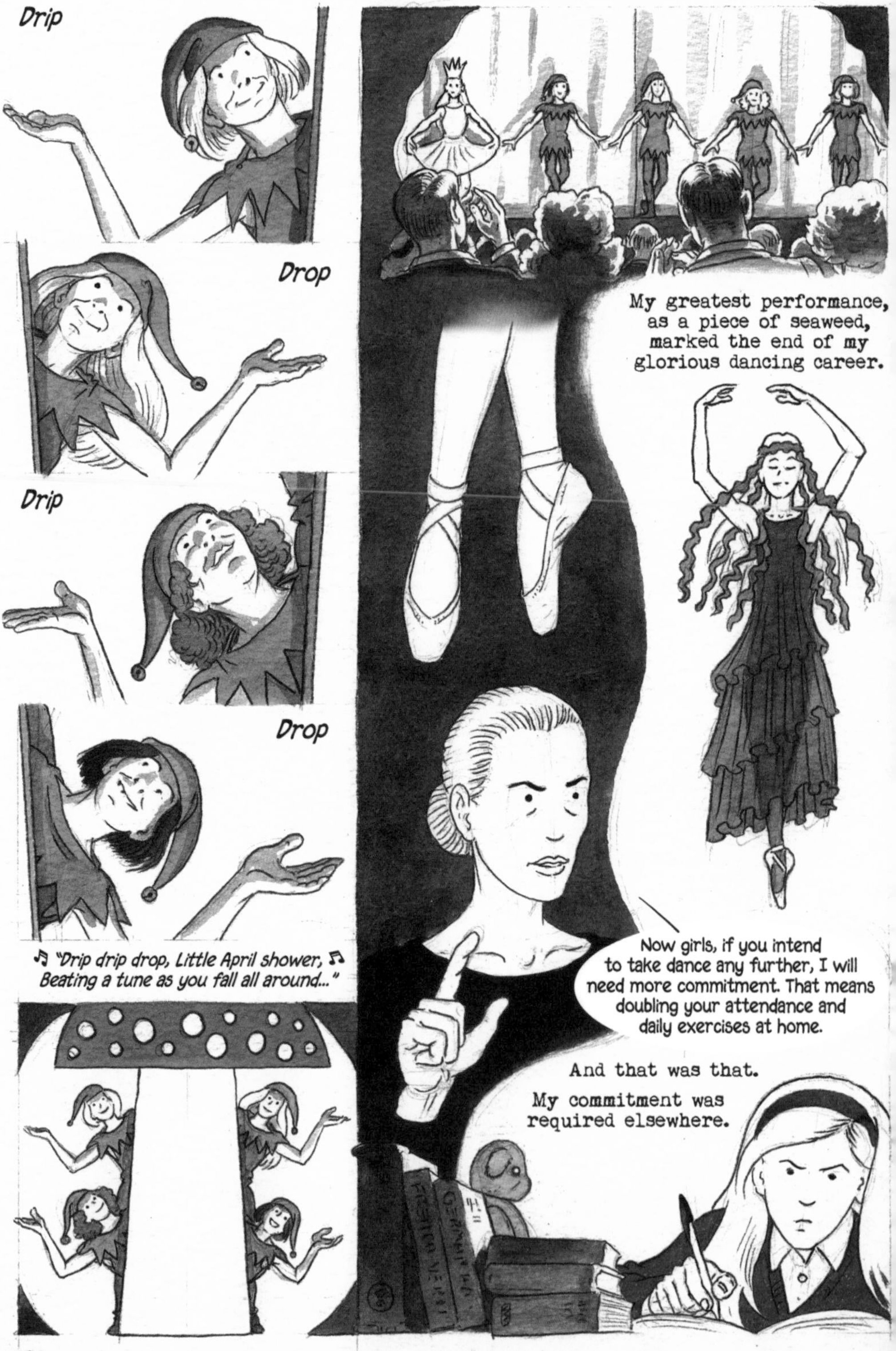
Drip
Drop
Drip
Drop
♫ "Drip drip drop, Little April shower, ♫
Beating a tune as you fall all around..."
My greatest performance, as a piece of seaweed, marked the end of my glorious dancing career.
Now girls, if you intend to take dance any further, I will need more commitment. That means doubling your attendance and daily exercises at home.
And that was that.
My commitment was required elsewhere.

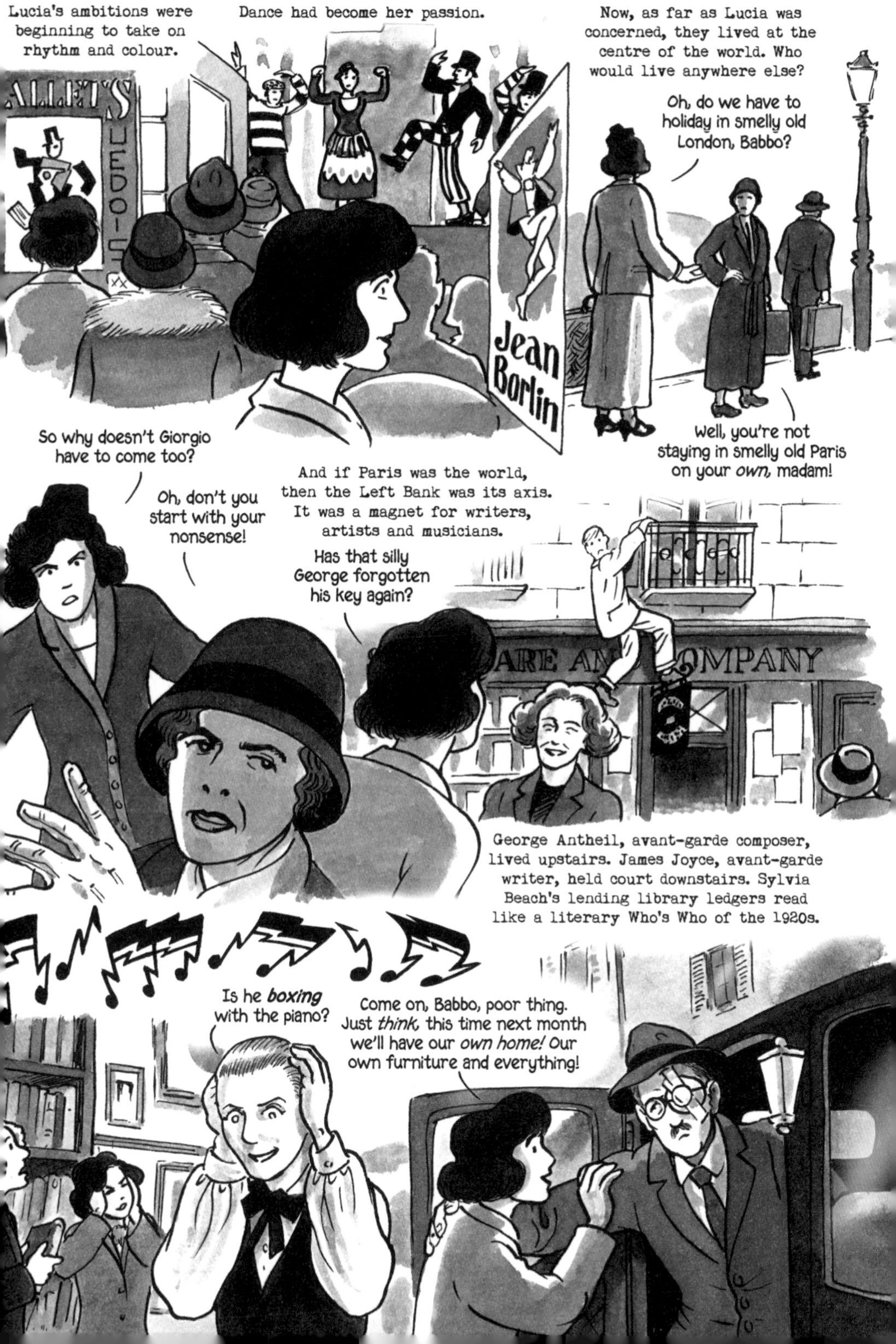

Lucia's ambitions were beginning to take on rhythm and colour.
Dance had become her passion.
Jean Borlin
Now, as far as Lucia was concerned, they lived at the centre of the world. Who would live anywhere else?
Oh, do we have to holiday in smelly old London, Babbo?
Well, you're not staying in smelly old Paris on your *own*, madam!
So why doesn't Giorgio have to come too?
Oh, don't you start with your nonsense!
And if Paris was the world, then the Left Bank was its axis. It was a magnet for writers, artists and musicians.
Has that silly George forgotten his key again?
George Antheil, avant-garde composer, lived upstairs. James Joyce, avant-garde writer, held court downstairs. Sylvia Beach's lending library ledgers read like a literary Who's Who of the 1920s.
Is he *boxing* with the piano?
Come on, Babbo, poor thing. Just *think*, this time next month we'll have our *own home!* Our own furniture and everything!

2 square Robiac

Will we **really** have our own telephone?

Yes indeed.

How **modern!** I can't wait!

Paris was a magnet for dancers too. In October 1925, Josephine Baker brought the Charleston to Paris in the Revue Nègre at the Théâtre des Champs-Elysées.

The following month, Margaret Morris – advocate of dance therapy and one of Lucia's heroes – established her school.

10 Avenue de la Bourdonnais

Lucia, how lovely to see you again.

I'm so **thrilled** to be here!

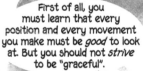

First of all, you must learn that every position and every movement you make must be *good* to look at. But you should not *strive* to be "graceful".

Does a *panther* strive to be graceful? Does a *tiger?* **No.** *Real* grace and good-looking movements can only be the outcome of **health** and **strength.**

Lucia blossomed. Her home life was settled, for the first time since they arrived in Paris. Her mind and body were focused on dance. Life was good.

Your progress has been **excellent,** Lucia. **Well done!** What are your plans *now?* What are you going to *do* with your considerable talents?

I'm not sure.

Why don't you speak with your tutors, Lois and Hélène? You may be able to join their troupe, if that appeals to you.

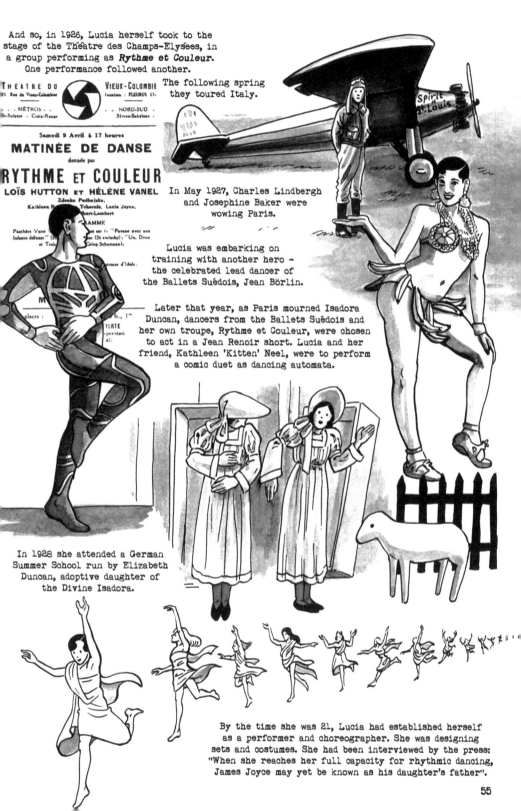

And so, in 1926, Lucia herself took to the stage of the Théâtre des Champs-Elysées, in a group performing as *Rythme et Couleur*. One performance followed another.

The following spring they toured Italy.

THÉÂTRE DU VIEUX-COLOMBIE
21, Rue du Vieux-Colombier   location : FLEURUS 57.

·· MÉTROS ··   ·· NORD-SUD ··
St-Sulpice · Croix-Rouge   Sèvres-Babylone ·

Samedi 9 Avril à 17 heures

MATINÉE DE DANSE
donnée par

RYTHME ET COULEUR
LOÏS HUTTON ET HÉLÈNE VANEL
Zdenka Podhajska,
Kathleen N...   Tcherník, Lucia Joyce,
...bert-Lambert

...RAMME

Panthère Verte ...
Infante défunte " (R... ...tes (St...winsky) ; " Us, Deux
et Trois ... Grieg-Schumann).
...reuses d'idole ·

places :   fr., 1re
...VERTE
...qmentatic
87 :

In May 1927, Charles Lindbergh and Josephine Baker were wowing Paris.

Lucia was embarking on training with another hero – the celebrated lead dancer of the Ballets Suédois, Jean Börlin.

Later that year, as Paris mourned Isadora Duncan, dancers from the Ballets Suédois and her own troupe, Rythme et Couleur, were chosen to act in a Jean Renoir short. Lucia and her friend, Kathleen 'Kitten' Neel, were to perform a comic duet as dancing automata.

In 1928 she attended a German Summer School run by Elizabeth Duncan, adoptive daughter of the Divine Isadora.

By the time she was 21, Lucia had established herself as a performer and choreographer. She was designing sets and costumes. She had been interviewed by the press: "When she reaches her full capacity for rhythmic dancing, James Joyce may yet be known as his daughter's father".

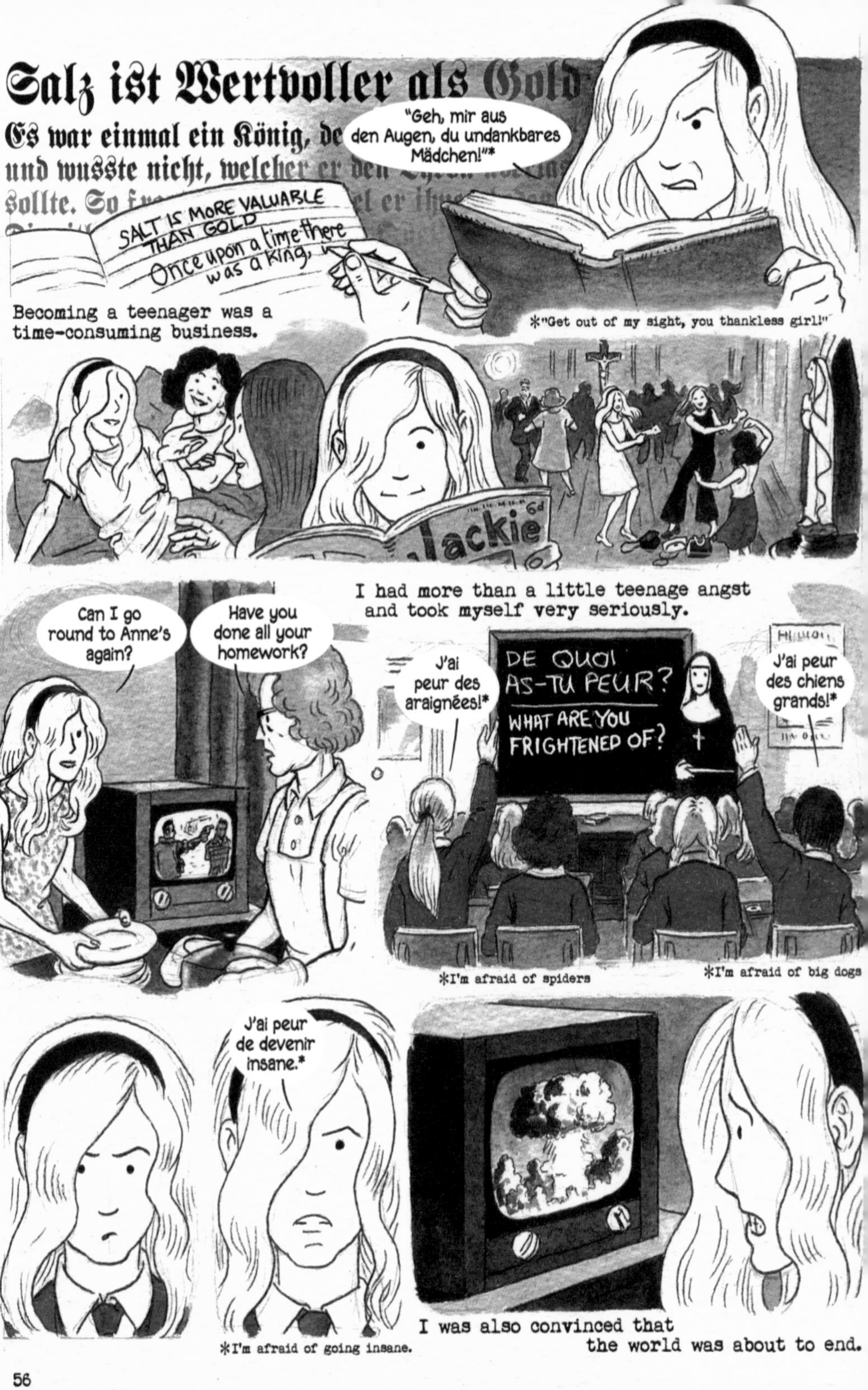
Salz ist Wertvoller als Gold
Es war einmal ein König, de
und wusste nicht, welcher er den
sollte.
"Geh, mir aus den Augen, du undankbares Mädchen!"*
SALT IS MORE VALUABLE THAN GOLD
Once upon a time there was a king,
Becoming a teenager was a time-consuming business.
*"Get out of my sight, you thankless girl!"
Jackie
6d
Can I go round to Anne's again?
Have you done all your homework?
I had more than a little teenage angst and took myself very seriously.
DE QUOI AS-TU PEUR?
WHAT ARE YOU FRIGHTENED OF?
J'ai peur des araignées!*
J'ai peur des chiens grands!*
*I'm afraid of spiders
*I'm afraid of big dogs
J'ai peur de devenir insane.*
*I'm afraid of going insane.
I was also convinced that the world was about to end.

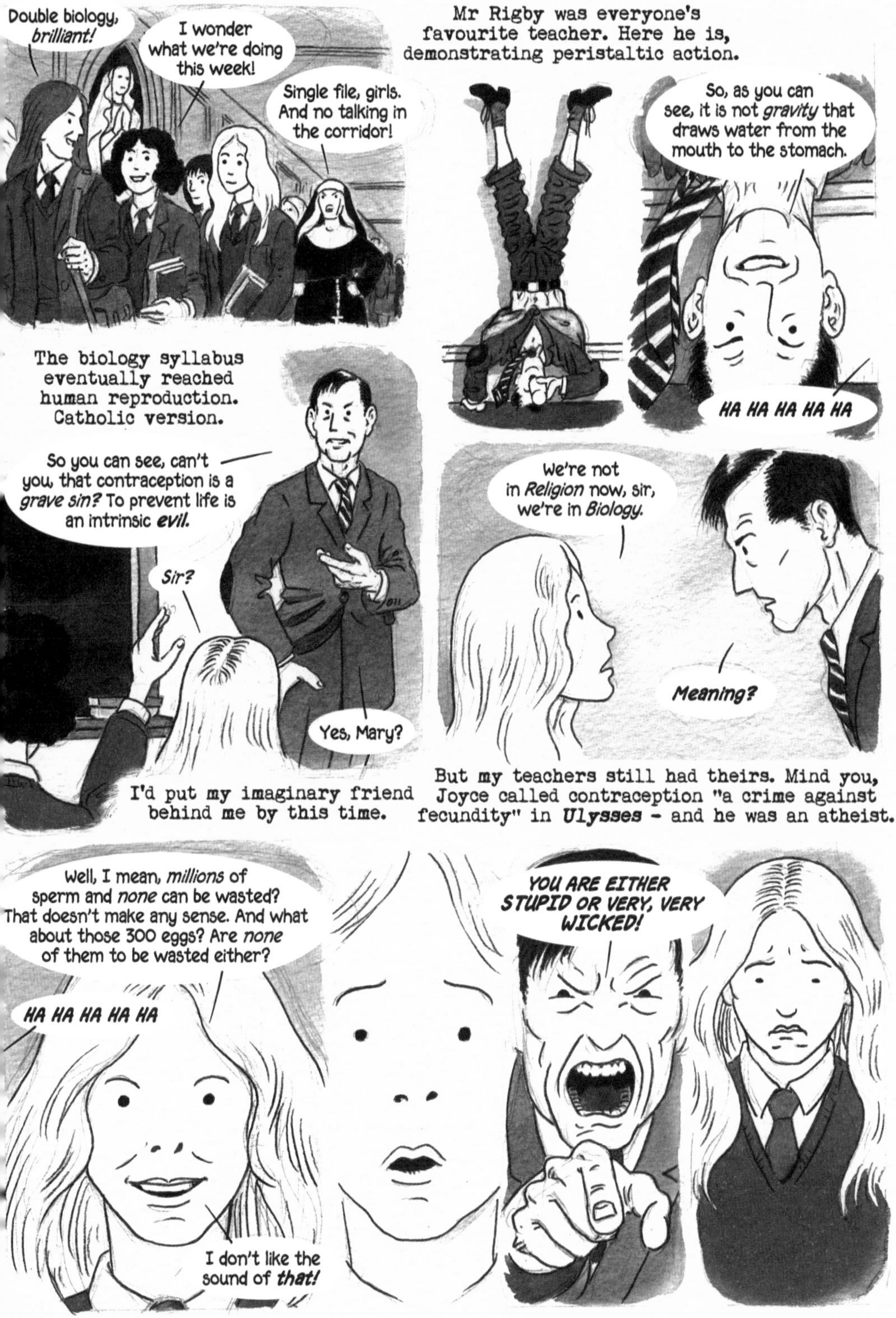
Double biology, *brilliant!*
I wonder what we're doing this week!
Single file, girls. And no talking in the corridor!
Mr Rigby was everyone's favourite teacher. Here he is, demonstrating peristaltic action.
So, as you can see, it is not *gravity* that draws water from the mouth to the stomach.
HA HA HA HA HA
The biology syllabus eventually reached human reproduction. Catholic version.
So you can see, can't you, that contraception is a *grave sin?* To prevent life is an intrinsic **evil.**
Sir?
Yes, Mary?
We're not in *Religion* now, sir, we're in *Biology.*
Meaning?
I'd put my imaginary friend behind me by this time.
But my teachers still had theirs. Mind you, Joyce called contraception "a crime against fecundity" in **Ulysses** - and he was an atheist.
Well, I mean, *millions* of sperm and *none* can be wasted? That doesn't make any sense. And what about those 300 eggs? Are *none* of them to be wasted either?
HA HA HA HA HA
I don't like the sound of ***that!***
YOU ARE EITHER STUPID OR VERY, VERY WICKED!

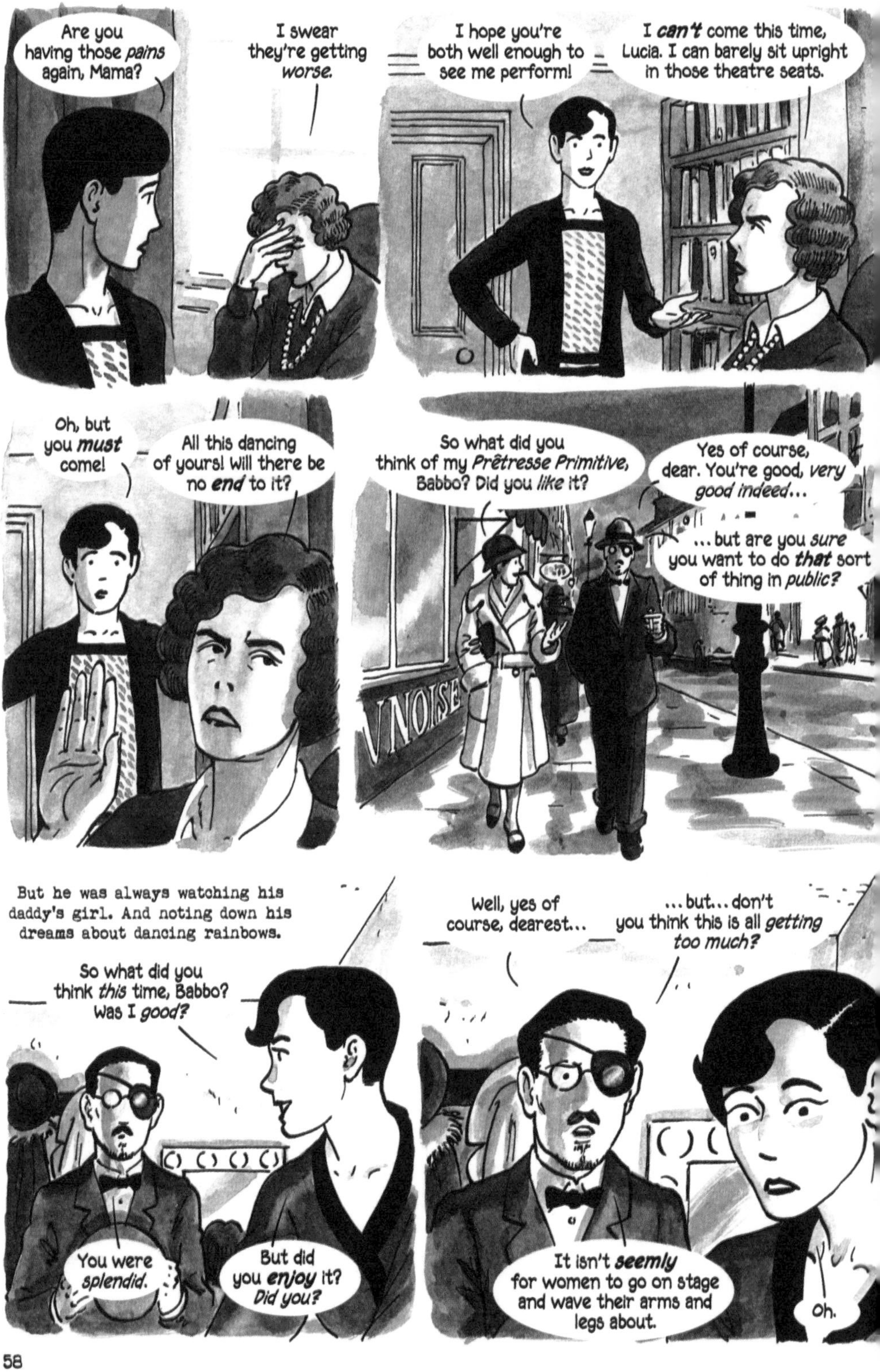

Are you having those pains again, Mama?
I swear they're getting worse.
I hope you're both well enough to see me perform!
I can't come this time, Lucia. I can barely sit upright in those theatre seats.
Oh, but you must come!
All this dancing of yours! Will there be no end to it?
So what did you think of my Prêtresse Primitive, Babbo? Did you like it?
Yes of course, dear. You're good, very good indeed...
...but are you sure you want to do that sort of thing in public?
VNOISE
But he was always watching his daddy's girl. And noting down his dreams about dancing rainbows.
So what did you think this time, Babbo? Was I good?
You were splendid.
But did you enjoy it? Did you?
Well, yes of course, dearest...
...but... don't you think this is all getting too much?
It isn't seemly for women to go on stage and wave their arms and legs about.
Oh.

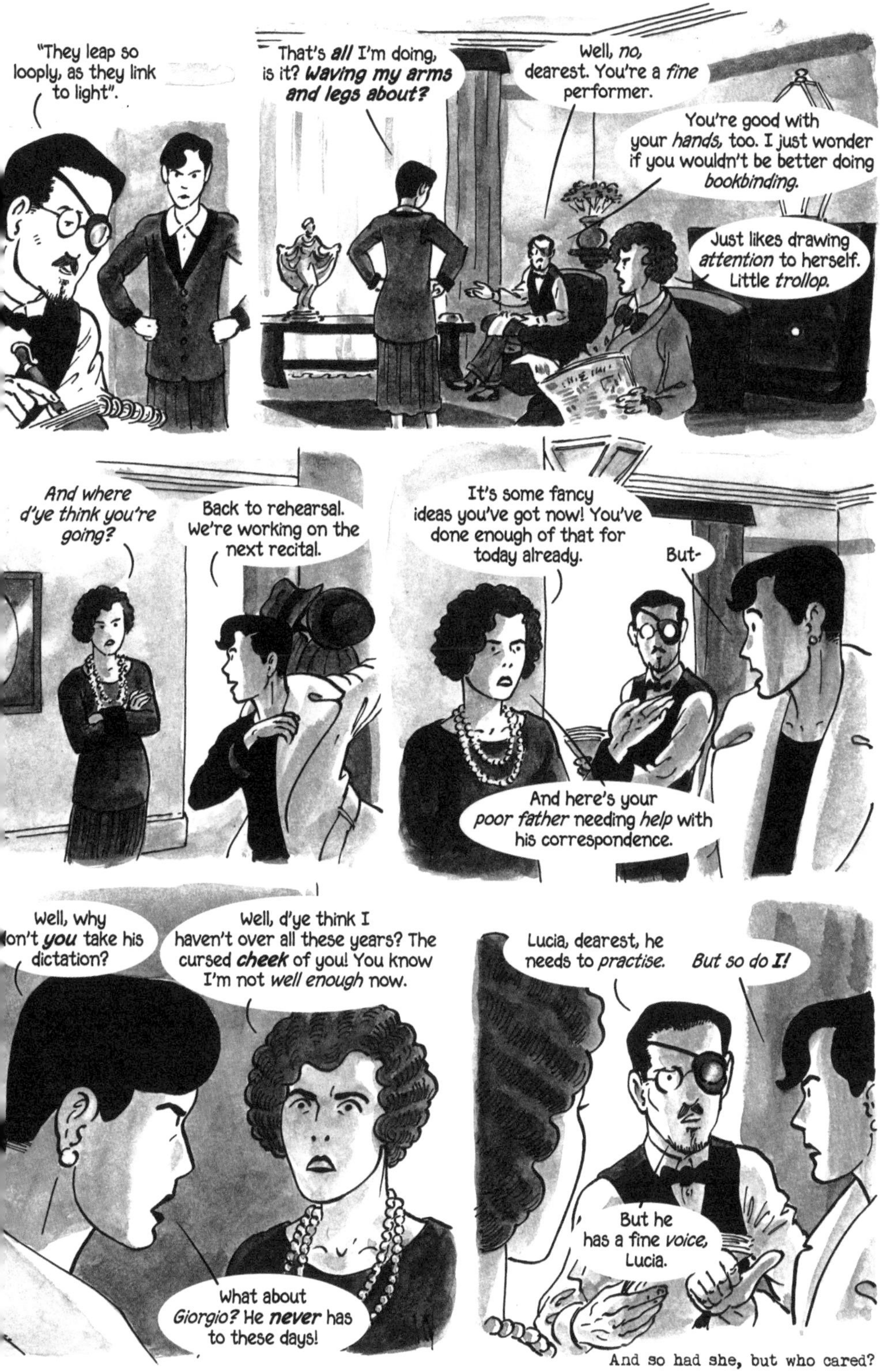
"They leap so looply, as they link to light".
That's *all* I'm doing, is it? ***Waving my arms and legs about?***
Well, *no,* dearest. You're a *fine* performer.
You're good with your *hands,* too. I just wonder if you wouldn't be better doing *bookbinding.*
Just likes drawing *attention* to herself. Little *trollop.*
And where d'ye think you're going?
Back to rehearsal. We're working on the next recital.
It's some fancy ideas you've got now! You've done enough of that for today already.
But-
And here's your *poor father* needing *help* with his correspondence.
Well, why don't ***you*** take his dictation?
Well, d'ye think I haven't over all these years? The cursed ***cheek*** of you! You know I'm not *well enough* now.
What about *Giorgio?* He ***never*** has to these days!
Lucia, dearest, he needs to *practise.*
*But so do **I!***
But he has a fine *voice,* Lucia.

And so had she, but who cared?

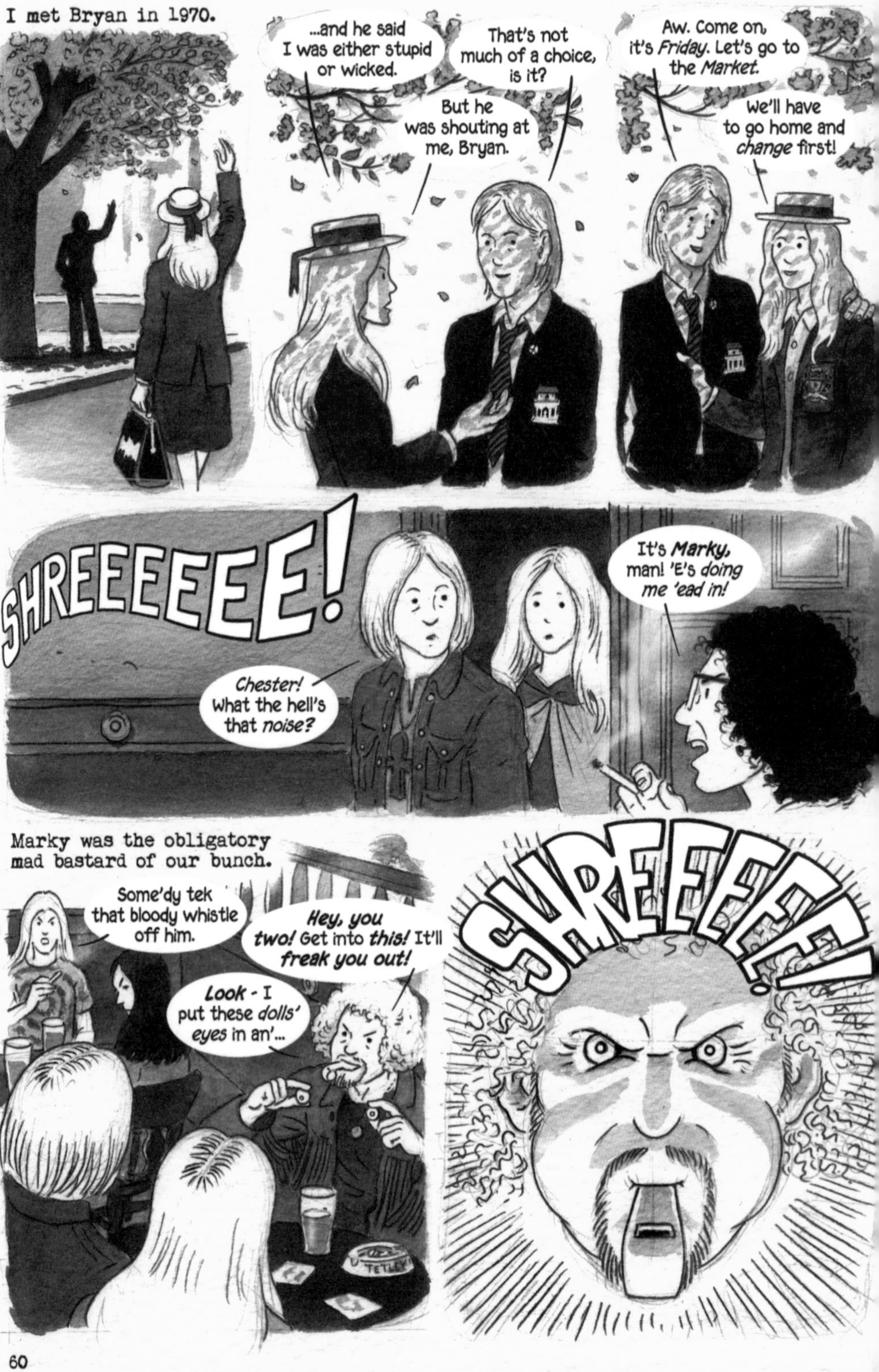
I met Bryan in 1970.
...and he said I was either stupid or wicked.
But he was shouting at me, Bryan.
That's not much of a choice, is it?
Aw. Come on, it's *Friday*. Let's go to the *Market*.
We'll have to go home and *change* first!
SHREEEEEE!
Chester! What the hell's that *noise?*
It's ***Marky,*** man! 'E's *doing me 'ead in!*
Marky was the obligatory mad bastard of our bunch.
Some'dy tek that bloody whistle off him.
Hey, you two! Get into ***this!*** It'll ***freak you out!***
Look - I put these *dolls' eyes* in an'...
SHREEEEEE!
TETLEY

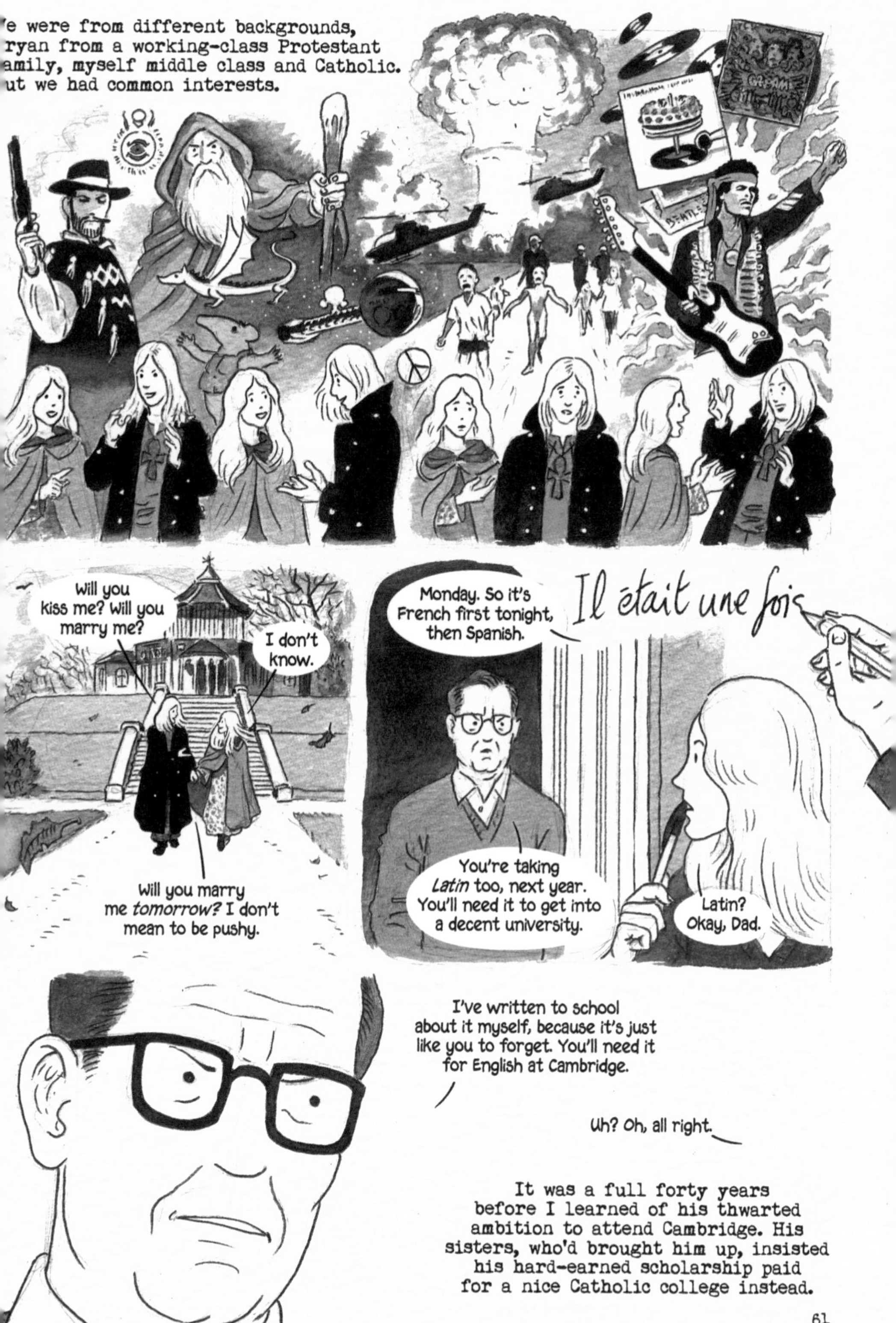
'e were from different backgrounds,
ryan from a working-class Protestant
amily, myself middle class and Catholic.
ut we had common interests.
Will you kiss me? Will you marry me?
I don't know.
Will you marry me *tomorrow?* I don't mean to be pushy.
Monday. So it's French first tonight, then Spanish.
Il était une fois
You're taking *Latin* too, next year. You'll need it to get into a decent university.
Latin? Okay, Dad.
I've written to school about it myself, because it's just like you to forget. You'll need it for English at Cambridge.
Uh? Oh, all right.
It was a full forty years before I learned of his thwarted ambition to attend Cambridge. His sisters, who'd brought him up, insisted his hard-earned scholarship paid for a nice Catholic college instead.

In October 1928, James had a new devotee - a willing scribe and all-purpose errand boy.

He soon became a daily visitor.

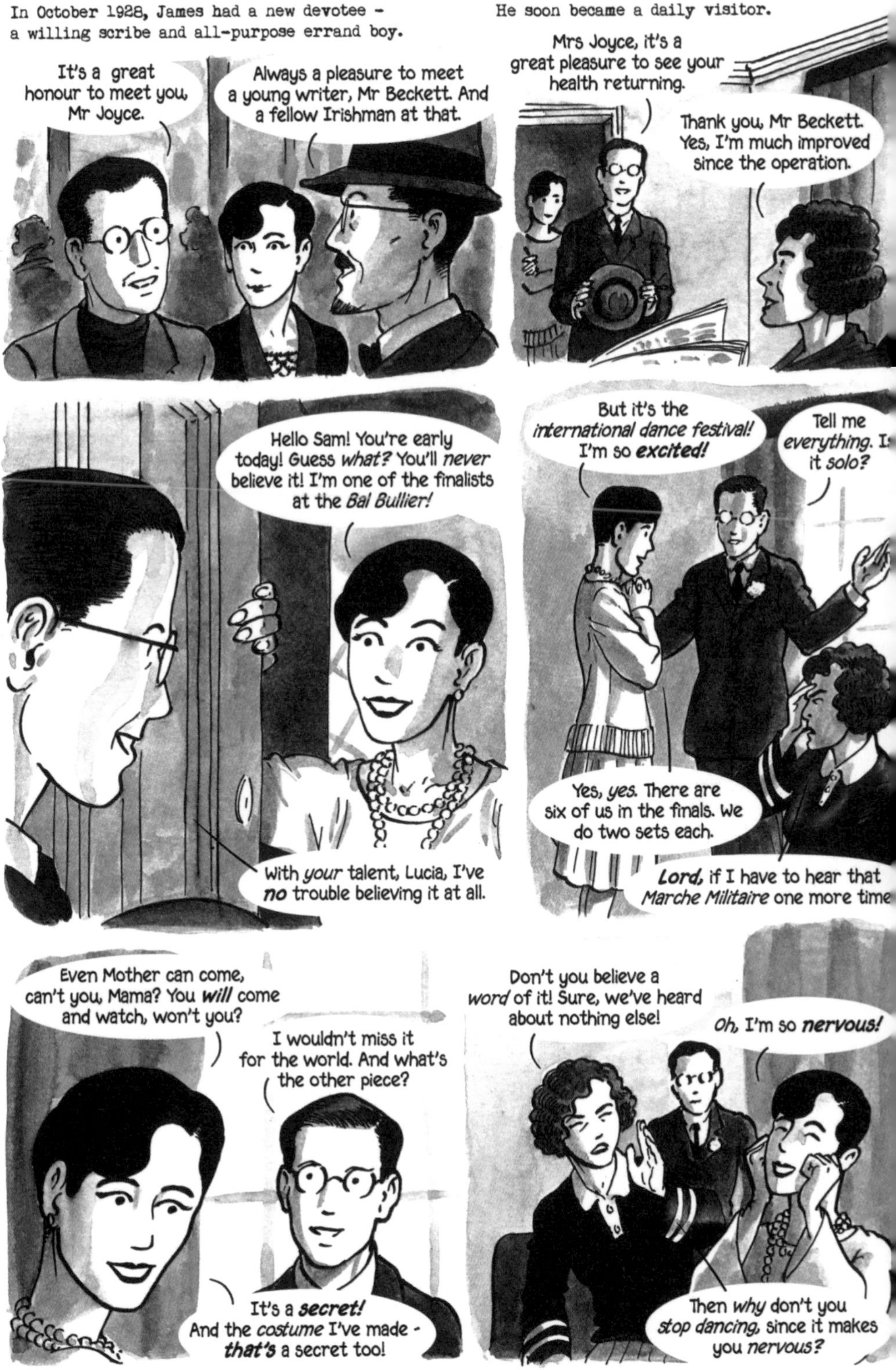

It's a great honour to meet you, Mr Joyce.
Always a pleasure to meet a young writer, Mr Beckett. And a fellow Irishman at that.
Mrs Joyce, it's a great pleasure to see your health returning.
Thank you, Mr Beckett. Yes, I'm much improved since the operation.
Hello Sam! You're early today! Guess *what?* You'll *never* believe it! I'm one of the finalists at the *Bal Bullier!*
With *your* talent, Lucia, I've **no** trouble believing it at all.
But it's the *international dance festival!* I'm so ***excited!***
Tell me *everything*. Is it *solo?*
Yes, *yes*. There are six of us in the finals. We do two sets each.
Lord, if I have to hear that *Marche Militaire* one more time
Even Mother can come, can't you, Mama? You ***will*** come and watch, won't you?
I wouldn't miss it for the world. And what's the other piece?
It's a ***secret!*** And the *costume* I've made - ***that's*** a secret too!
Don't you believe a *word* of it! Sure, we've heard about nothing else!
Oh, I'm so ***nervous!***
Then *why* don't you *stop dancing,* since it makes you *nervous?*

al Bullier,
8th May 1929

"This very remarkable artist - subtle and barbaric tout ensemble. Barbaric, she performed forcefully in the Marche Militaire by Schubert ...subtle in her chosen piece, Feu Follet by the English composer, Donald."

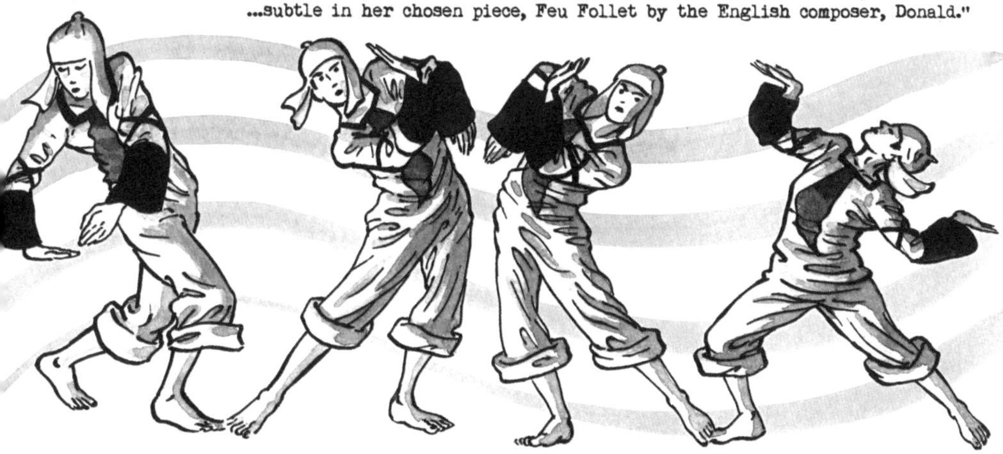

The audience loved her, though she didn't win. Her father decided to celebrate anyway. Any excuse for a party.

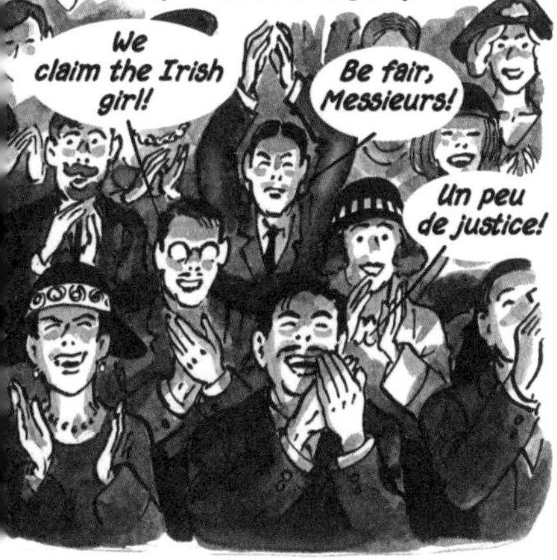

We claim the Irish girl!
Be fair, Messieurs!
Un peu de justice!

Lucia accepted an invitation from one of the judges, a Hungarian dancer called Madika, to study with her as preparation for the next international competition the following year.

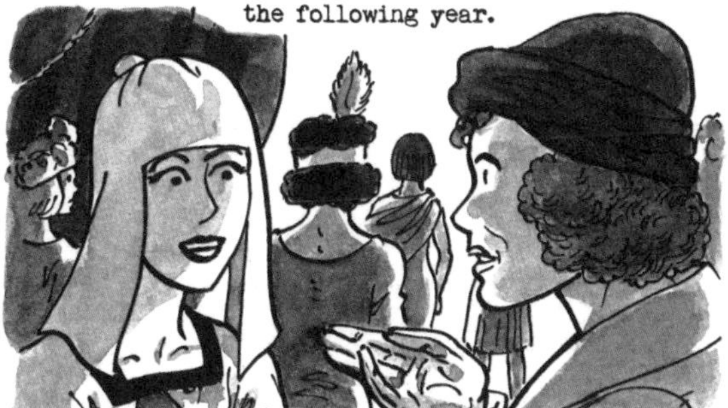

She had embarked on further dance training already. Training with Börlin had made her realise that a modernist dancer needs to know what rules she is breaking.

Accordingly, at the age of 21, she took up classical ballet with Lubov Egorova, former star of the Russian Ballet.

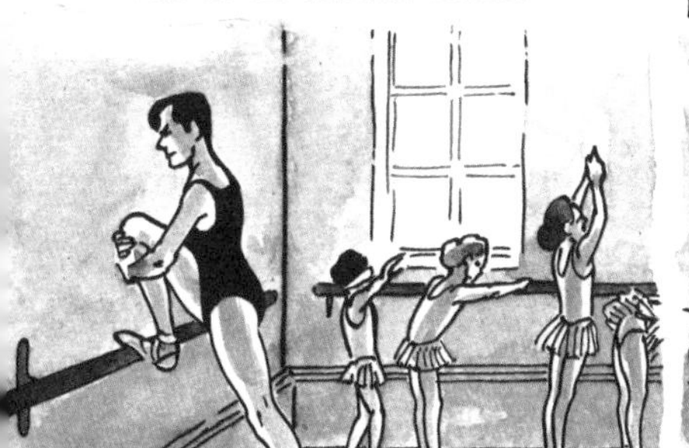

Lubov Egorova's studio, rue de La Rochefoucauld

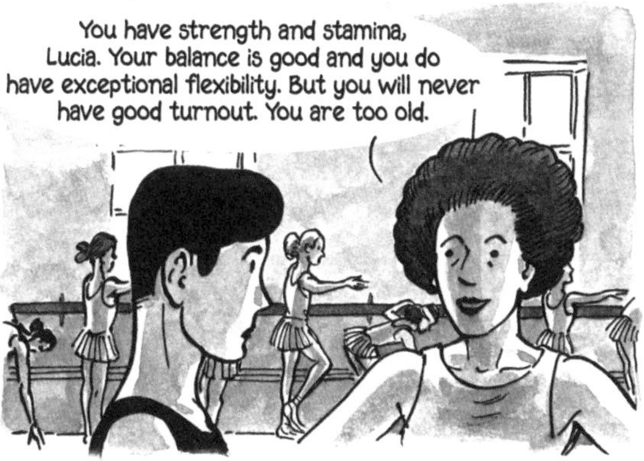

You have strength and stamina, Lucia. Your balance is good and you do have exceptional flexibility. But you will never have good turnout. You are too old.

Two years previously, Egorova had taken on Scott Fitzgerald's wife as an even older student. Zelda Fitzgerald's only novel, ***Save Me the Waltz***, contains a fictionalised account of her ordeal.

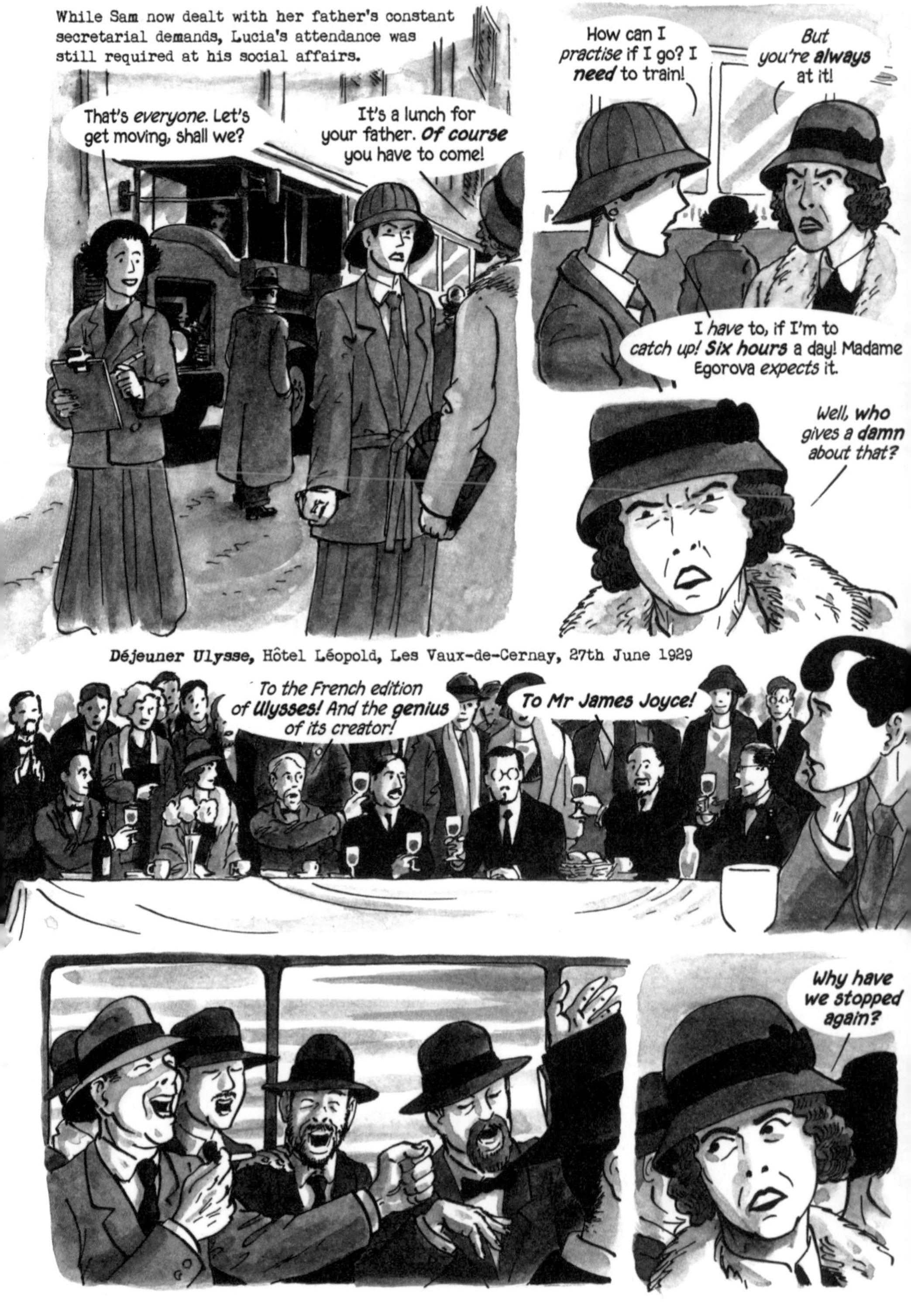
While Sam now dealt with her father's constant secretarial demands, Lucia's attendance was still required at his social affairs.
That's *everyone*. Let's get moving, shall we?
It's a lunch for your father. ***Of course*** you have to come!
How can I *practise* if I go? I ***need*** to train!
*But you're **always** at it!*
I *have* to, if I'm to *catch up!* ***Six hours*** a day! Madame Egorova *expects* it.
*Well, **who** gives a **damn** about that?*
Déjeuner Ulysse, Hôtel Léopold, Les Vaux-de-Cernay, 27th June 1929
*To the French edition of **Ulysses!** And the **genius** of its creator!*
To Mr James Joyce!
Why have we stopped again?

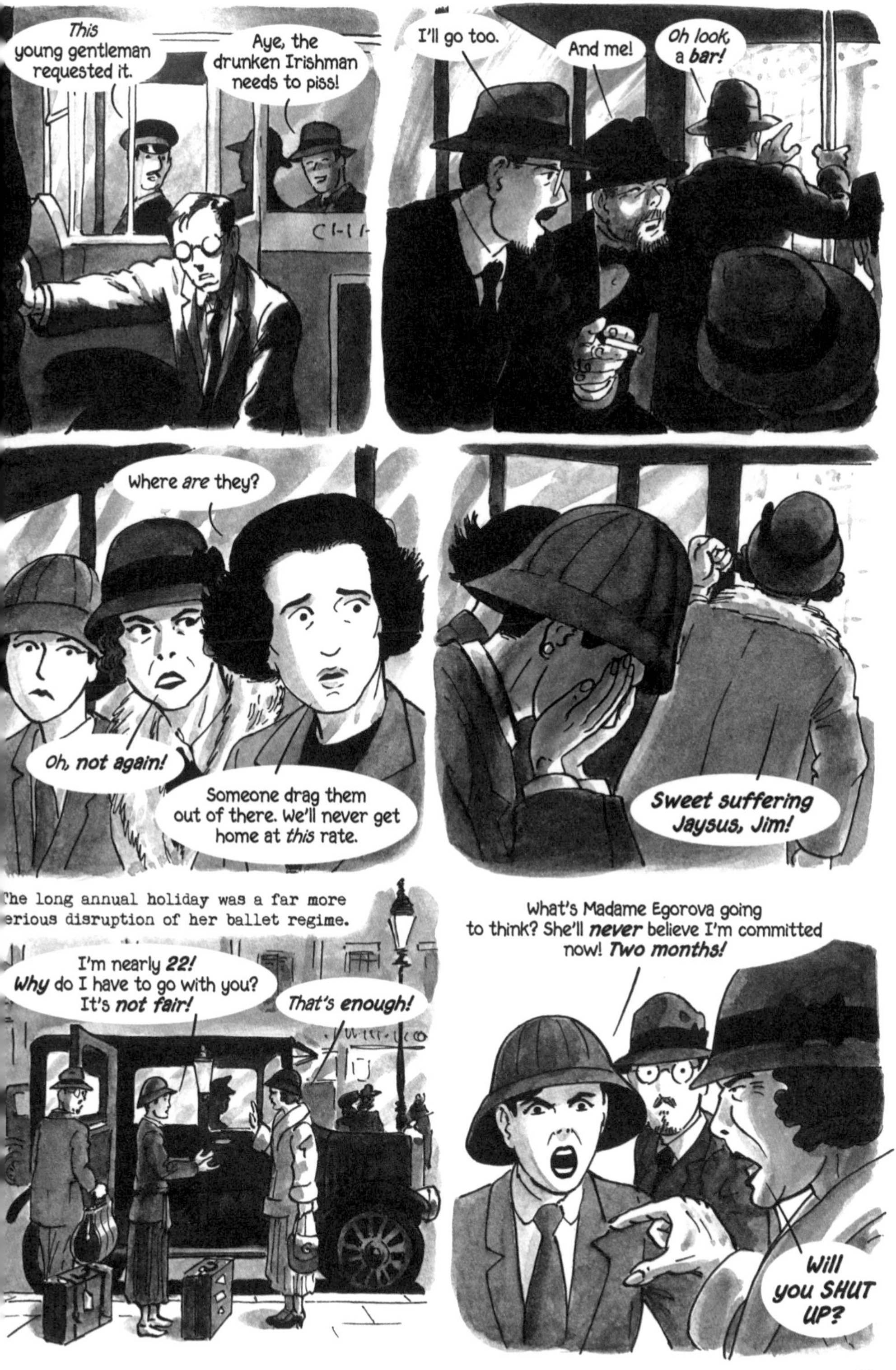
This young gentleman requested it.
Aye, the drunken Irishman needs to piss!
I'll go too.
And me!
Oh look, a *bar!*
Where *are* they?
Oh, not again!
Someone drag them out of there. We'll never get home at *this* rate.
Sweet suffering Jaysus, Jim!
The long annual holiday was a far more erious disruption of her ballet regime.
I'm nearly ***22! Why*** do I have to go with you? It's ***not fair!***
That's ***enough!***
What's Madame Egorova going to think? She'll ***never*** believe I'm committed now! ***Two months!***
Will you SHUT UP?

The trip was a delight for her convalescent mother. Shopping in London followed by summer at the seaside. And, like all their holidays, it was a research expedition for her father.

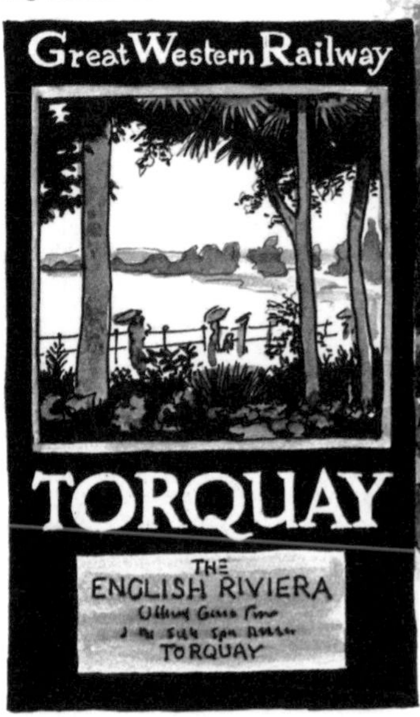
Great Western Railway
TORQUAY
THE ENGLISH RIVIERA
TORQUAY

But Lucia was falling behind.

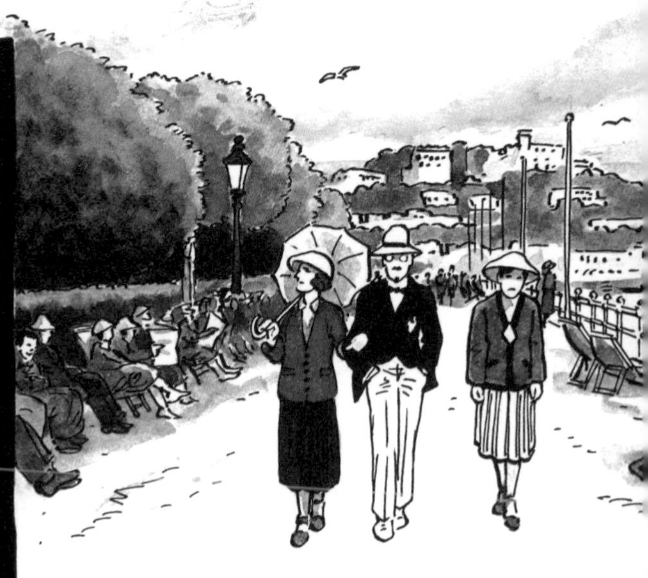

Her renewed regime was punishing. In the month of the Wall Street Crash, Lucia was going through her own crisis.

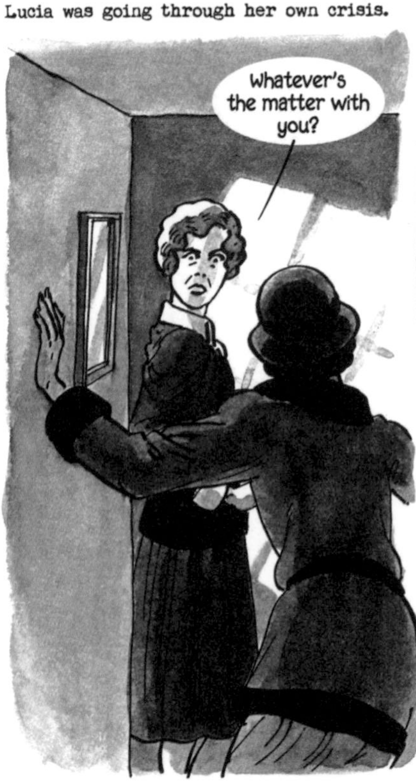
Whatever's the matter with you?

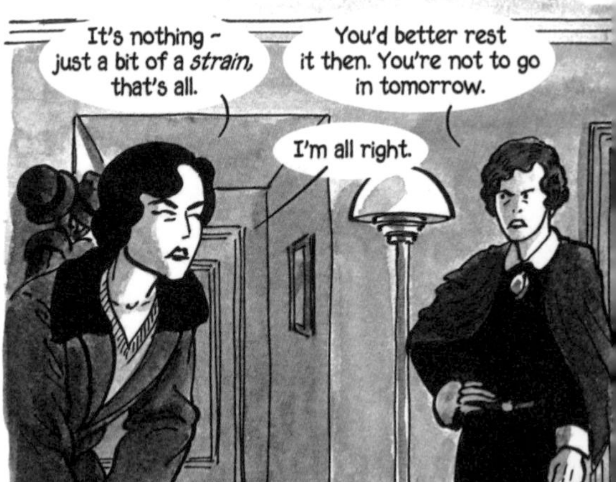
It's nothing - just a bit of a *strain*, that's all.
You'd better rest it then. You're not to go in tomorrow.
I'm all right.

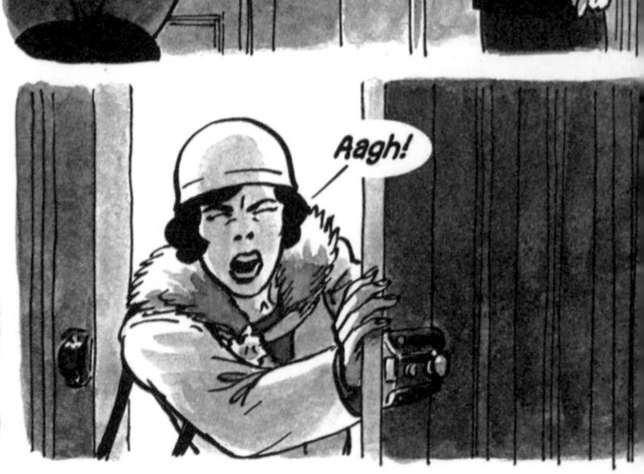
Aagh!

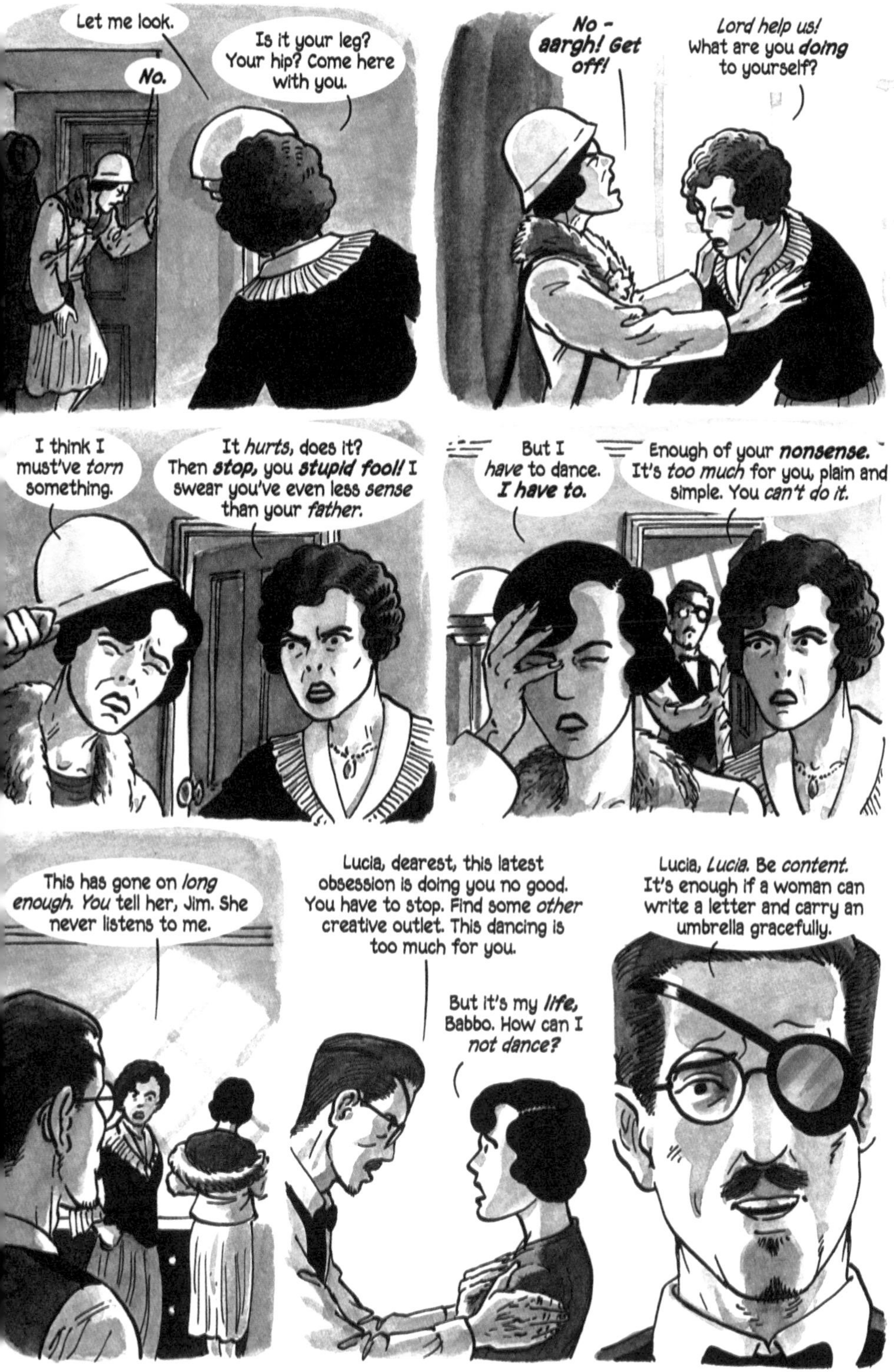

Let me look.
No.
Is it your leg? Your hip? Come here with you.
No - aargh! Get off!
Lord help us! What are you doing to yourself?
I think I must've torn something.
It hurts, does it? Then stop, you stupid fool! I swear you've even less sense than your father.
But I have to dance. I have to.
Enough of your nonsense. It's too much for you, plain and simple. You can't do it.
This has gone on long enough. You tell her, Jim. She never listens to me.
Lucia, dearest, this latest obsession is doing you no good. You have to stop. Find some other creative outlet. This dancing is too much for you.
But it's my life, Babbo. How can I not dance?
Lucia, Lucia. Be content. It's enough if a woman can write a letter and carry an umbrella gracefully.

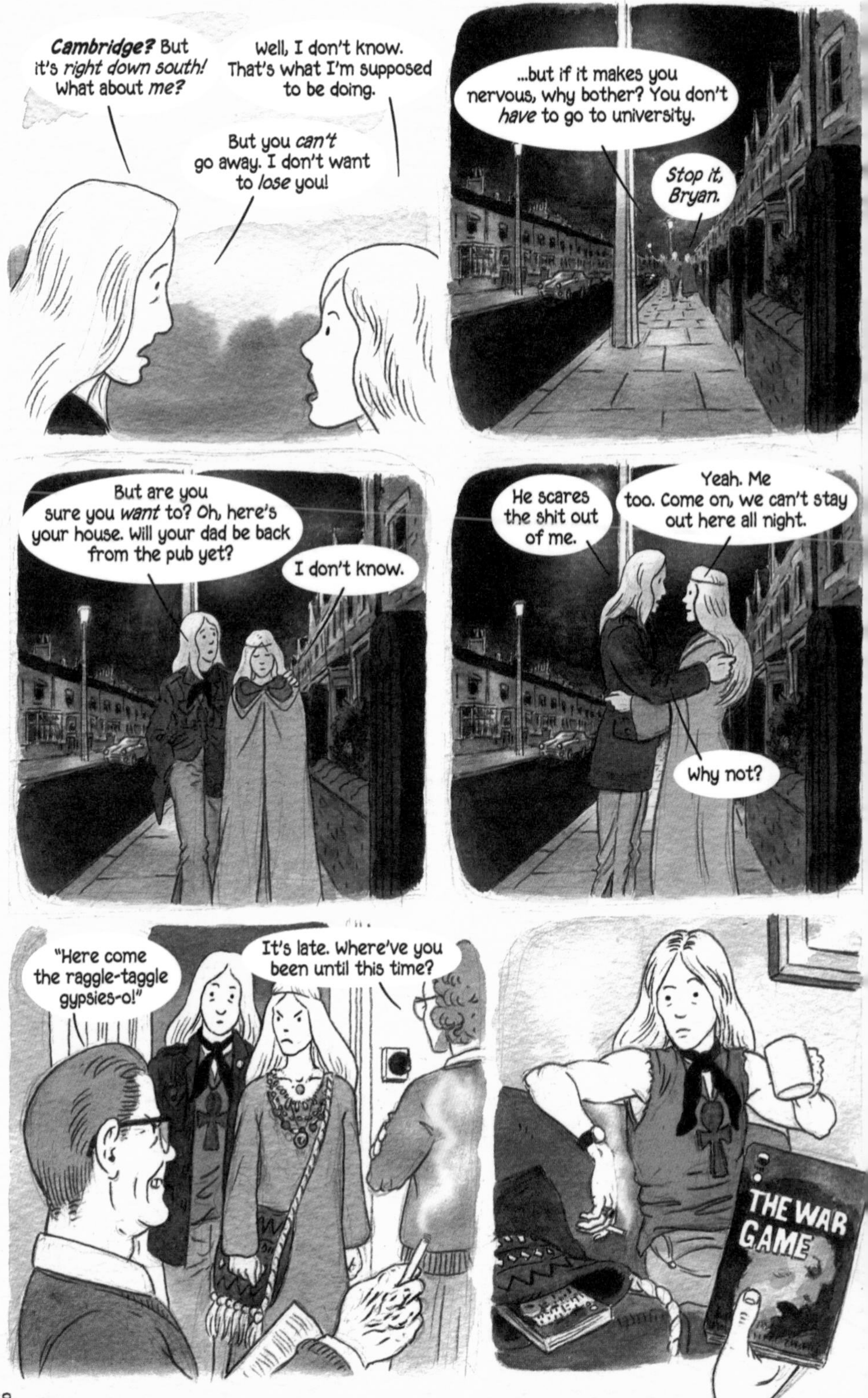
Cambridge? But it's *right down south!* What about *me?*
Well, I don't know. That's what I'm supposed to be doing.
But you *can't* go away. I don't want to *lose* you!
...but if it makes you nervous, why bother? You don't *have* to go to university.
Stop it, Bryan.
But are you sure you *want* to? Oh, here's your house. Will your dad be back from the pub yet?
I don't know.
He scares the shit out of me.
Yeah. Me too. Come on, we can't stay out here all night.
Why not?
"Here come the raggle-taggle gypsies-o!"
It's late. Where've you been until this time?
THE WAR GAME

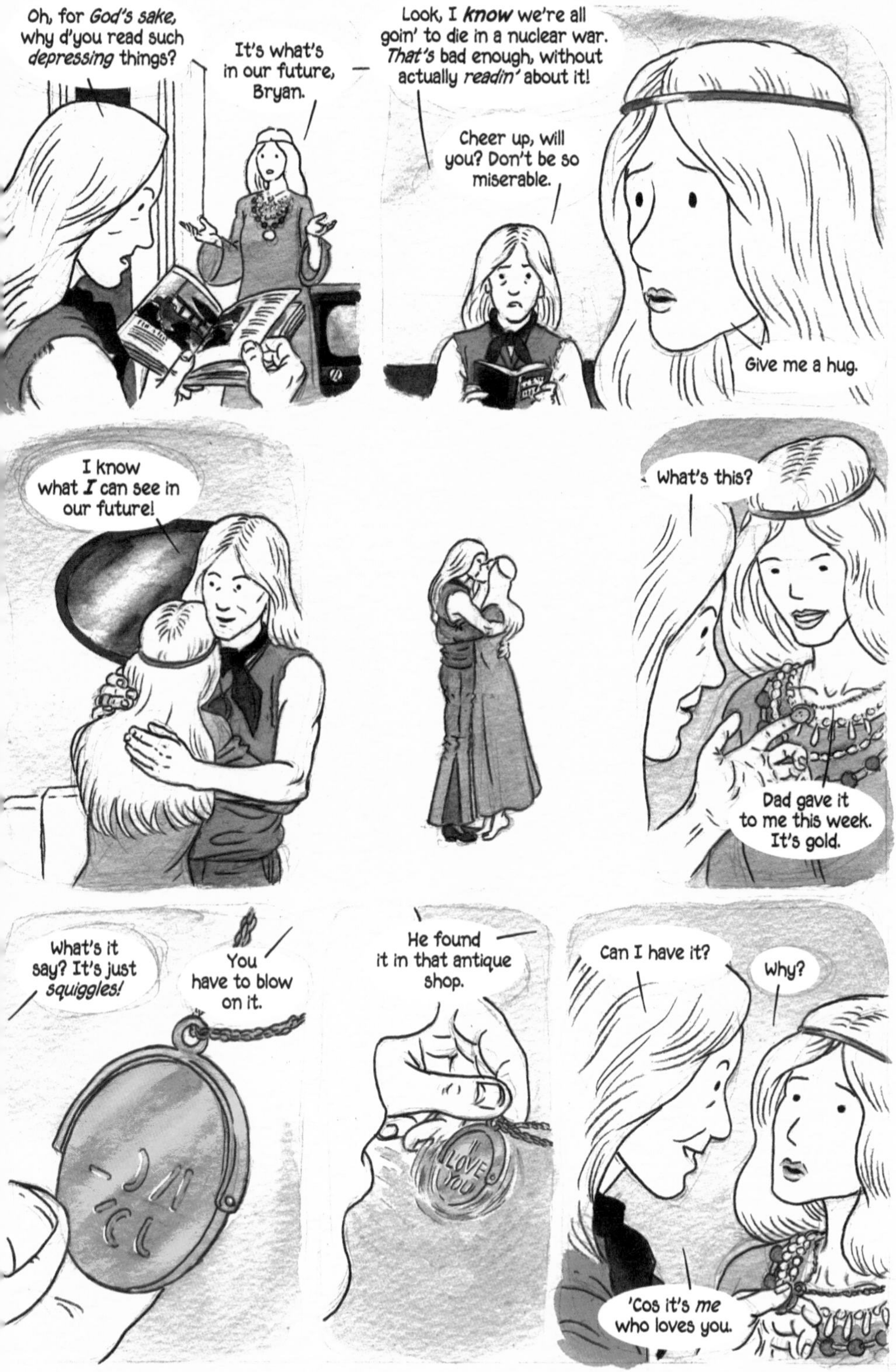
Oh, for *God's sake,* why d'you read such *depressing* things?
It's what's in our future, Bryan.
Look, I **know** we're all goin' to die in a nuclear war. *That's* bad enough, without actually *readin'* about it!
Cheer up, will you? Don't be so miserable.
Give me a hug.
I know what *I* can see in our future!
What's this?
Dad gave it to me this week. It's gold.
What's it say? It's just *squiggles!*
You have to blow on it.
He found it in that antique shop.
I LOVE YOU
Can I have it?
Why?
'Cos it's *me* who loves you.

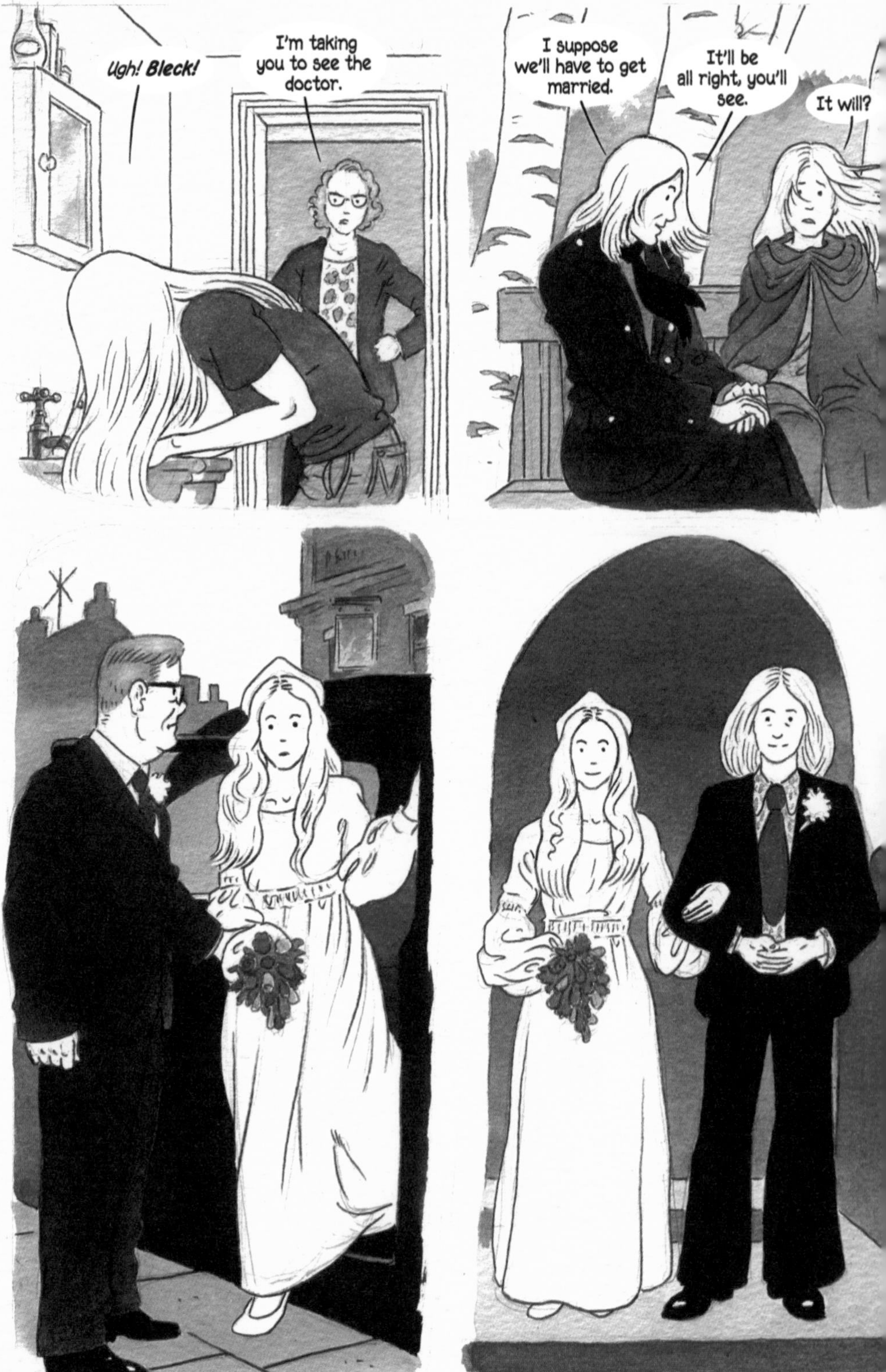
Ugh! Bleck!
I'm taking you to see the doctor.
I suppose we'll have to get married.
It'll be all right, you'll see.
It will?

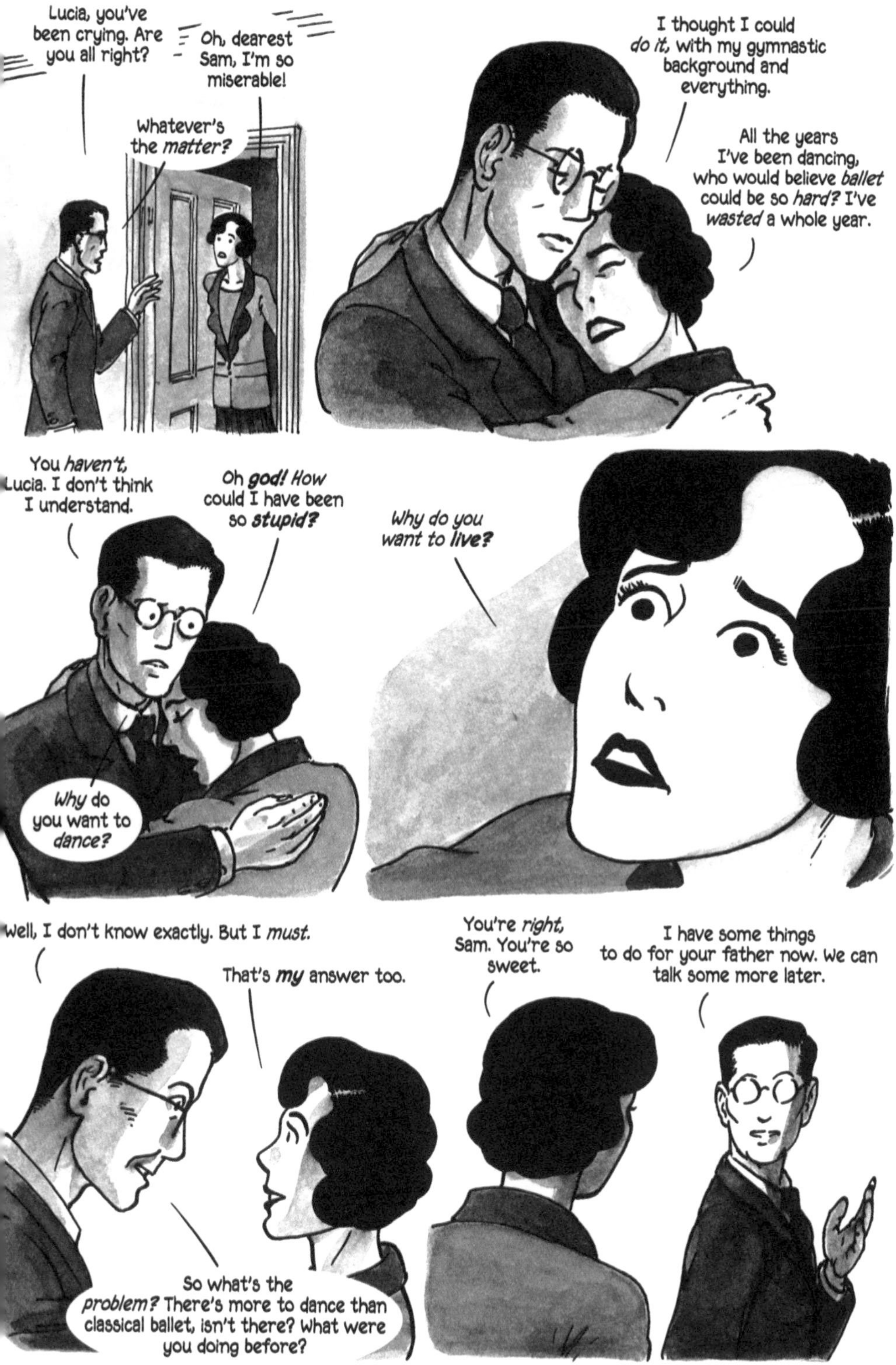
Lucia, you've been crying. Are you all right?
Oh, dearest Sam, I'm so miserable!
Whatever's the *matter?*
I thought I could *do it,* with my gymnastic background and everything.
All the years I've been dancing, who would believe *ballet* could be so *hard?* I've *wasted* a whole year.
You *haven't,* Lucia. I don't think I understand.
Oh **god!** How could I have been so **stupid?**
Why do you want to *dance?*
*Why do you want to **live?***
Well, I don't know exactly. But I *must.*
That's ***my*** answer too.
So what's the *problem?* There's more to dance than classical ballet, isn't there? What were you doing before?
You're *right,* Sam. You're so sweet.
I have some things to do for your father now. We can talk some more later.

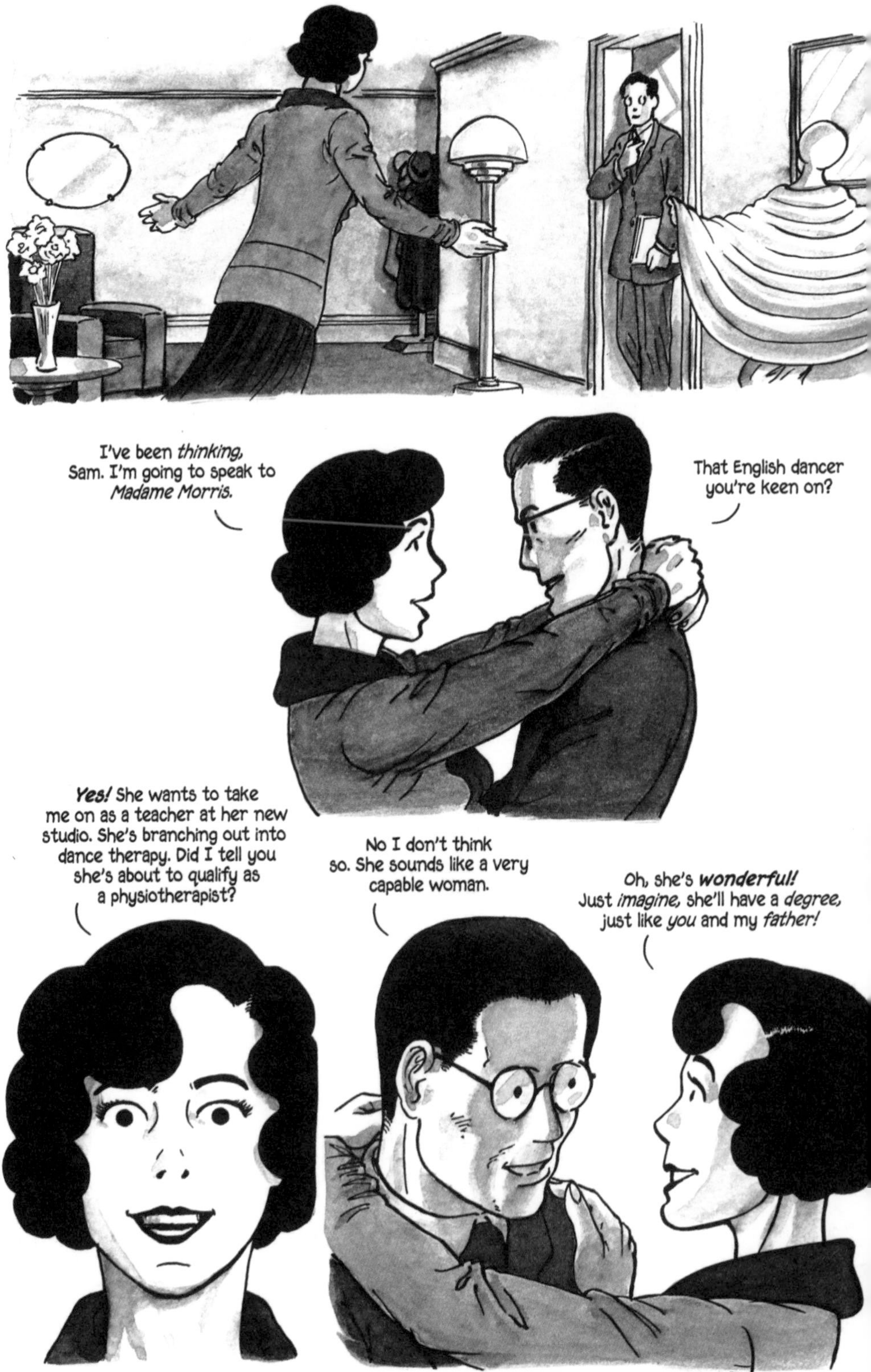
I've been *thinking,* Sam. I'm going to speak to *Madame Morris.*
That English dancer you're keen on?
Yes! She wants to take me on as a teacher at her new studio. She's branching out into dance therapy. Did I tell you she's about to qualify as a physiotherapist?
No I don't think so. She sounds like a very capable woman.
Oh, she's ***wonderful!*** Just *imagine,* she'll have a *degree,* just like *you* and my *father!*

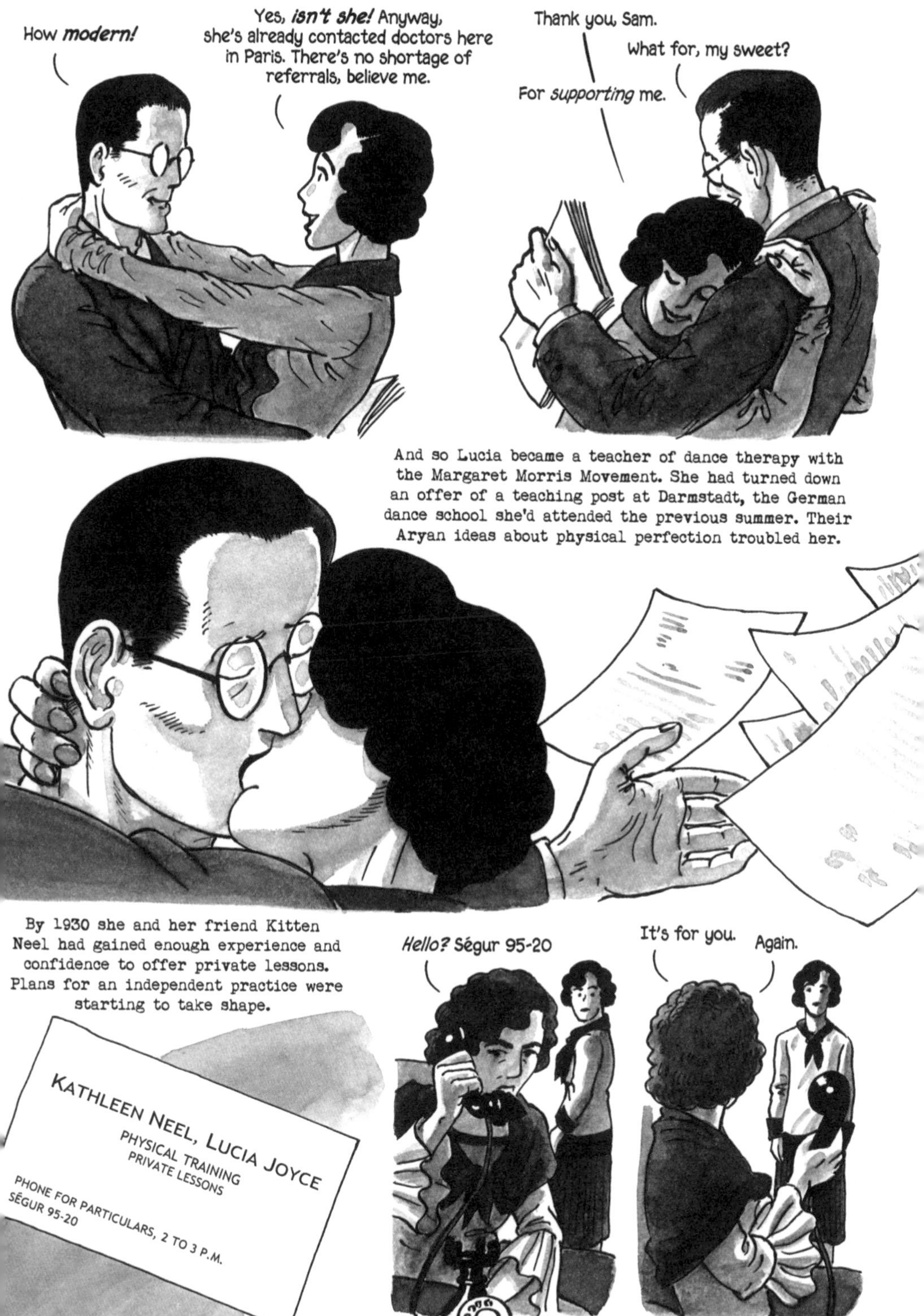
How *modern!*
Yes, ***isn't she!*** Anyway, she's already contacted doctors here in Paris. There's no shortage of referrals, believe me.
Thank you, Sam.
What for, my sweet?
For *supporting* me.
And so Lucia became a teacher of dance therapy with the Margaret Morris Movement. She had turned down an offer of a teaching post at Darmstadt, the German dance school she'd attended the previous summer. Their Aryan ideas about physical perfection troubled her.
By 1930 she and her friend Kitten Neel had gained enough experience and confidence to offer private lessons. Plans for an independent practice were starting to take shape.
KATHLEEN NEEL, LUCIA JOYCE
PHYSICAL TRAINING
PRIVATE LESSONS
PHONE FOR PARTICULARS, 2 TO 3 P.M.
SÉGUR 95-20
Hello? Ségur 95-20
It's for you.
Again.

We settled in Preston after we married. Bryan was now a student there. But I moved back home for about a month before the baby was due. My mother had insisted. She was concerned that I wouldn't receive the support I needed otherwise.

I had **very little** idea what was going to happen, just that it was going to be rough.

I think it's started, Mum.

I'll drive you in before I go to school. I think it might be a bit soon, though.

Billinge Hospital
MATERNITY UNIT

See you tonight.

I could tell that much from my mother's face.

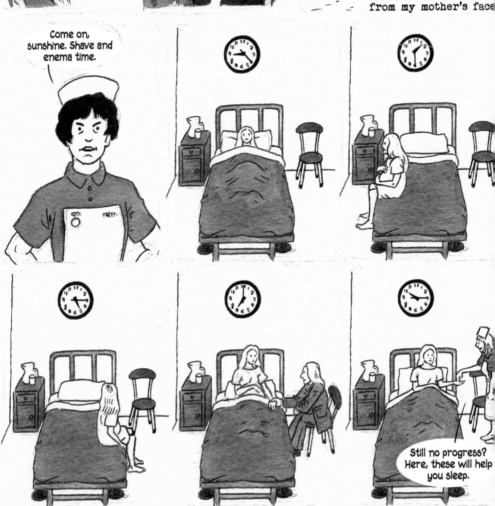

Come on, sunshine. Shave and enema time.

Still no progress? Here, these will help you sleep.

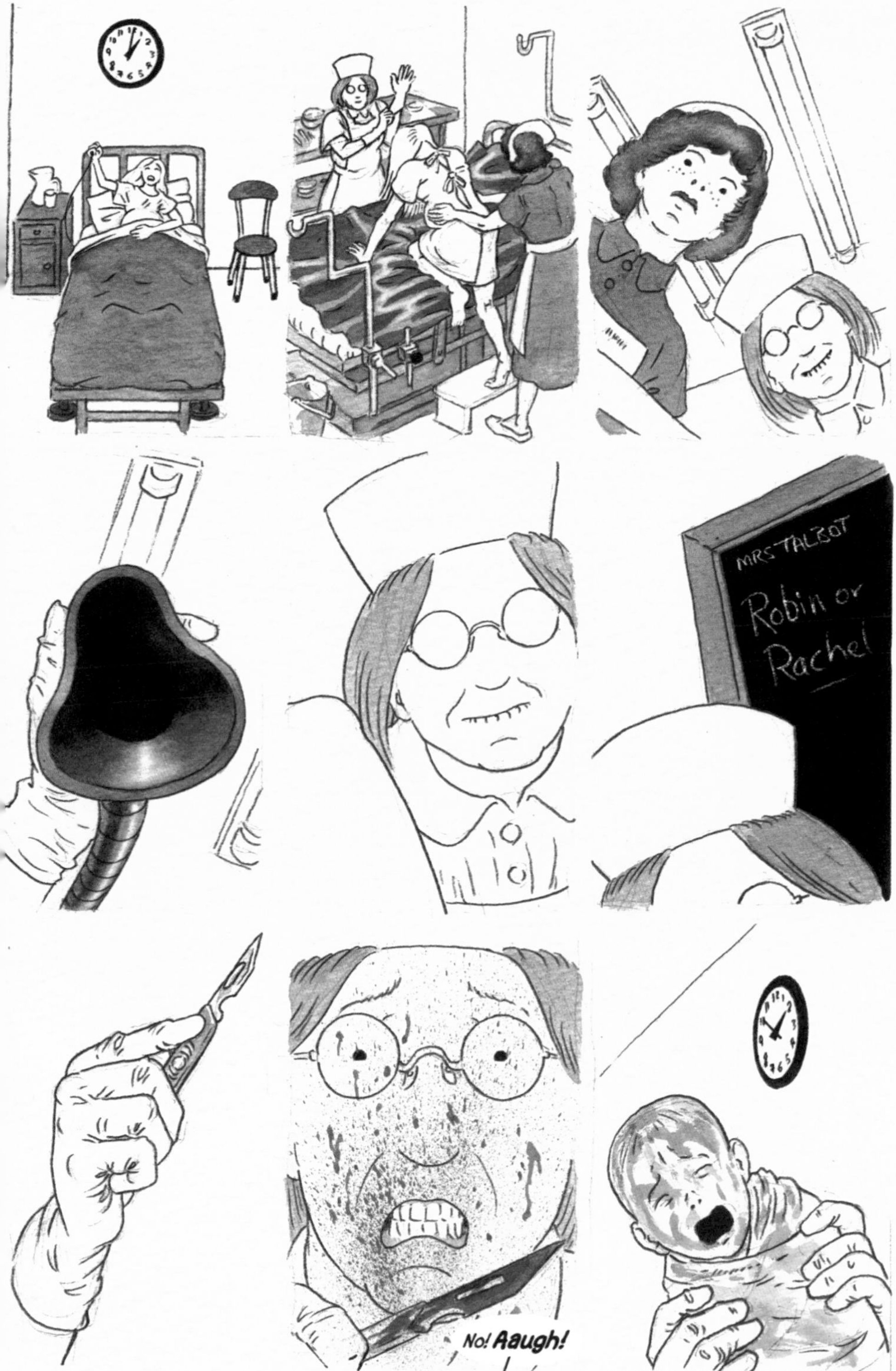
MRS TALBOT
Robin or Rachel
No! Aaugh!

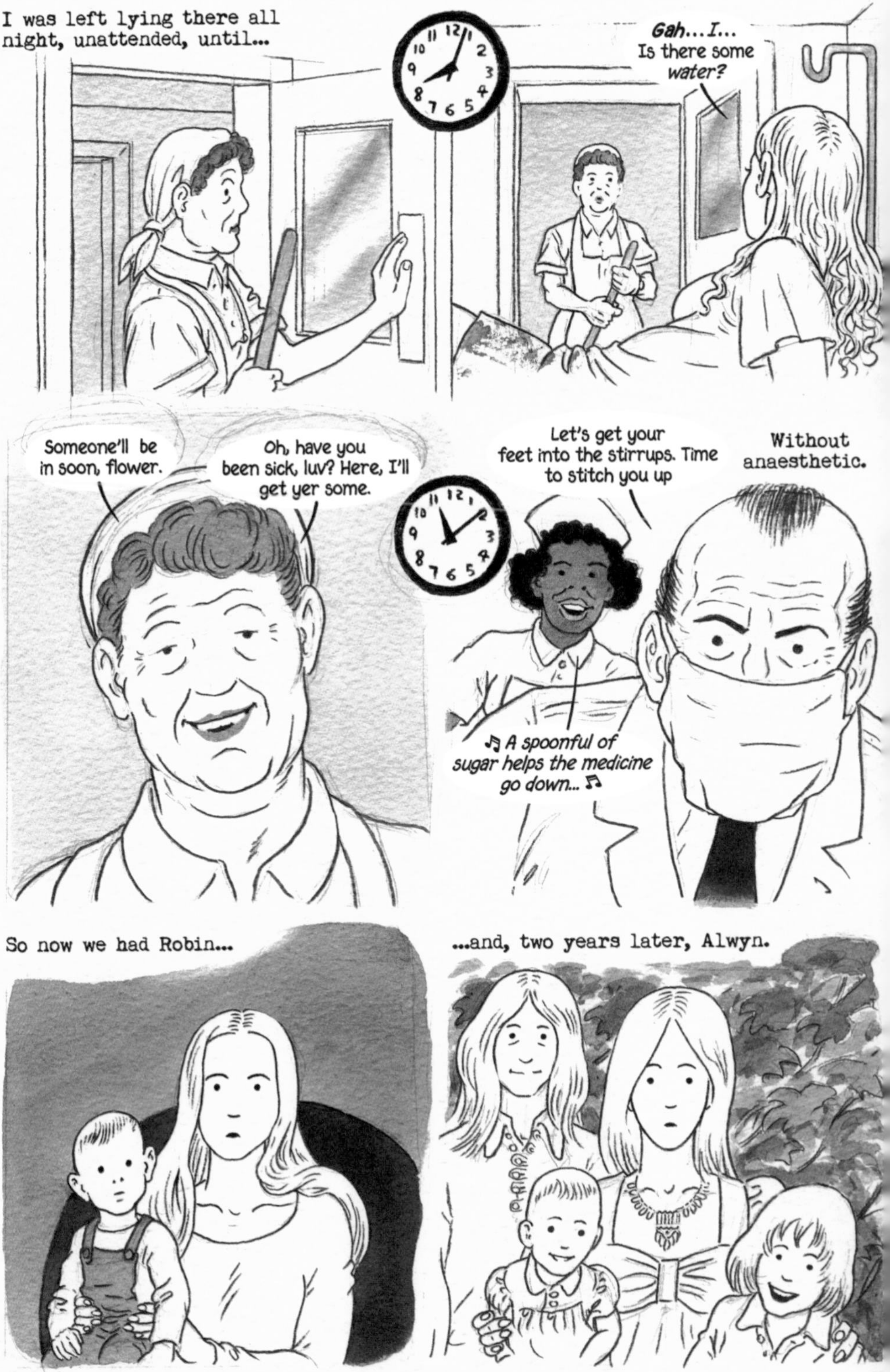
I was left lying there all night, unattended, until...
Gah... I... Is there some water?
Someone'll be in soon, flower.
Oh, have you been sick, luv? Here, I'll get yer some.
Let's get your feet into the stirrups. Time to stitch you up
Without anaesthetic.
♫ A spoonful of sugar helps the medicine go down... ♫
So now we had Robin...
...and, two years later, Alwyn.

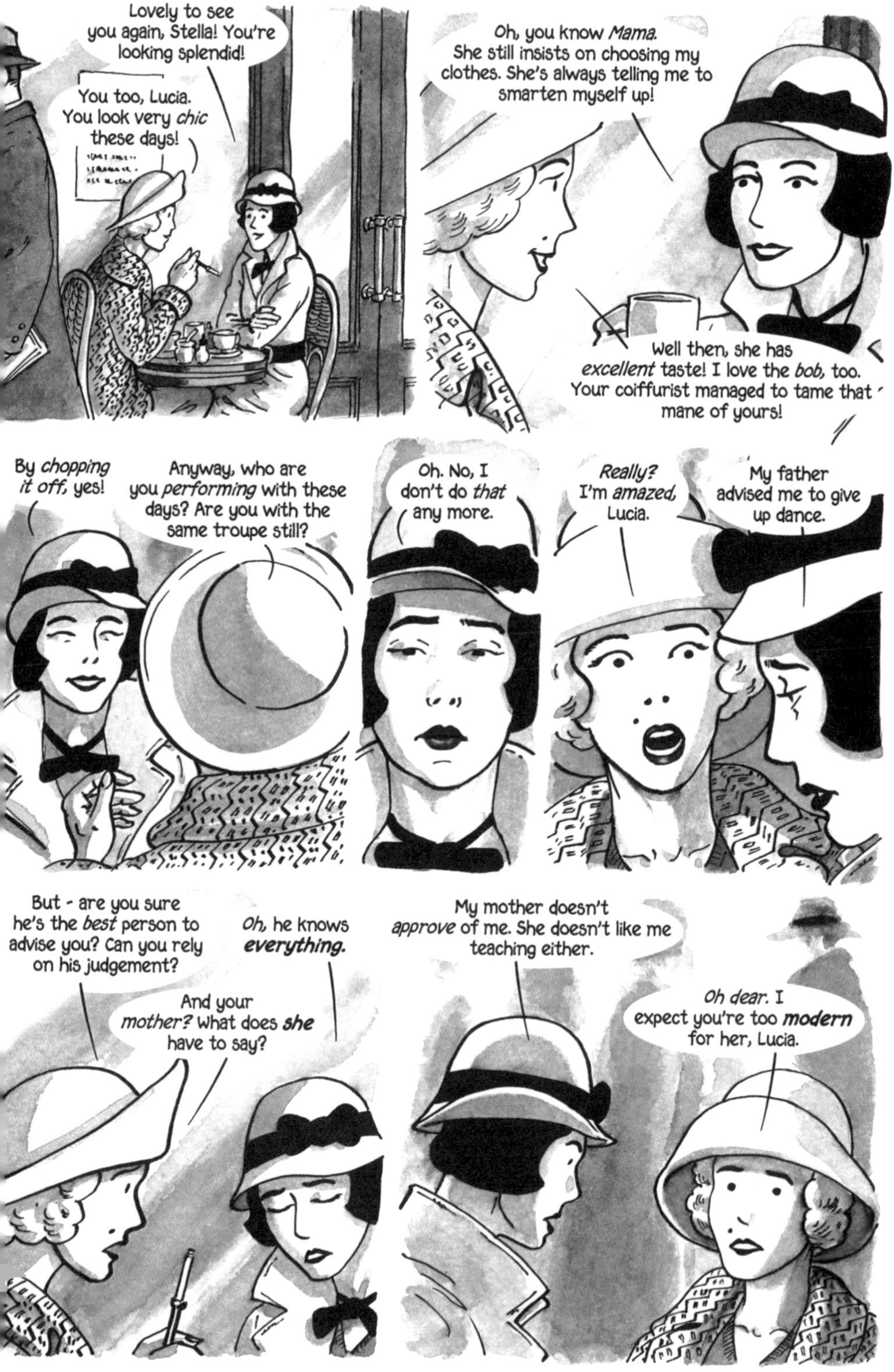
Lovely to see you again, Stella! You're looking splendid!
You too, Lucia. You look very *chic* these days!
Oh, you know *Mama*. She still insists on choosing my clothes. She's always telling me to smarten myself up!
Well then, she has *excellent* taste! I love the *bob*, too. Your coiffurist managed to tame that mane of yours!
By *chopping it off*, yes!
Anyway, who are you *performing* with these days? Are you with the same troupe still?
Oh. No, I don't do *that* any more.
Really? I'm *amazed*, Lucia.
My father advised me to give up dance.
But - are you sure he's the *best* person to advise you? Can you rely on his judgement?
Oh, he knows ***everything.***
And your *mother?* What does ***she*** have to say?
My mother doesn't *approve* of me. She doesn't like me teaching either.
Oh dear. I expect you're too **modern** for her, Lucia.

Lucia had established a professional life for herself. Unfortunately everything else was starting to fall apart.

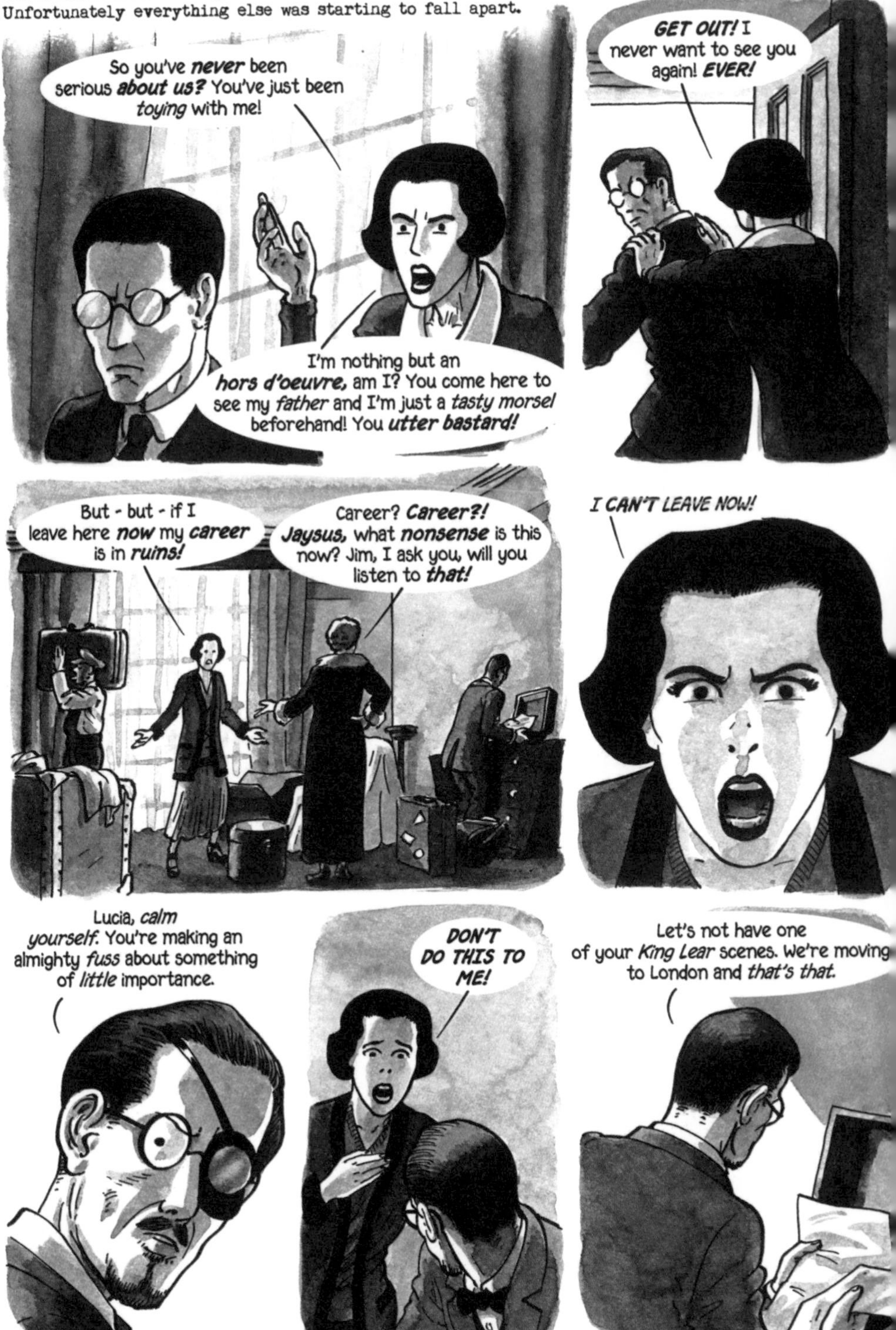
So you've never been serious about us? You've just been toying with me!
I'm nothing but an hors d'oeuvre, am I? You come here to see my father and I'm just a tasty morsel beforehand! You utter bastard!
GET OUT! I never want to see you again! EVER!
But - but - if I leave here now my career is in ruins!
Career? Career?! Jaysus, what nonsense is this now? Jim, I ask you, will you listen to that!
I CAN'T LEAVE NOW!
Lucia, calm yourself. You're making an almighty fuss about something of little importance.
DON'T DO THIS TO ME!
Let's not have one of your King Lear scenes. We're moving to London and that's that.

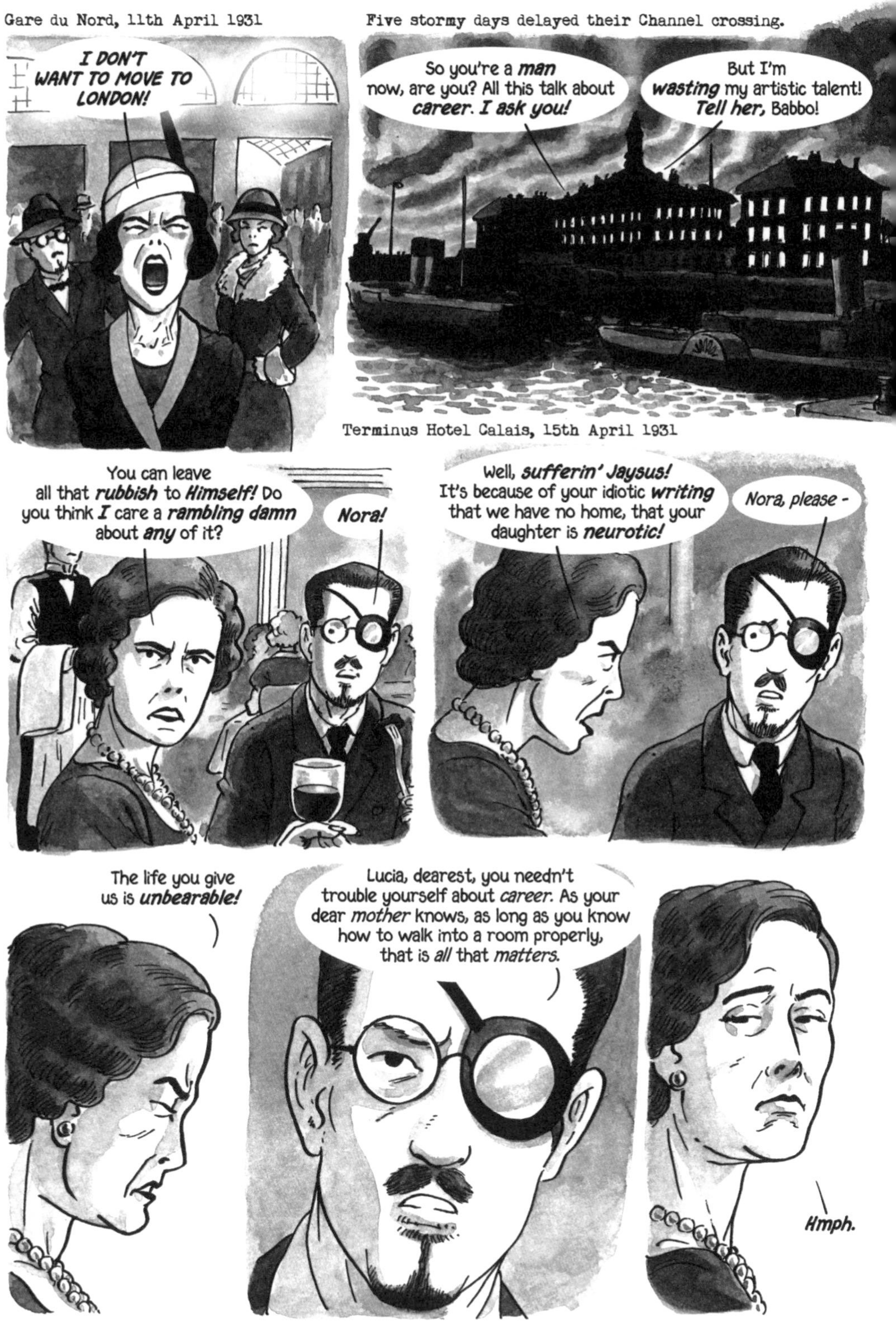

Gare du Nord, 11th April 1931
I DON'T WANT TO MOVE TO LONDON!
Five stormy days delayed their Channel crossing.
So you're a man now, are you? All this talk about career. I ask you!
But I'm wasting my artistic talent! Tell her, Babbo!
Terminus Hotel Calais, 15th April 1931
You can leave all that rubbish to Himself! Do you think I care a rambling damn about any of it?
Nora!
Well, sufferin' Jaysus! It's because of your idiotic writing that we have no home, that your daughter is neurotic!
Nora, please -
The life you give us is unbearable!
Lucia, dearest, you needn't trouble yourself about career. As your dear mother knows, as long as you know how to walk into a room properly, that is all that matters.
Hmph.

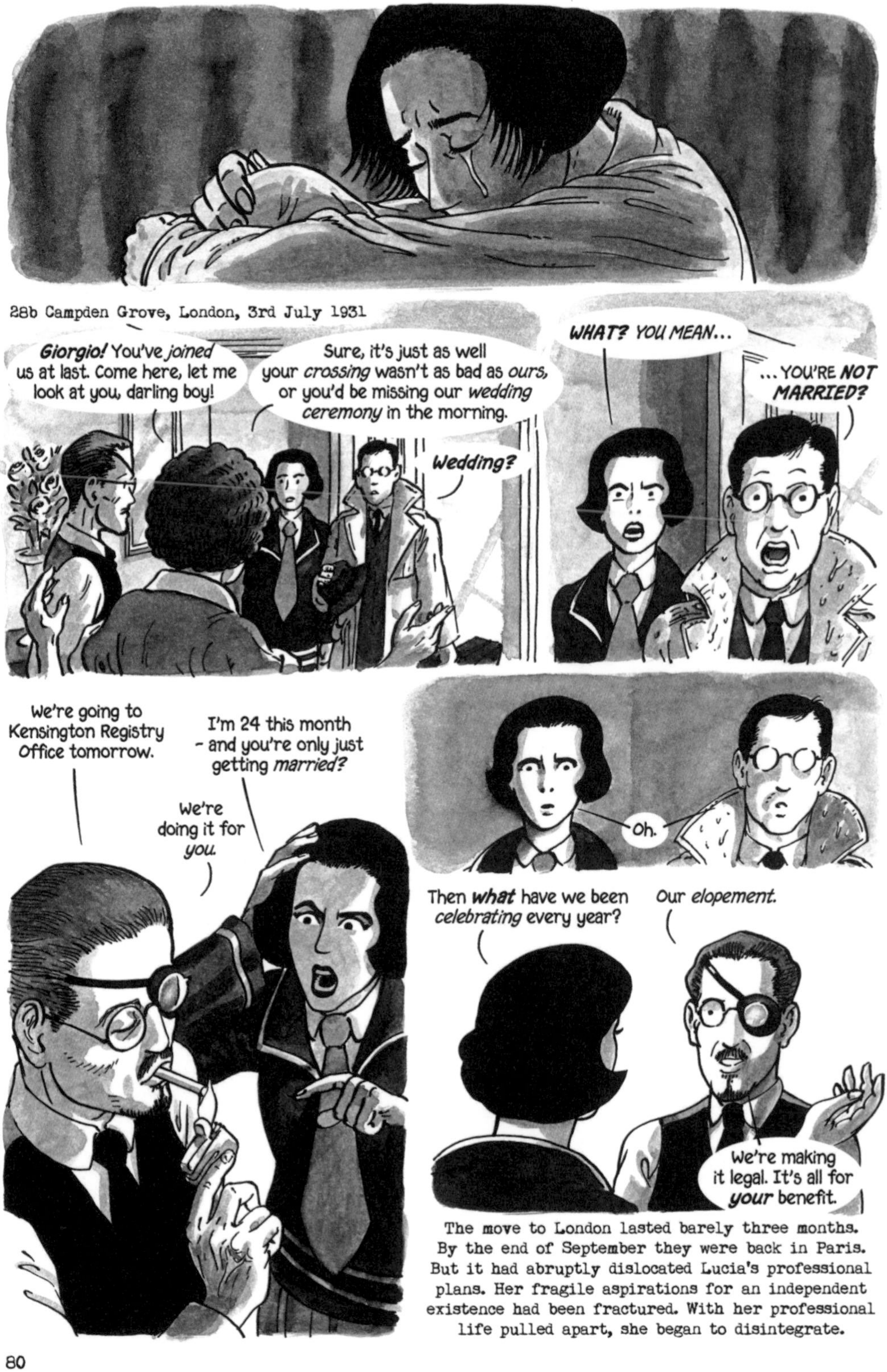
28b Campden Grove, London, 3rd July 1931
Giorgio! You've joined us at last. Come here, let me look at you, darling boy!
Sure, it's just as well your crossing wasn't as bad as ours, or you'd be missing our wedding ceremony in the morning.
Wedding?
WHAT? YOU MEAN...
...YOU'RE NOT MARRIED?
We're going to Kensington Registry Office tomorrow.
I'm 24 this month - and you're only just getting married?
We're doing it for you.
Oh.
Then what have we been celebrating every year?
Our elopement.
We're making it legal. It's all for your benefit.
The move to London lasted barely three months. By the end of September they were back in Paris. But it had abruptly dislocated Lucia's professional plans. Her fragile aspirations for an independent existence had been fractured. With her professional life pulled apart, she began to disintegrate.

No longer a dancer, her performances began to take on other forms. Strident. Discordant.

4 avenue Pierre Premier de Serbie, Paris, 25th September 1931

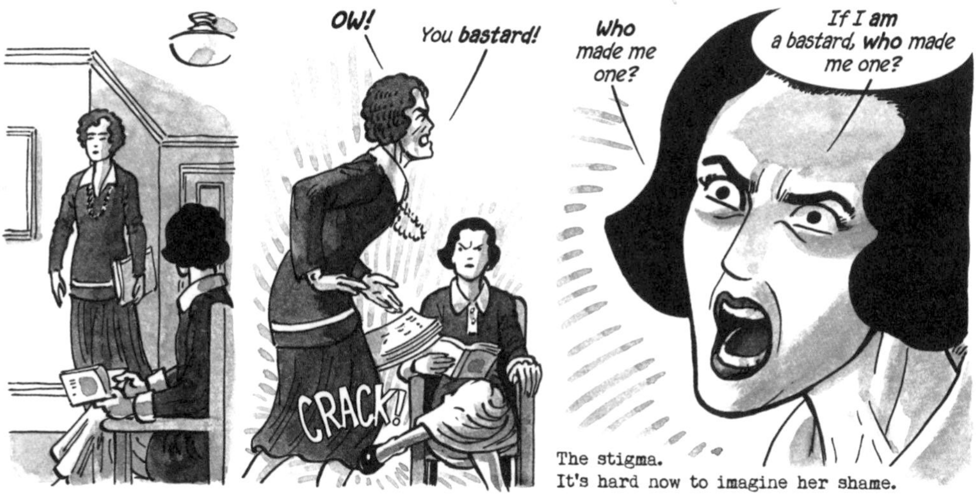
OW!
You bastard!
CRACK!
Who made me one?
If I am a bastard, who made me one?
The stigma.
It's hard now to imagine her shame.

2 Avenue St Philibert, 2nd February 1932

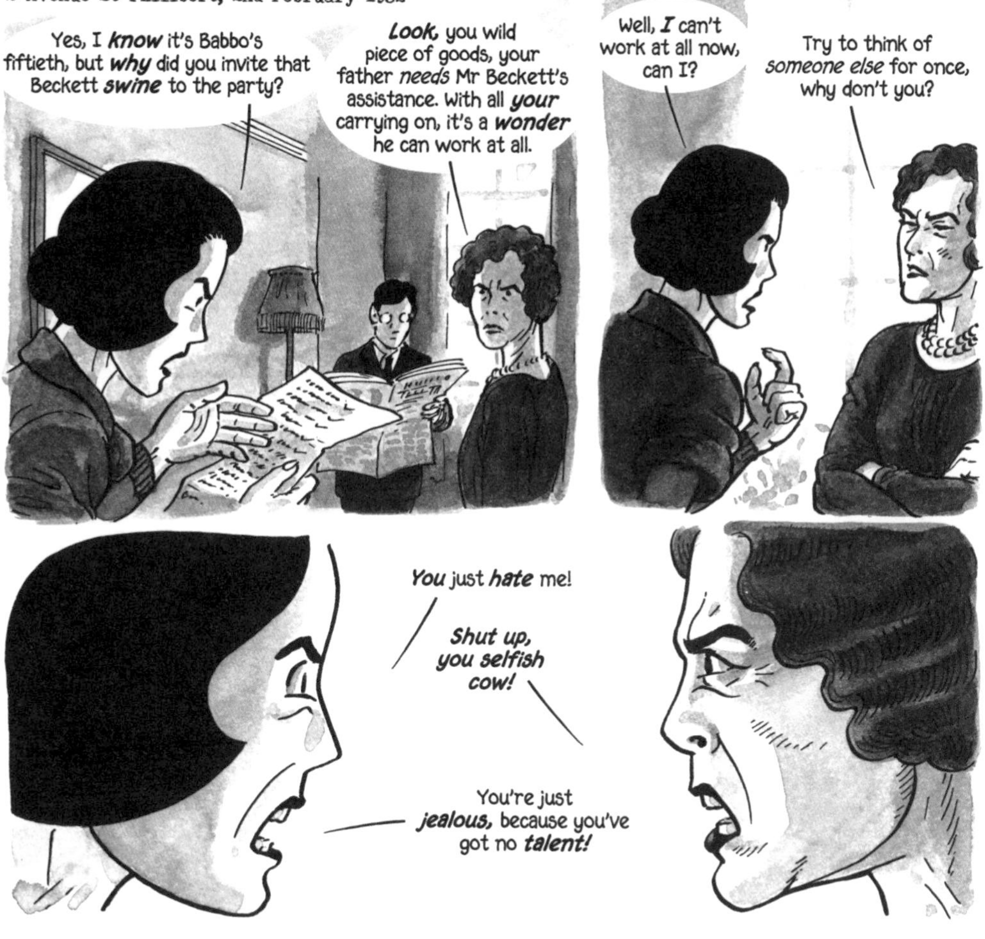
Yes, I know it's Babbo's fiftieth, but why did you invite that Beckett swine to the party?
Look, you wild piece of goods, your father needs Mr Beckett's assistance. With all your carrying on, it's a wonder he can work at all.
Well, I can't work at all now, can I?
Try to think of someone else for once, why don't you?
You just hate me!
Shut up, you selfish cow!
You're just jealous, because you've got no talent!

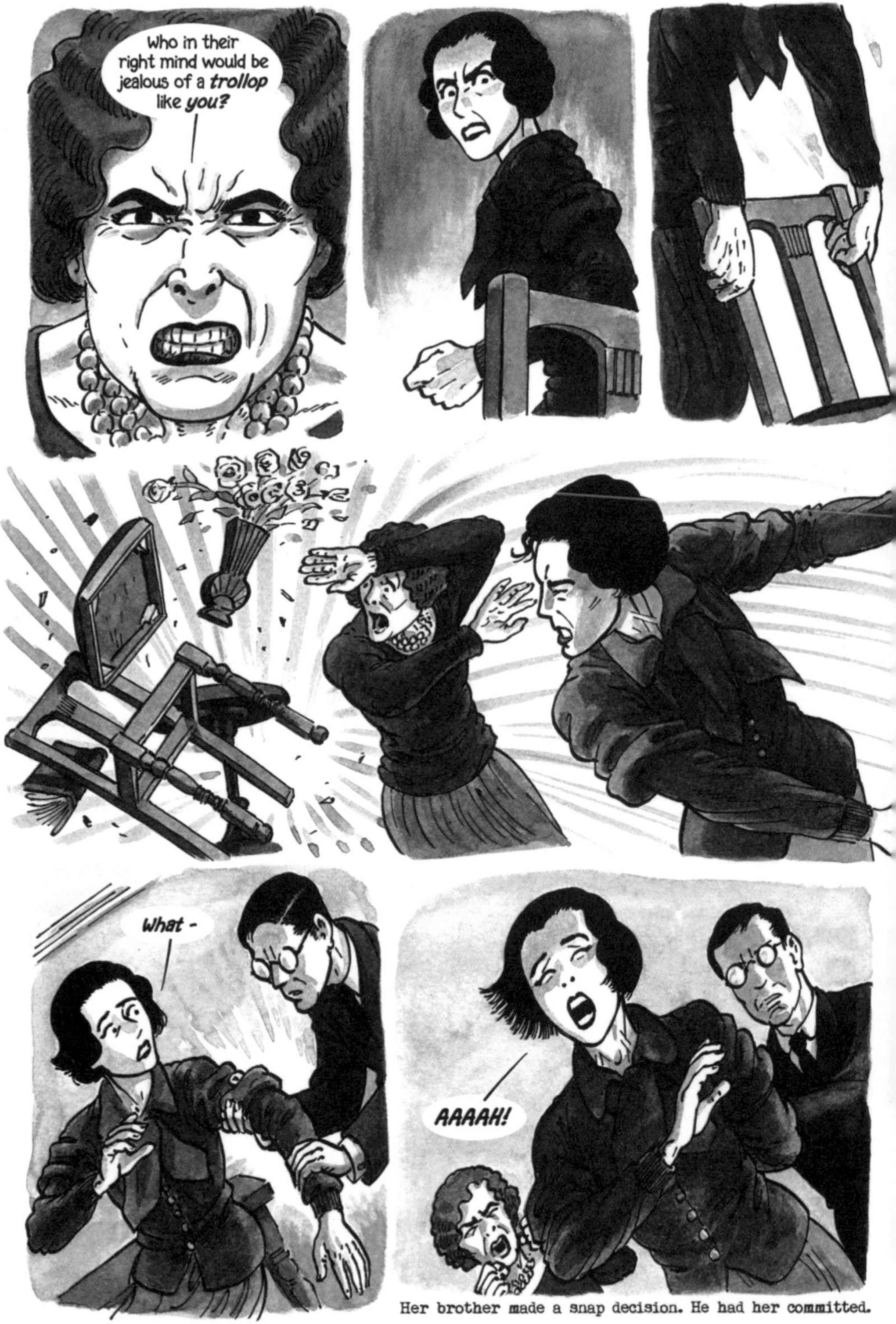
Who in their right mind would be jealous of a *trollop* like *you?*
What -
AAAAH!
Her brother made a snap decision. He had her committed.

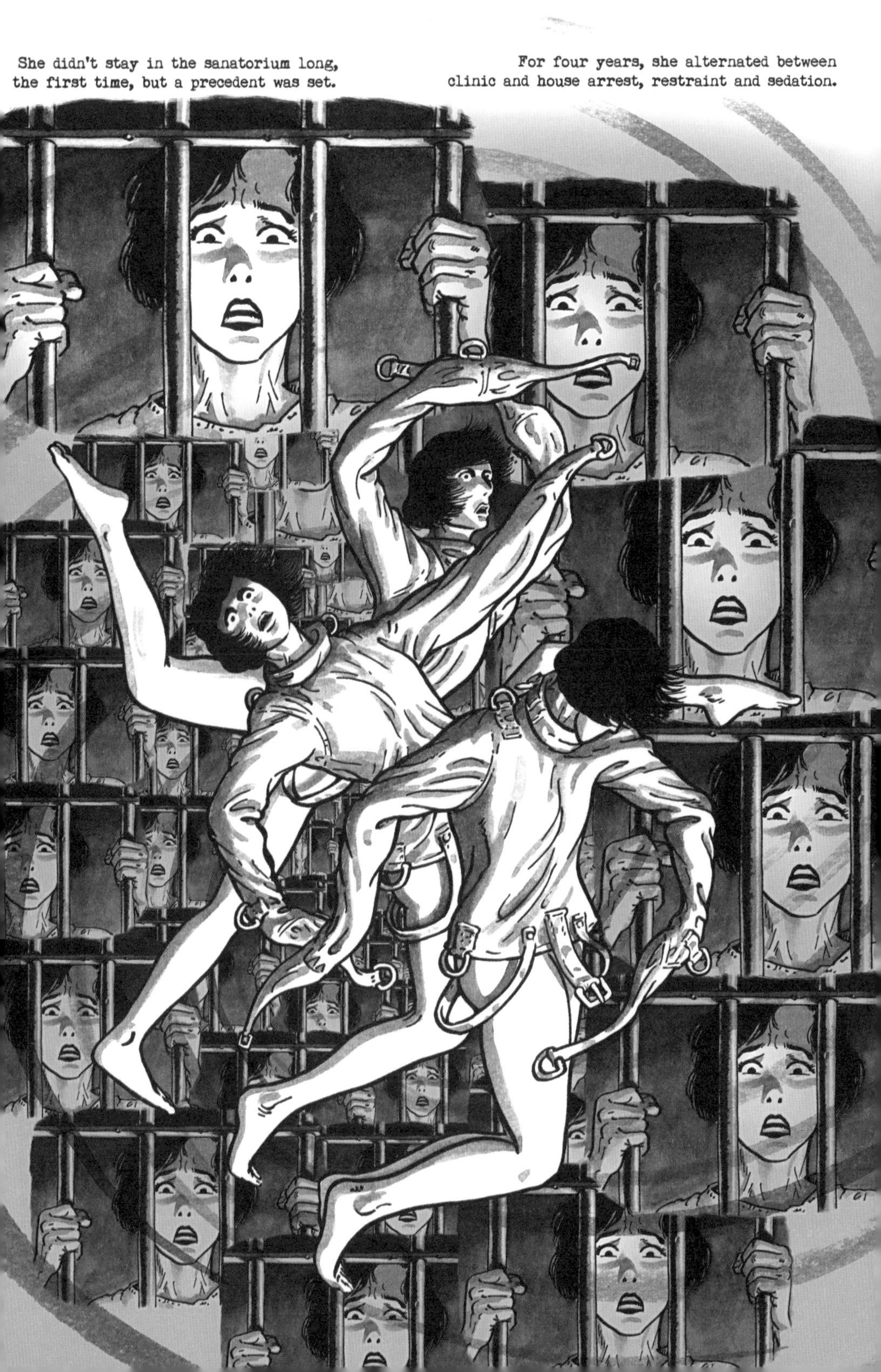
She didn't stay in the sanatorium long, the first time, but a precedent was set.
For four years, she alternated between clinic and house arrest, restraint and sedation.

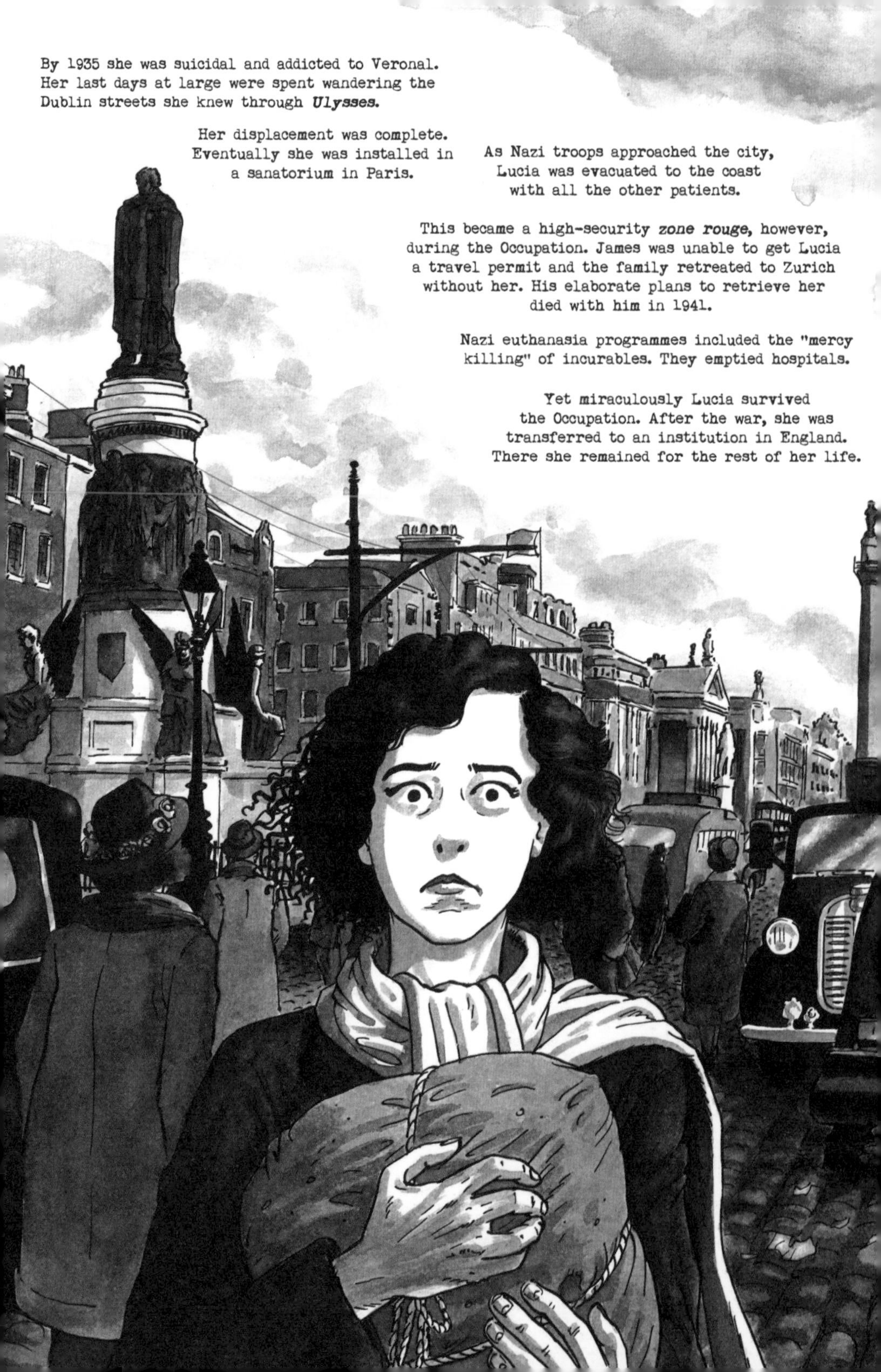

By 1935 she was suicidal and addicted to Veronal. Her last days at large were spent wandering the Dublin streets she knew through *Ulysses.*
Her displacement was complete. Eventually she was installed in a sanatorium in Paris.
As Nazi troops approached the city, Lucia was evacuated to the coast with all the other patients.
This became a high-security *zone rouge*, however, during the Occupation. James was unable to get Lucia a travel permit and the family retreated to Zurich without her. His elaborate plans to retrieve her died with him in 1941.
Nazi euthanasia programmes included the "mercy killing" of incurables. They emptied hospitals.
Yet miraculously Lucia survived the Occupation. After the war, she was transferred to an institution in England. There she remained for the rest of her life.

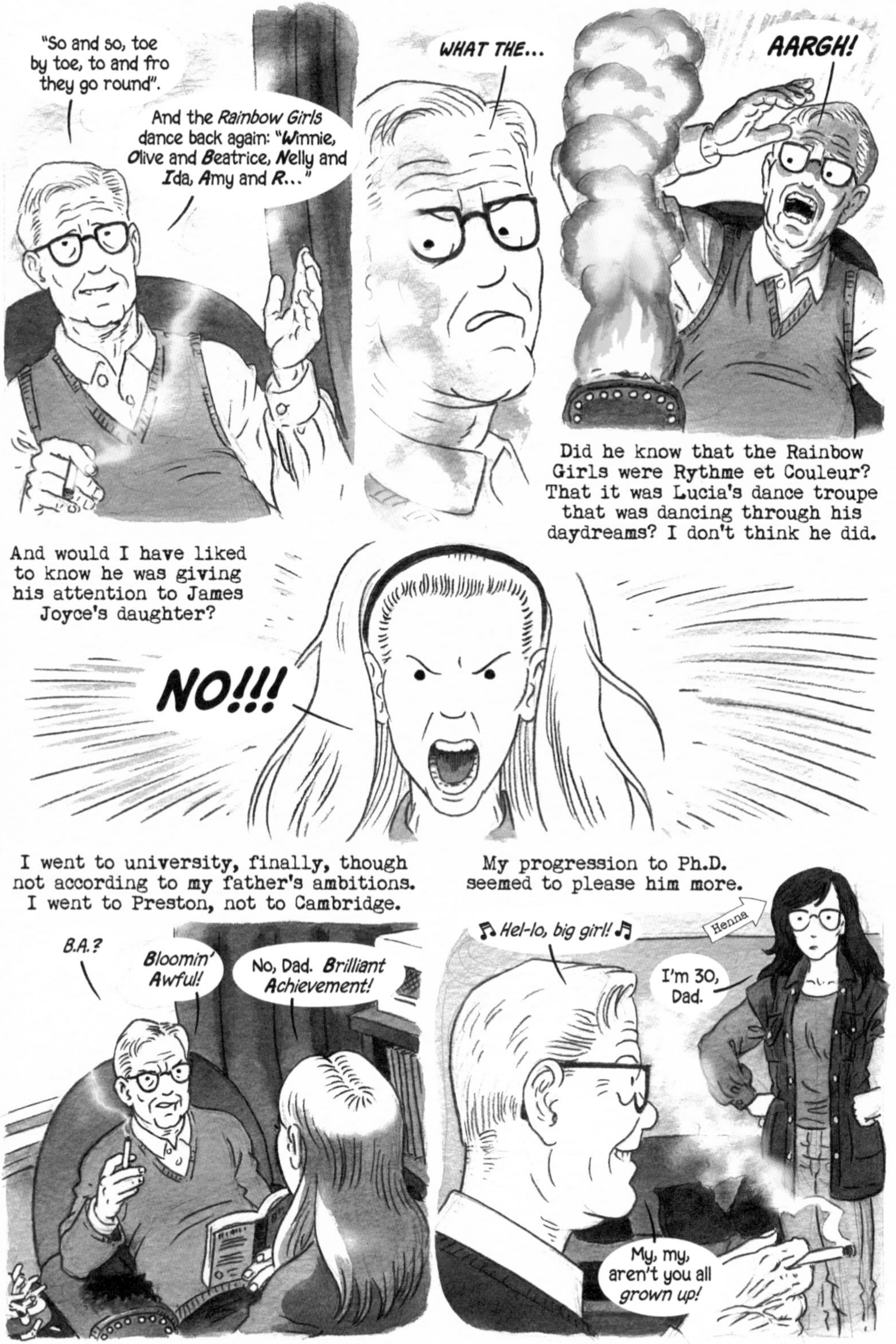
"So and so, toe by toe, to and fro they go round".
And the *Rainbow Girls* dance back again: "Winnie, Olive and Beatrice, Nelly and Ida, Amy and R..."
WHAT THE...
AARGH!
Did he know that the Rainbow Girls were Rythme et Couleur? That it was Lucia's dance troupe that was dancing through his daydreams? I don't think he did.
And would I have liked to know he was giving his attention to James Joyce's daughter?
NO!!!
I went to university, finally, though not according to my father's ambitions. I went to Preston, not to Cambridge.
B.A.?
Bloomin' Awful!
No, Dad. *Brilliant Achievement!*
My progression to Ph.D. seemed to please him more.
♫ Hel-lo, big girl! ♫
Henna
I'm 30, Dad.
My, my, aren't you all *grown up!*

And, as none of us lives happily ever after, the time came when we buried him. An American Joycean flew over for the ceremony.

Would you like a drink, Adeline? The Market Hotel's just here.

She was devastated.

Mary, your father was a wonderful man. The man with the flashing eyes! So warm, so encouraging – he was an inspiration to us all!

Then who should walk in but Wigan's biggest nutcase – the last thing on earth the grieving woman needed.

Bryan! Great to see you, man! Mary!

Oh my God! Not now!

What you two doing back in Wigan?

Funeral tomorrow.

My dad.

Oh, man!

This is Adeline Glasheen. She's come over from the States. Adeline, this is... er, Marky.

Pleasure to meet you. I knew Mr Atherton - he was the most inspirational teacher I ever had!

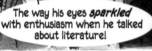

The way his eyes sparkled with enthusiasm when he talked about literature!

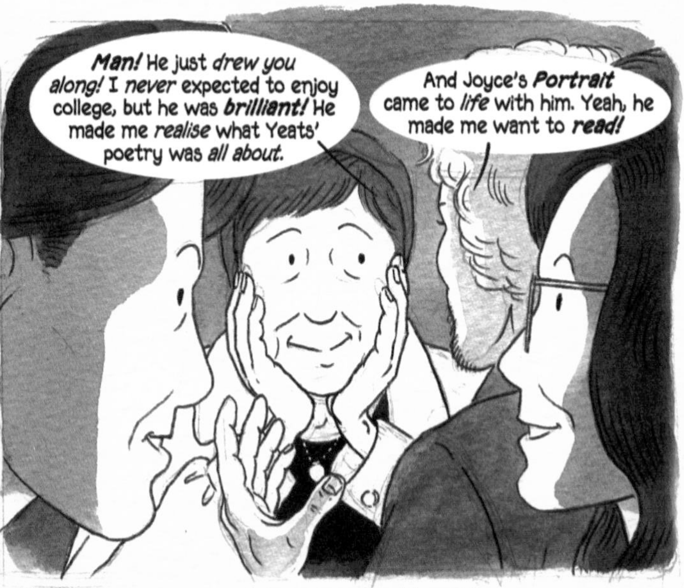
Man! He just drew you along! I never expected to enjoy college, but he was brilliant! He made me realise what Yeats' poetry was all about.
And Joyce's Portrait came to life with him. Yeah, he made me want to read!

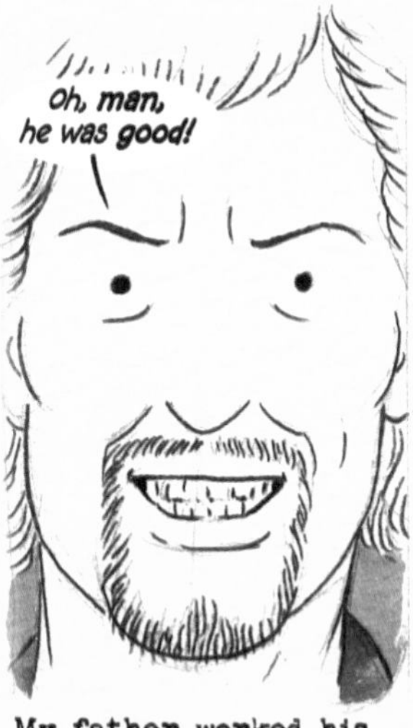
Oh, man, he was good!

My father worked his charm everywhere, it seems. Just very rarely at home.

Then we gave him a send-off, with a son at each corner of his coffin.

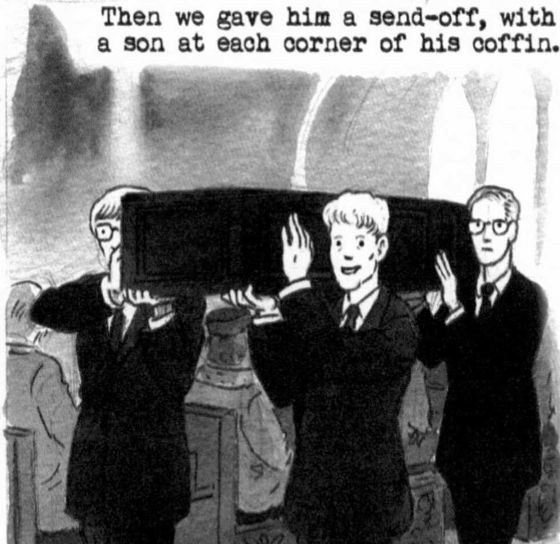

Bryan's mum was shocked.

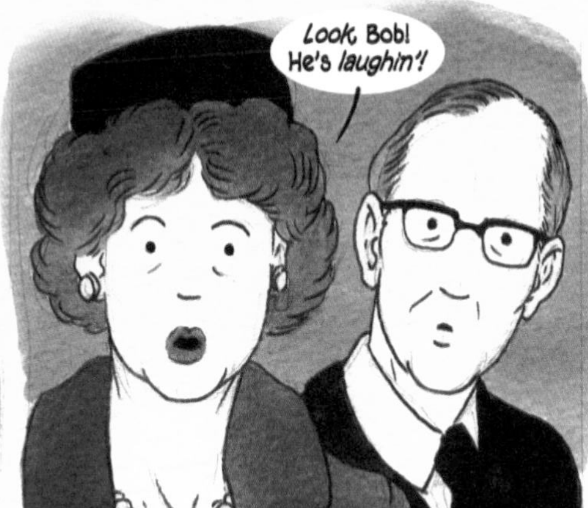
Look, Bob! He's laughin'!

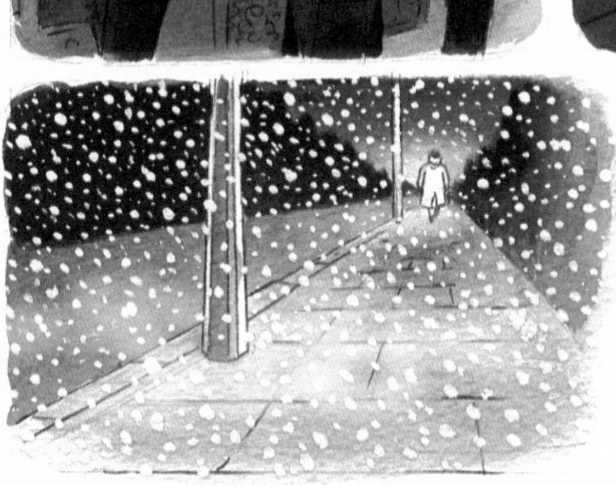

Our mother moved into a "granny flat", where she lived another four years. When her time was up, she seemed to know.

It was just before Christmas. She wrote out cheques to each of her children, then walked to the Post Office and paid all her bills. Then she went back home, sat down and died.

Merry Christmas, Mum.

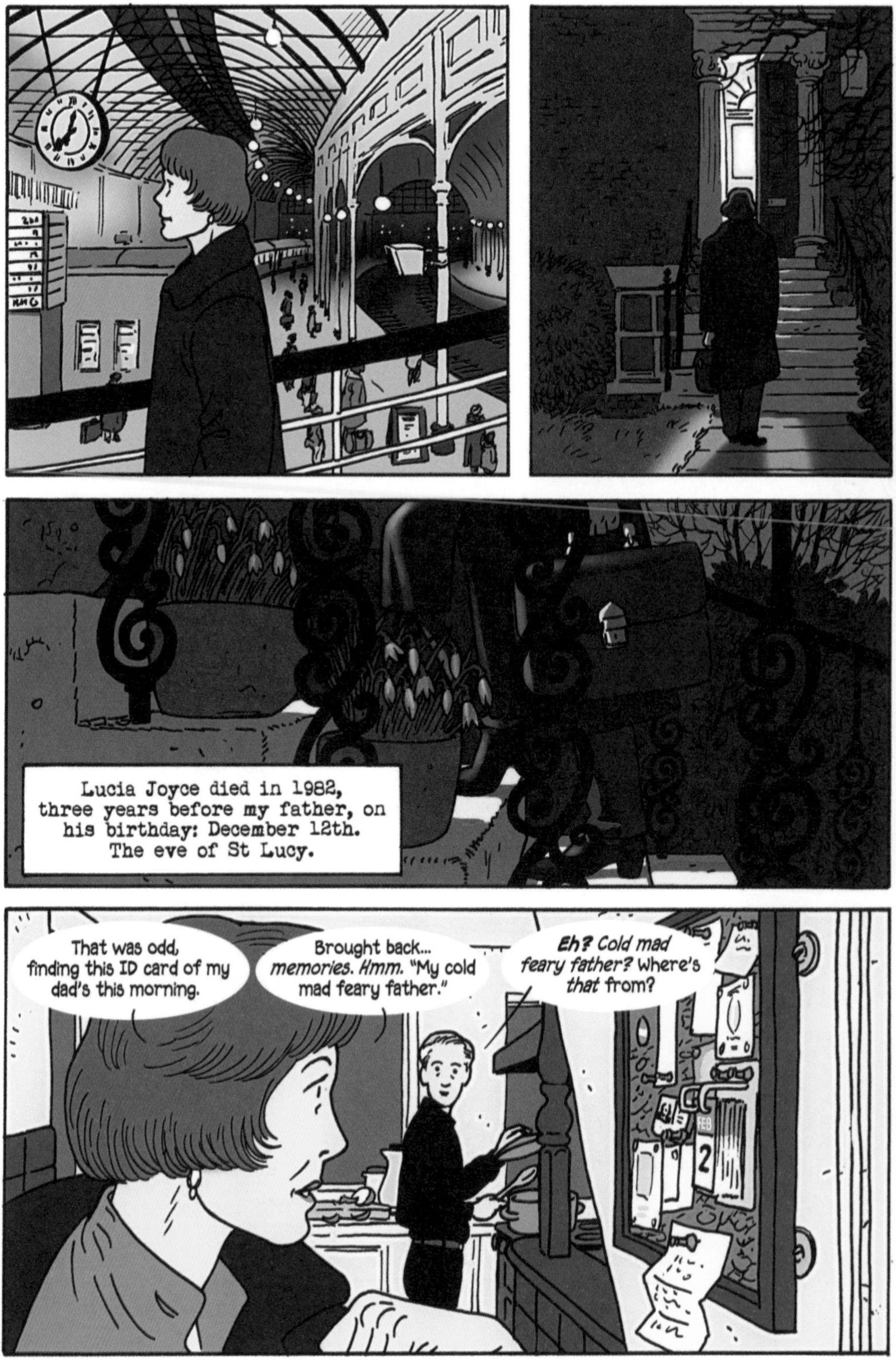
Lucia Joyce died in 1982, three years before my father, on his birthday: December 12th. The eve of St Lucy.
That was odd, finding this ID card of my dad's this morning.
Brought back... *memories. Hmm.* "My cold mad feary father."
Eh? Cold mad feary father? Where's *that* from?
FEB
2

sad and weary I go back to you, my cold father, my cold mad father, my cold mad feary father, till the near sight of the mere size of him, the moyles and moyles of it, moananoaning, makes me ...ltsick and I rush, my only, into your arms. I see them ... those therrble prongs! Two more. Onetwo ... My leaves have drifted from me. ... emind me of. Lff! ... you

OF THE GUILD OF UNDERGRADUATES

THE UNIVERSITY OF LIVERPOOL

FACULTY OF ARTS

No.

...of Study shown on the...

...ourse is permissible without the sanc... the Dean.
...mmunicate any change of Address to the Chief Clerk, Academic Department.

...iste...

STANLEY DUMBELL,
Registrar.

CHORUS

"Oh, whack fol the dah now dance to your partner

Around the flure your trotters shake

Isn't it the truth I told you?

Lots of fun at Finnegan's Wake"

Grand... (and) national 13

575 City & Suburban

481

583

610

PARIS,
1922-1939.

58 Santoy

90 antepost

628 194

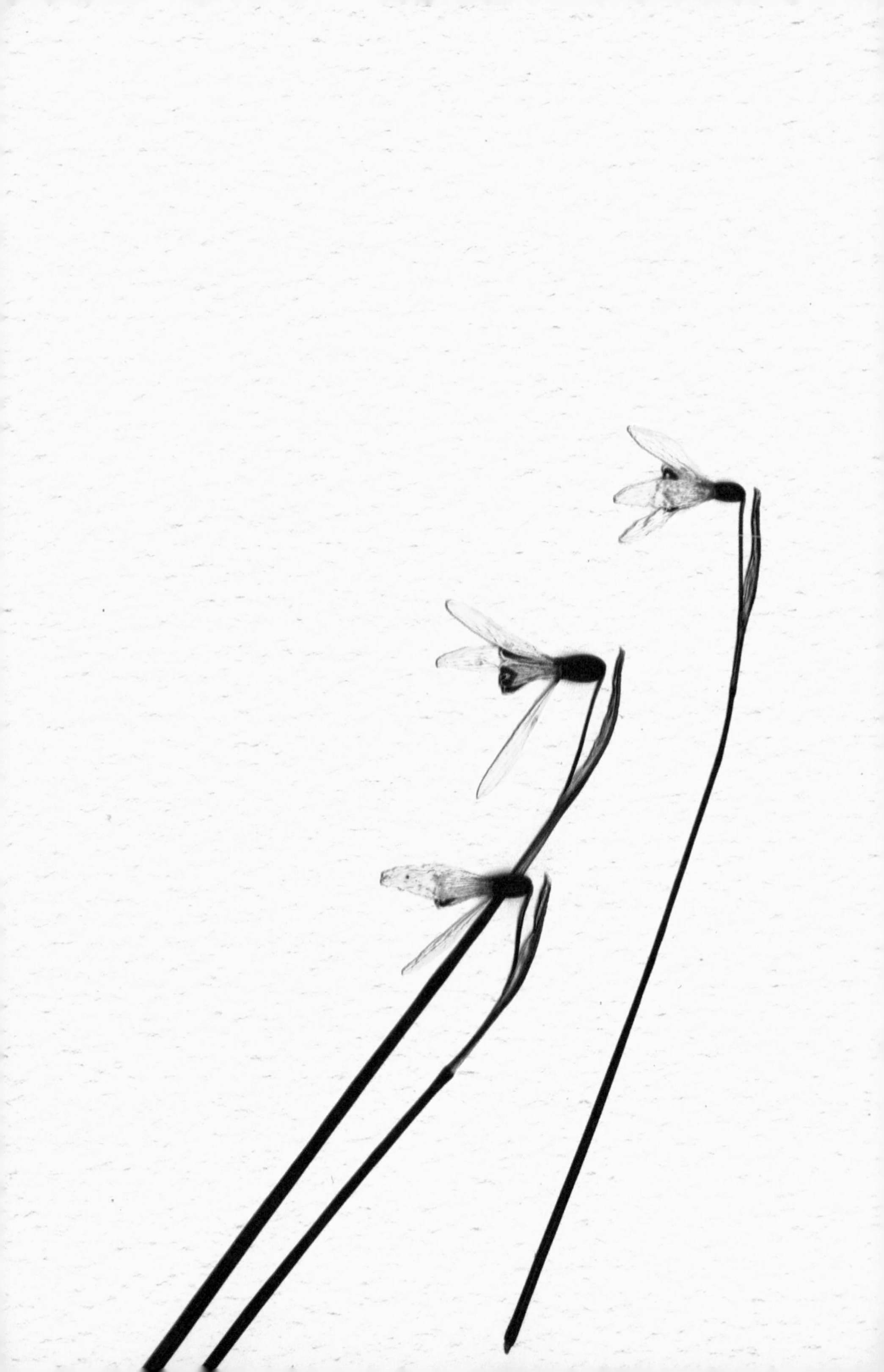

Mary Talbot is an internationally acclaimed scholar
who has published widely on language, gender and power,
particularly in relation to media and consumer culture. Her
recent books include *Language and Gender* (2nd edition) and *Media
Discourse: Representation and Interaction*, though she continues
to be best known for her critical investigation of the
'synthetic sisterhood' offered by teen magazines. Dr Talbot
has worked in higher education for over twenty-five years
and *Dotter of her Father's Eyes* is the first work she
has undertaken in the graphic novel format. She is
currently scripting a historical graphic novel.

Bryan Talbot has worked on underground comics, science
fiction and superhero stories such as *Judge Dredd* and *Batman:
Legends of the Dark Knight*, Vertigo titles including *Hellblazer*,
Sandman and *Fables* and has written and drawn several Eagle and
Eisner Award-winning graphic novels. In 2009 he was awarded a
Doctorate in Arts. He is currently drawing *Grandville Bête Noire*,
the third volume in his series of steampunk detective thrillers.

Photograph by kind permission of the *Sunderland Echo*

Source books

Aubert, Jacques and Senn, Fritz (eds) 1985 *James Joyce*. Paris: Editions de l'Herne

Ellman, Richard 1982 *James Joyce*. Oxford: Oxford University Press

Fitch, Noel Riley 1985 *Sylvia Beach and the Lost Generation: A History of Literary Paris in the Twenties and Thirties*. New York: Norton

Joyce, Lucia 1985 "Charlie et les Gosses," in Aubert and Senn eds.

Hager, Bengt 1990 *Ballets Suedois*. (trans. Ruth Sharman) London: Thames & Hudson

Lawson, Joan 1994 *Beginning Ballet*. (2nd edn) London: A & C Black

McAuliffe, Jody 2005 "Lucia Joyce as Cordelia and the Fool," *Journal of Modern Literature* 28(3): 170–182

Maddox, Brenda 1988 *Nora: A Biography of Nora Joyce*. Harmondsworth: Penguin

Maroger, Dominique 1985 "Lucia et la Danse," in Aubert and Senn eds.

Maroger, Dominique 1985 "Dernière Rencontre avec Lucia," in Aubert and Senn eds.

Norburn, Roger 2004 *A James Joyce Chronology*. Basingstoke: Palgrave Macmillan

Rickett-Young, Linda 1996 *Essential Guide to Dance*. London: Hodder & Stoughton

Royal Academy of Dancing 1993 *Step-by-Step Ballet Class: An Illustrated Guide to the Official Ballet Syllabus*. London: Ebury Press

Shloss, Carol Loeb 2003 *Lucia Joyce: To Dance in the Wake*. London: Bloomsbury

Trewhitt, Bev and Hastie, Jim (eds.) 1997 *Margaret Morris, Modern Dance Pioneer*. New York: International Association of Margaret Morris Movement Ltd

Academic books by Mary M Talbot

Fictions at Work

Language and Gender

Media Discourse: Representation and Interaction

Language, Intertextuality and Subjectivity:
Voices in the Construction of Consumer Femininity

All the World and Her Husband:
Women in Twentieth-Century Consumer Culture
(with Maggie Andrews)

Language and Power in the Modern World
(with David Atkinson and Karen Atkinson)

Other books by Bryan Talbot

Brainstorm

The Adventures of Luther Arkwright

Heart of Empire

The Tale of One Bad Rat

Alice in Sunderland

The Art of Bryan Talbot

The Naked Artist (Prose)

Grandville

Grandville Mon Amour

Metronome
(Writing as Veronique Tanaka)

Cherubs
(With Mark Stafford)

Nemesis the Warlock Vols 1 & 2
(With Pat Mills)

Sandman: Fables and Reflections
(With Neil Gaiman, Stan Wock and Mark Buckingham)

The Dead Boy Detectives and the Secret of Immortality
(With Ed Brubaker and Steve Leialoha)

Published by Jonathan Cape 2012

4 6 8 10 9 7 5

Copyright   Bryan Talbot and Mary M Talbot 2012

Bryan Talbot and Mary M Talbot have asserted
their rights under the Copyright, Designs and Patents
Act 1988 to be identified as the author of this work

This book is sold subject to the condition that it shall not,
by way of trade or otherwise, be lent, resold, hired out,
or otherwise circulated without the publisher's prior
consent in any form of binding or cover other than that
in which it is published and without a similar condition,
including this condition, being imposed on the
subsequent purchaser

First published in Great Britain in 2012 by
Jonathan Cape
Random House, 20 Vauxhall Bridge Road,
London SW1V 2SA

www.rbooks.co.uk

Addresses for companies within The Random House Group
Limited can be found at: www.randomhouse.co.uk/offices.htm

The Random House Group Limited Reg. No. 954009

A CIP catalogue record for this book
is available from the British Library

ISBN 9780224096089

The Random House Group Limited makes every effort to ensure
that the papers used in its books are made from trees that have been
legally sourced from well-managed and credibly certified forests. Our
paper procurement policy can be found at: www.randomhouse.co.uk/paper.htm

Printed and bound in Great Britain by
Butler Tanner and Dennis, Frome, Somerset

.245· Chaucer ?   ŏŏg ·

Her leaves souvenir souvenir

our love of libel 523

Page
625 line 17 from top   for 'dear.' read 'dear!'
625 line 29 from top   for 'remember.' read 'remember!'
626 line 6 from top   for 'arrohs.' read 'arrohs!'
627 line 7 from top   for 'part.' read 'part!'
628 line 8   after 'morning' insert comma
628 line 9 from top   for 'fair.' read 'fair!'

576–
577 arthur's read immate friend 23   Gill 440

H. Hogg 480–

69   617   366/2

§ Heidelburgh 408

Head ache 433   Boggs

Second copy presently § N·3

Milly Bloom
Snotty   450   bemolly

J's father . 443.   Chet 593 · 633

S   M 222

                        Panto.
                        dame) 548
                        Sinbad)
Broylan   45 Cend Broylan   Cinderella 440

Jail p.141.
Q 405.2D : thou jehovial
Counterfeit Kevin 483 ? Gide?   256 That little

Mangans 3 cows. 380–   28   Englands

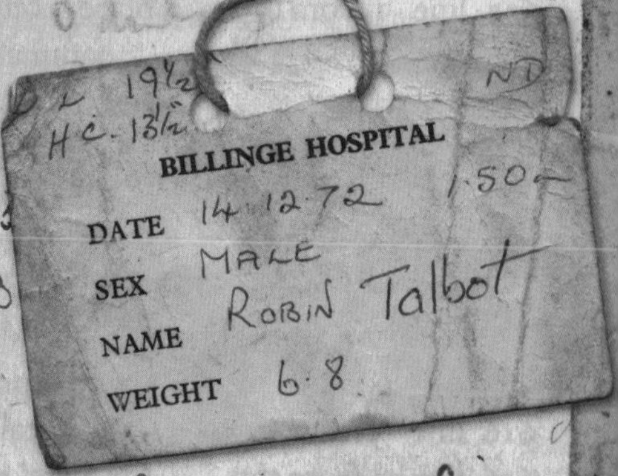

BILLINGE HOSPITAL
DATE 14·12·72   1·50
SEX   MALE
NAME ROBIN Talbot
WEIGHT 6·8

19½
Hc·13¼   ND